AṢṬĀVAKRAGĪTĀ

Aṣṭāvakragītā

(The Song of the Self Supreme)

The Classical Text of Ātmādvaita by Aṣṭāvakra with an Introductory Essay, Sanskrit Text, English Translation, Annotation and Glossarial Index

RADHAKAMAL MUKERJEE

MOTILAL BANARSIDASS PUBLISHERS
PRIVATE LIMITED • DELHI

7th Reprint: Delhi, 2014
(First published in 1971 by MLBD as
"The Song of the Self Supreme : Aṣṭāvakragītā')

ISBN: 978-81-208-1366-3 (Cloth)
ISBN: 978-81-208-1367-0 (Paper)

MOTILAL BANARSIDASS
41 U.A. Bungalow Road, Jawahar Nagar, Delhi 110 007
8 Mahalaxmi Chamber, 22 Bhulabhai Desai Road, Mumbai 400 026
203 Royapettah High Road, Mylapore, Chennai 600 004
236, 9th Main III Block, Jayanagar, Bengaluru 560 011
Sanas Plaza, 1302 Baji Rao Road, Pune 411 002
8 Camac Street, Kolkata 700 017
Ashok Rajpath, Patna 800 004
Chowk, Varanasi 221 001

published by JP Jain for Motilal Banarsidass Publishers (P) Ltd,
41 U.A. Bungalow Road, Jawahar Nagar, Delhi-110007

CONTENTS

INTRODUCTORY ESSAY

The Importance and Background of the Text

The *Aṣṭāvakra Gītā* is a unique text among the world's contemplative classics dealing systematically with the mystical experiences of the Self on its way to transcendence, peace and bliss. There are few ancient treatises in East or West which evince such profound and lively concern with the Supreme Self as the ultimate reality, embodied in mystical insight and experience, and written with such spiritual imagination and poetic fervour. It may, indeed, be compared with the *Dialogues of Plato*, the *Tao Teh King* and the *Bhagavad Gītā* that all record universal insights and experiences of meditation which belong to the heritage of entire mankind.

Aṣṭāvakra' s teaching in respect of the cosmic Self is presented in the form of his dialogue with Janaka, the magnificent King of Videha, about whom we read so much in the *Rāmāyaṇa*, the *Mahābhārata* and *Bṛhadāraṇyaka Upaniṣad*. Although the evidence is not clear and definite, Aṣṭāvakra of this text is probably the same as the holy sage of the eight-curved body of the *Mahābhārata*; while Janaka, his disciple here, is identical with the renowned King-seer (rājarṣi) of Videha and father of Sītā, spouse of Rāmacandra, in both the epics. It is the same King-seer whom Yājñavalkya teaches the birth of the Supreme Self in the *Bṛhadāraṇyaka Upaniṣad* (IV, 2, 4; 3, 1) and who stimulates a metaphysical debate between this sage-teacher and a group of Brāhmaṇa *ṛṣis* in the same *Upaniṣad* (III, 1, 1). It is noteworthy that he is also depicted as the splendid model of the wise man in the *Bhagavad Gītā* (III, 20, 25).

The Trio : Aṣṭāvakra, Yājñavalkya and Janaka

In the *Mahābhārata* we find Janaka making the following oft-quoted observation. "Infinite is, indeed, my wealth of which nothing is mine. If Mithilā is burnt, nothing that is mine is burnt" (Śāntiparva, VII, 1). In the *Aṣṭāvakra Gītā* *'me nāsti kiñcana athavā me sarvam'* (II, 14) is similarly echoed by Janaka. The spirit of the magnificent trio, Aṣṭāvakra, Yājñavalkya and Janaka ,is identical—the quest and vision of the Self (*ātmā-Brahma-anusandhāna-anubhava*). The true self, as taught by both Aṣṭāvakra and Yājñavalkya to King Janaka, is infinite:*Ākāśaṁ ātmā*, says Yājñavalkya in the *Bṛhadāraṇyaka Upaniṣad* (III, 2, 13); "boundless as Space is the Self; the phenomenal world is like a water-pot", observes Aṣṭāvakra (VI, 1). The Self is all pervasive, formless, subtle, boundless and stainless as the sky. "That great unborn Self who is undecaying, undying, immortal, fearless Brahman" (*Bṛhadāraṇyaka Upaniṣad*, IV, 4, 25). In the *Aṣṭāvakra Gītā* we read, "May be a king or a beggar, he shines who is unattached". King Janaka in both the epics is the fully liberated, unattached being (*jīvanmukta*) who carries on in a disinterested manner his duties of life for the integration of the world-order (what the *Bhagavad Gītā* calls *Lokasaṁgraha*), unaffected by the human condition. He is, therefore, the most appropriate disciple for being instructed in the truth of the supreme self by Aṣṭāvakra in our text, leading to his withdrawal into the silence and bliss of the Absolute.

The Aṣṭāvakra Legend in the Mahābhārata

The legend about Aṣṭāvakra is fully given in the *Mahābhārata* (*Vanaparva*, 132-134). The sage was born a cripple, crooked on eight parts of his body, due to the curse of his father, the great ṛṣi Kahoḍa. While he had been in his mother's womb, he became so learned and wise that he expostulated with his father who had been reading the whole night. The enraged father cursed the embryo. This was the cause of the eightfold twisting of Aṣṭāvakra's limbs as he came out of his mother's body. Later on, Kahoḍa went to the court of Janaka where he was defeated in an intellectual duel with Vandin. As a result he was immersed into the ocean. For years nobody in his family knew about this.

When Aṣṭāvakra was only twelve, he came to ascertain from Śvetaketu about the fate of his father. He and Śvetaketu then journeyed to the court of Janaka for challenging Vandin in a philosophical debate. Aṣṭāvakra there declared to Janaka from whom he sought permission for entering into the intellectual combat, "I have come before the Brāhmins to expound the doctrine of the unity of Brahman (*Brahmādvaitam*)" (*Mahābhārata, Vanaparva* 133; 18). Vandin was duly defeated in the philosophical debate and merged into the ocean, whence Kahoḍa reappeared. The father let his son bathe in the river Samaṅga. Aṣṭāvakra's limbs were immediately made straight, but he was ever called Aṣṭāvakra.

It is worth while to refer to the intellectual disquisition between Aṣṭāvakra and Vandin as given in the epic. The former obviously enters into the controversy with the object of proving the supremacy of the *Upaniṣadic* creed, although the meaning of his argument is hidden behind a citation of the numerals in which the controversialists are seriously engaged.

The Significance of Number Thirteen

As the intellectual combat proceeds, the various numerals, one to thirteen, are successively brought out for denoting the supreme principle of the universe. Vandin, citing from the first to the twelfth number and referring to various categories, beings and things, suddenly stopped after the first-half of his śloka on the thirteenth number. Aṣṭāvakra thereupon completed the full śloka relating to thirteen. The implication is that the self which is essentially non-dual, free and unconditioned becomes subject to happiness and sorrow and the cycle of birth and deaths through the thirteen viz., the ten organs of sense and activity, and intelligence, mind and ego-sense. Through wisdom, the Self not only should transcend happiness and sorrow as well as the twelve *śīlas* (viz., *dharma*, truth, self-restraint, penance, good-will, modesty, forgiveness, exemption from envy, sacrifice, charity, concentration and control over the senses) but also surmount the thirteen. This is liberation in life, according to Aṣṭāvakra, who recovers the supreme *Upaniṣadic* truth, "I am Brahman" (*ahaṁ brahmāsmi*), and the Self is all that exists (*sarvaṁ* ātmā), which was eclipsed by the specious arguments of the sophist Vandin. The latter only uses "words of subtlety" and cannot indeed get past thirteen.

When Aṣṭāvakra composes the second half of the *śloka* on thirteen, he makes the remark, "Thirteen sacrifices are presided over by Keśī (which is an epithet of Kṛṣṇa); and thirteen are devoured by *Atichandas* (the longer metres) of the *Veda*". The Supreme Self, as Kṛṣṇa-Vāsudeva, presides over the sacrifices offered by the body, senses, mind and ātman (*Adhiyajña* of the *Bhagavad Gītā*, VIII, 2, 4)—thirteen in number—and enables man to surmount the metres of the Vedas, and realize the supreme Brahman or Ātman. Accordingly, the teaching of *Brahmādvaita* or *Atmādvaita* is duly expounded, as promised by Aṣṭāvakra when he obtained his entry into Mithilā, the city of Janaka, for the duel with Vandin.

Winternitz in his *History of Indian Literature* refers to number of riddles and litanies from Christianity and Hinduism. Aṣṭāvakra's arrangement of the categories of truths according to numbers is a noteworthy example of number puzzle and prayer in Hinduism.

A much later legend is also recorded in the *Viṣṇupurāṇa* (V, 38; 71-84) that as the sage was performing penances with his body under waters, the nymphs of heaven offered hymns to him. On this Aṣṭāvakra gave them the boon that they would obtain Puruṣottama for husband. But as he came out of the waters the nymphs seeing his uncouth form laughed. The sage cursed that they would be the wives of Puruṣottama and then fall into the hands of robbers. The symbolism underlying the twisted body of the sage is that it is ātman-knowledge rather than the physical appearance of the body which alone counts. Even the ugliest human frame can be illumined by the radiance of wisdom of the self, (*ātmajyotiḥ*) absolute and supreme.

The Aṣṭāvakra Gītā and the Bhagavad Gītā : Possible Date of Our Gītā

The *Aṣṭāvakra Gītā* in its style and composition closely resembles the epics. It belongs to the intellectual and spiritual climate of the age of Janaka and Yājñavalkya prior to the systematisation of philosophical thought. Like the *Bhagavad Gītā* (c. 6th Century B.C) it is simple and easy and at the same time pregnant and forceful. Like it, it also avoids philosophical discussions and focuses on the spiritual reality, insisting on tattvajñāna or ontological truth. Its date may be assigned to the period immediately after the *Bhagavad Gītā*, to c. 5th, 4th century B.C. and before the rise of the great philosophical schools and the formulation of the philosophical *sūtras*

(c. 2nd to 1st Century B.C.). It is very much nearer to the *Bhagavad Gītā* and such later *Upaniṣads* as the *Śvetāśvatara*, *Muṇḍaka* and *Māṇḍūkya Upaniṣads* than to the *Brahmasūtras* (c. 2nd Century B.C.). All these were composed in a mystical milieu and emphasized intuitive illumination and transcendence. There is a slight reference in the text to the Buddhist speculation in respect of the non-existence (XVIII, 42, 63) and to the Śūnyam or void (XX, 1), while one of its common similes of the ocean as the Self and its waves as the external world is used in an important context by Aśvaghoṣa (c. 1st Century A.D.), the founder of Mahāyāna idealism. Like the *Bhagavad Gītā*, the *Aṣṭāvakra Gītā* preceded the formation of the Buddhist as well as of Hindu philosophical system. While the *Muṇḍaka Upaniṣad* and the *Bhagavad Gītā* refer to the Vedānta, the *Aṣṭāvakra Gītā* does not mention the term. Its several references to *dvaita* and *advaita*, however, clearly indicate acquaintance with the advaita Vedantic speculation of the times. "Rare is the man who knows the Self as the One without a second as well the Ruler of the Universe. He is completely free from fear" (IV. 6). This echoes the supreme monism of the *Upaniṣads*. Surely does Aṣṭāvakra, like the seer of the *Muṇḍaka Upaniṣad*, realize that the completeness and certitude of the knowledge of the Self can emerge only from Vedānta and *Vijñāna* (*vedānta-vijñāna-suniścitārthāḥ, Muṇḍaka Upaniṣad*).

Unlike the *Bhagavad Gītā*, the *Aṣṭāvakra Gītā* shows no interest in the personal God but goes back to the older Upaniṣadic monistic idealism. The Self, according to Aṣṭāvakra, is the ultimate reality, ineffable, eternal and universal. There is hardly any ancient Indian text like the *Aṣṭāvakra Gītā* which depicts so eloquently and profoundly, yet so poetically, the grandeur, the beauty, the bliss and the incomprehensibility of the Self. According to the *Bṛhadāraṇyaka Upaniṣad*, "Where everything indeed has become the Self itself, whom and by what should one think ?" By what can we know the Universal Knower ?", (II, 4, 12-14). The Self is stainless and perfect, beyond meaning and word. It is not only the transcendent and the unthinkable but also the serene, the blissful, the beautiful and the beloved (XVIII, 35). The *summum bonum* of man's life is to attain the Self, but, as Aṣṭāvakra points out, the Self is not jīva, nor is it an object to be attained (II, 22), the Self already abides and abides for eternity (XVIII, 4). He must, therefore, be instinctually and constantly established in himself giving up duties and goals of life, yogic discipline and prayer, and even *samādhi* itself (XII, 1-8).

The Grandeur of the Self in the Aṣṭāvakra Gītā

Aṣṭāvakra's originality lies in giving a remarkably imaginative and poetic expression to the quest of the Self, absolute and supreme. In the world's religious literature there can be found no grander exposition of the status of the Self as given in chapters VI, XV, and XX. According to the *Bhagavad Gītā*, the phenomenal self of man is a fragment of the Supreme God—the ultimate reality (XV, 7). Radhakrishnan observes that many names are given to this divine essence of the soul—"apex, ground, abyss, spark, fire, inner light". To these we may add That, Tao, darkness. void (*śūnya*), transcendence and Being. There is a universal emphasis of the transcendent aspect of this real Self in the major religions of mankind. In Aṣṭāvakra while the Self is posited as pure absolute, unconditioned and inalienably possessed of its own unity and bliss, he denies any process or opposition which jeopardizes or obscures the infinite and indivisible reality in the cosmic process. This is, of course, based on the blend of Upaniṣadic monistic notions with hallowed yogic experiences that the sage transmits from the past. The transcendent and boundless absolute Self is, according to Aṣṭāvakra, like the ocean; the phenomenal world is like its waves. Due to the winds of mind or notions of finiteness, the things and beings of the universe rise and fall, jostle, play and interact with one another like the waves, all in the ocean of the unborn, changeless Self (II, 4, 23-25; VI, 2; XV, 7, 11). There is neither gain nor loss of the infinite, oceanic Self, due to the fluctuations of the waves of phenomena, the body, senses, mind and the universe—the cosmic becoming. We have already mentioned that Aṣṭāvakra's favourite simile of the ocean of being and the waves of the mind and the phenomenal world reappears in the metaphysical monism of Aśvaghoṣa (c. 100 A.D.), one of the founders of Mahāyāna Buddhism. To Aṣṭāvakra neither knowledge nor duty, neither renunciation nor yoga discipline and *Samādhi* can reveal the range and depth of the self. For in truth the unborn Self alone exists, and all that exists is the Self. The Self, incomprehensible and marvellous, is in all cosmic beings and things, as all comic beings and things are in the Self(III 5, XV, 6). Meditate on the Self and the Self is transformed into forms or modes of the mind. "A man who reflects on the inconceivable Self resorts only to a form or mode of his thought. Hence abandoning that thought, thus verily do I abide in myself" (XII, 7). There is therefore, no *jīva* nor Brahman, no acceptance nor denial nor dissolution, neither unity nor duality. Such is the lofty teaching of the *Aṣṭāvakra Gītā*.

Aṣṭāvakra's New Concepts and Epithets Relating to Ātman

Aṣṭāvakra coins several new words and phrases for bringing home the new teaching relating to self-knowledge and self-transcendence : *svāsthya*, *svasthi* or *svasthaḥ* which now mean health or well-being, but denote eternal self-abidance in Aṣṭāvakra. It may be, however, noted that svasthi with bhava is an epithet of Śiva. Aṣṭāvakra identifies the *nirupādhi*, *svastha* Self, free from any limitations, with Śiva (XX, 13). Gauḍapāda in his *Māṇḍūkya Kārikā* uses the same term (*svasthaḥ*) for the establishment of self in the Self along with his favourite epithet *aja* or unborn (III, 47) or *ātma Saṁsthā*. (III 34). The *Bhagavad Gītā* uses the word *svastha* only once, meaning one who dwells in his real Self (XIV, 24). The *Tejobindu Upaniṣad* says, *svayameva prabhuḥ svasvarūpe svayaṁ svasthe sa jīvanmukta ucayati*, using the epithets of *svasvarūpa* and *svasthaḥ* together for the definition of the *jīvanmukta* (IV, 31,32). Aṣṭāvakra's cognate, oft-repeated terms are: *svarūpa*, *Svasvarūpa*, *svapada* and *svarūpastha* and his peculiar adjectives of the self are: *nirvibhāga* (indivisible), *nīrasa* (passionless) *nirvimarśa* (free from reasoning) and *niḥsvabhāva* (free from natural attributes or human nature). Patañjali's term kaivalya (aloneness) is used by him only thrice in the sense of absoluteness of the Self (XI, 6, XVII. 18, XX, 4). It may be noted that the *Bhagvad Gītā* does not use the term *kevala* or *kaivalya* in this sense at all.

To Aṣṭāvakra there is no universe nor cosmic process. There is only being, no becoming. *I alone am.* Nothing is ever born because the Self is the only formless and unimmitable entity—the ultimate reality (I. 18). This is not the Buddhist *śūnyavāda* or nihilism but *ekātmavāda* or *kevala ātmādvaita* in a radical form denying any form, appearance or function. Life and death are equally appearances belonging to subjectivity. *Jīvanmukti* or liberation while living is formulated by Aṣṭāvakra as the goal. Man must accept life and its tasks resulting from actions in previous births, but his pure and serene Self stands aloof. With his tranquil mind fixed in *citsvarūpa* he lives and acts with all his body released from natural conditions ((XVIII, 13, 22, 25-26). At the same time Aṣṭāvakra rejects this cherished Vedantic ideal by saying, "To the ever undifferentiated Self, what is liberation in life and what is liberation in death?" (XX, 4). For "nothing exists in his yogic vision" (XVIII, 80). The Self, according to Aṣṭāvakra, ever is, and has neither birth nor death, neither freedom nor bondage. It does not spring out of anything or *akiñcanabhava* (XIII, 1) neither comes and goes anywhere (II, 12, XV, 9) and from it nothing springs (XX, 14). It is simply non-dual and abides encompassing the universe, having no beginning nor end. This certainly anticipates Gauḍapāda's doctrine of *ajātavāda* by many centuries (*Māṇḍūkya Kārikā*, III, 20, 36, 47-48)

The Recovery of Upaniṣadic Monism by Aṣṭāvakra

Śaṅkara claims that the absolutist-creed (*advaita*) was recovered from the Vedas by Gauḍapāda, dated according to Vidhusekhara Bhattacharya about 500 A.D. and according R.D. Karmarkar about 600 A.D. Long before Gauḍapāda's *Kārikā*, Aṣṭāvakra rehabilitated the Upaniṣadic creed in a bold and clear form, identifying the Self with the ultimate reality and denying orders or dimensions of reality. It is noteworthy that Aṣṭāvakra only once slightly hints at the doctrine of *Māyā*. "In the phenomenal world that lasts until the dawning of self-knowledge *Māyā* prevails (i.e. relativist consciousness tainted by *Māyā*) (XVIII, 73). The *Bṛhadāraṇyaka Upaniṣad* makes mention of *māyā* only once (III, 5,19,) and *Śvetāśvatara Upaniṣad* thrice (IV, 10, V, 5 and VI, 12). As a matter of fact the Upaniṣadic meaning of the term *māyā* is something different from what it obtained in later Indian thought. There is no antinomy between *māyā* or *avidyā* and knowledge or *tattva* in Aṣṭāvakra but rather a difference in viewpoint. *Māyā* creates the false image like the unreal mother-of-pearl, mistaken for the silver, the snake mistaken for the rope and the sun-beam mistaken for the water (II, 9). Similarly the universe appears in the Self as a false image, Aṣṭāvakra says, through *ajñāna* or ignorance. In a similar manner Śaṅkara speaks of the whole world appearing like a city's image, reflected in a looking-glass. The city exists entirely in the Self, but through māyā appears outside. *Māyā*, then, is the looking-glass that reflects the unreality and *not* the unreality itself. In I, 10, we read that the image reflected in a looking-glass is unreal. The looking-glass exists within and outside the mere reflection. And so does the Self exist inside and outside, encompassing the body, mind and the phenomenal world—mere appearances. Aṣṭāvakra insists that the wise one should realise that the universe is mere appearance only existing up to the dawning of self-knowledge (III, 11, XVIII, 73).

It is clear that the oppositions between the Self and *māyā* between *jīva* and *Iśvara* and between *vidyā* (knowledge) and *avidyā* (ignorance), stressed so much by later Indian thought, fade away in Aṣṭāvakra's conception of the Self as beyond all opposites, ever-effulgent, stainless and unborn (XX, 2, 11). His position accordingly is often paradoxical. Especially at the end of XVIII (90-100) and in the final chapters XIX and XX, does he wax eloquent as he dismisses the distinctions between knowledge and ignorance, freedom and bondage, eternity and death, partness and wholeness, being and non-being when the Self and nothing but the Self shines and illumines both the outer and inner self. Indian spiritual experience through the ages has indeed revelled in such paradoxes by abolishing all modalities of the real, and derived supreme satisfaction from the realisation that there can be no definition of the Self, God or the Absolute except in paradoxical statements.

Ātmānubhava or Mystical Experience

Our sage makes ontology entirely mystical through a profound synthesis between man's reason and suprarational intuition. He does not give any arguments in support of his ontological position. Only mystical experience provides here the proof of the absoluteness of the Self. To say that:

"You encompass the universe as the universe enters into you. You are in reality the embodiment of pure conciousness. Do not give way to the pettiness of the finite mind,' (I, 16), or "O pure intelligence, do not agitate your mind with (the thoughts of) affirmation and denial. Silencing these, abide in your own Self—the embodiment of bliss itself" (XV, 19).

It is to rely exclusively on the mystical experience that blends profound insight with perennlal joy and peace. he Self is eternally dear, blissful and glorious. Aṣṭāvakra elegantly salutes the Self thus:"Adoration to the One, the embodiment of bliss and effulgence, with the dawning of knowledge of which one's delusion of the world becomes verily a dream" (XVIII, 1).

In India direct or immediate mystical insight is called *anubhava, svarūpa darśana* or *sākṣātkāra.* Gauḍapāda calls this supra-mundane intuition or *lokatatvajñāna* (*Māṇḍūkya Kārikā*, IV, 87-88). According to Vidyāraṇya, *anubhava* means a particular mode of the mind, which has for its result the intuition of Brahman or ātman. Non-duality establishes itself through the mental mode destroying itself as well as the phenomenal world. The metaphor used in this context is that of the powder of the clearing nut (*kaṭaka*) when mixed in muddy Ganges water precipitating itself as well as the mud. Accordingly, as the Self is revealed in *Anubhava* or *sākṣātkāra*, all plurality vanishes. Śaṅkara explains this by saying that when Brahman or Ātman is known through the concentration of mind or Brahman or Ātman in devotion and meditation (*samādhāna*), all duality, such as the distinction of the meditative and the meditated, is destroyed. "Brahman and Ātman is not known until this distinction is resolved, what has been resolved cannot be revived". *anubhava* rests on the dissolution of all pairs of opposites and not merely of the opposition between *jīva* and Brahman, freedom and bondage. It offers also not merely a clear, undoubted, all-encompassing awareness but also a boundless feeling of joy and peace that are not otherwise experienced.

The Use of Upaniṣadic Mahāvākyas by Aṣṭāvakra

Śaṅkara stresses that the yogī's *anubhava* or integral experience in which the truth of the Self or Brahman must culminate is generated by the great Vedānta formulae. The *Upaniṣadic mahāvākyas* that Aṣṭāvakra uses for meditation in order to produce the direct experience of ātman are several, e.g. The "Self is all that exists" (*ātmā eva idaṁ sarvam*) in IV, 4, XV, 15, XVIII, 9; "The Self is the prime cause of all" (*kāraṇātmā eva sarvam*) in II, 5, 10, XV, 14; "The Self is pure intelligence" (*avikalpaḥ hi ātmā cidrūpaḥ*) in I, 3, II, 19; "The Self is supreme, unutterable bliss in itself" (*ānanda ātmā*) in I, 10, XV, 19, XVI, 2; "I am Brahman" (*ahaṁ Brahmāsmi*) in I, 20, XVIII, 8, 28, 37; "Thou art that" (*tattvamasi*) in XV, 7; and "The Self is beyond all the states of consciousness—waking, sleep, slumber and ecstasy (*Māṇḍūkya Upaniṣad*) in XVIII, 94, XIX, 5. To Aṣṭāvakra the Self of the yogī experiencing *atmānubhava* is not merely the inaccessible, supreme *truth* but also the inexpressible, supreme *beauty and love* and the unsurpassable supreme *peace and joy* (III, 4, XVIII, 1, 3, 35).

Aṣṭāvakra's coinage of new terms and phrases for the transcendent Self is remarkably rich, original and poetic. Apart from his use of such familiar *Upaniṣadic* terms with reference to ātman as *śānta* (XVIII, 1), *śiva* (XX, 13), *sundara* (III, 4), *priya* (XVIII, 35), *pūrṇa svarasa vigraha* (XVIII, 67) and *advaya* or *advaita* (I, 20, II, 21, III, 6, XX, 7), we have a host of new pregnant epithets of ātman that do not occur even in the principal *Upaniṣads* and the *Bhagavad Gītā*. Some of these are given below:*akiñcanabhava* or unborn (XIII, 1), *miṣprapañca* or the self beyond relativity, (XVIII, 35); *nirvimarśa* or the self free from dicursive reasoning (XX, 9, XV, 20), *nirviśeṣa* or the self free from particularisation (XX, 4), *niḥsvabhāva* or the self as devoid of natural attributes (XVIII, ,9,XX, 5); *nirāyāsa* or the self as effortless (XVIII, 5); *nirindriya* or devoid of the sense-organs (XVIII, 95) and *nīrasa* or the self as flavourless (XVIII, 68). It is only in the later *Upaniṣads* that we encounter several other terms often repeated by Aṣṭāvakra:*nirañjana* (*Śvetāśvatara* VI, 19, *Māṇḍūkya* 1, 3), *niḥsaṅkalpa*, (*Maitri*, VI, 10, 30), *nirvikalpa* (*Tejobindu*, 6, *Nārāyaṇa*, 2), *nirālamba* (*Mukti*, I, 23), *nirguṇa* (*Gītā*, XIII, 14, 31, *Śvetāśvatara* VI, 11) *niṣkriya* (*Śvetāśvatara* VI, 12), *asaṅga* and *niḥsaṅga* (*asaṅga* of the *Upaniṣads*). Gauḍapāda, of course, has deployed the most considerable number of terms in a later age while expounding the absoluteness of the Self.

Anomalous Use of Terms of Theistic Import

It is remarkable that Aṣṭāvakra, though showing no theistic inclination at all links the ancient terms for the Lord or God with the Self. The Self, absolute and pure, is *Iśvara Parameśvara*, *Jagadīśvara*, *Bhagavān*, *Sākṣipuruṣa* and *Sarvanirmātā* (I, 12, IV, 6, XI, 2, XIV, 3 and XV, 8). Neither Gauḍapāda nor Śaṅkara of the later ages has done this. The key doctrine of Aṣṭāvakra is:"You are the essence of Supreme Knowledge. You are the Lord, you are the Self and you transcend nature" (*jñānasvarūpo bhagavānātmā tvaṁ prakṛteḥ paraḥ*, XV, 8). Much in a theistic manner he also strongly enjoins in this verse faithfulness or *śraddhā* as indispensable for the quest of the Self (XV, 8). Faithfulness or reverence to being (*ātmaprīti* or *ātmarati* of the *Bhagavad Gītā*) is not different in kind from faithfulness or reverence to the Lord, Kṛṣṇa-Vāsudeva. With the stress of the thought that the realisation of the Self is spontaneous and unborn the common way of theistic worship and grace of God does not, however, find any place in Aṣṭāvakra. The first verse of the *avadhūta Gītā* says "By God's grace (*īśvarānugraha*) alone there arises in men the desire for non-duality (*advaita-vāsanā*)". Contemplation of the non-relational impersonal, absolute Self, beyond the notion of duality and unity which is considered by Aṣṭāvakra as a delusion, supersedes God's mercy in his *Gītā*.

The apparent theistic fervour (XV, 8) is obviously due to the exalted position given to the Self or ātman as the transcendent principle. The same we find in the *Kauśītaki-Brāhmaṇa-Upaniṣad* which says : "This is truly the life-breath, the intelligent Self, bliss, ageless, immortal. He does not become great by good action nor small by evil action. This one, truly indeed causes him whom he wishes to lead up from these worlds to perform good actions. This one, indeed, also causes him whom he wishes to lead downward to perform bad action. He is the protector of the world, he is the sovereign of the world, he is the lord of all. He is myself, this one should know, he is myself, this one should know" (III, 8). Aṣṭāvakra has no scruples in using such terms for the supreme Self as *Īśvara*, *Parameśvara* and *Bhagavān* applied to the personal God, Kṛṣṇa Vāsudeva by the *Bhagavad Gītā*. This is due, no doubt, to the profound influence of the *Bhagavad Gītā* on the spiritual and intellectual climate of the time. But this does not imply at all any theism as embodied in contemporary Bhāgavatism, of which the *Bhagavad Gītā* is the principal scripture. The Ātman is merely acknowledged, revered and adored by Aṣṭāvakra as the highest principle—the all-pervading Lord of the universe, the creator and witness of all, who is also called *Paramātmā* or the Supreme and transcendent Self. He observes : "Rare is the individual who knows the non-dual Self as the Lord of the universe (*Jagadīśvara*). He does whatever comes to his mind and has no fear from anywhere" (IV, 6). Again, 'As I have known the supreme Self (*Paramātmā*) who is the eternal person as the witness (*Sākṣī-puruṣa*) and who is the Lord (*Īśvara*), I have no desire for bondage and liberation, nor anxiety for salvation" (XIV, 3).

It is noteworthy that Aṣṭāvakra seldom uses the term *Paramātman* or the supreme Self (II, 3, XIV, 3). In this he conforms to the *Bhagavad Gītā* where the term occurs only four times as contrasted with its very frequent use in the *Mahābhārata*. Aṣṭāvakra even uses the *Upaniṣadic* term Brahman sparingly. The few instances of use of the term Brahman are given below : In I, 20 the absolute Self is identified with the all-pervading Brahman. XVIII, 8, 16, 20, refer to the formula 'I am, Brahman' (*ahaṁ Brahmāsmi*) ; while XVIII, 37 mentions the self as enjoying the nature of the supreme Brahman (*parabrahma svarūpa bhāk*). The word *Puruṣa* or the Supreme Person with which we are so familiar in the *Upaniṣads* and the *Bhagavad Gītā* is used only once and that in the compound word *sākṣi-puruṣa* in the *Aṣṭāvakra Gītā* (XIV, 3).

Difference between the Aṣṭāvakra Gītā, the Upaniṣads and Bhagavad Gītā

Aṣṭāvakra does not agree with the general *Upaniṣadic* view that in the cosmic process, dualities and relativities arise which obscure the infinite, undivided Ātman or Brahman. He completely and unequivocally denies any second philosophical principle and any transformation of the Self which in its own nature is unborn, immutable and free from limitations. He rejects the dualism between *puruṣa* (Self) and *prakṛti* (not-self) of the *Sāṁkhya* philosophy, and makes the Self the prime cause, whence the phenomenal existence (*jagat-dvaitam*), beginning with *mahat* and manifested through mere name, springs (XVIII, 69). The supreme Self transcends *prakṛti* (*prakṛteḥ paraḥ* II, 1, XV, 8). While the *Bhagavad Gītā* makes *puruṣa* and *prakṛti* both subordinate to the Divine (*Puruṣottama*), the *Aṣṭāvakra Gītā* posits the pure, transcendent Self as the unique, integral and supreme principle, from which the creative forces emerge. The unborn and eternal Self is lifted above all empirical oppositions of creation and destruction, existence and non-existence, beginning and end, *jīva* and Brahman (XX, 6, 10). The Self is inalienably possessed of its own unity, luminousness and pervasiveness—the sole and eternal witness of the shifting play of *prakṛti* together with the modes (*guṇas*). With his uncompromising mystical doctrine of the indivisibility and beatitude of Self, Aṣṭāvakra rejects the subsequent Buddhist nihilism—the doctrine of those who think that nothing is (XVIII, 42) and fix themselves on the void (XX, 1). Close to Buddhist *yogācāra* idealism, he is yet nearer the Upaniṣadic speculation in respect of the indefinability and incomprehensibility of the absolute Self, or Ātman.

We may clarify here the major differences between the *Aṣṭāvakra Gītā*, the *Upaniṣads* and the *Bhagavad Gītā* : First, Aṣṭāvakra stresses that the highest metaphysical reality is Ātman or Self rather than Brahman, *Puruṣa* or God (especially XV, 15, XVII, 2, XVIII 8, 9). He also emphatically discards any polarity and contradiction between the empirical self or Ātman governed by the *guṇas* and the transcendent Self, often called *Puruṣa* or Brahman by the *Upaniṣads* and *Paramātman* by the *Bhagavad Gītā* and the *Mahābhārata*. Thus Aṣṭāvakra is the exponent of radical Ātmādvaita Vedānta.

Secondly, he does not brook any second category besides the Ātman, and rejects the principle of *māyā*. The latter is linked in Śaṅkara's philosophy of the Vedānta with the transformation of the ultimate reality Brahman or Self and the streaming forth of the phenomenal world in all its manifoldness. Aṣṭāvakra neither accepts the Sāṁkhya dualism of

Puruṣa and *Prakṛti* nor follows the *Bhagavad Gītā* in regarding *māyā* as the making of the Supreme and subservient to Him. With him the unborn and the eternal Self is the one that exists. It is indivisible and continuous, and there cannot be two dimensions, orders or phases of reality, absolute and provisional or apparent. To him the universe only exists until the dawning of self-knowledge (*buddhi paryanta*). Uptill then *māyā* prevails (XVIII, 73). Truly the phenomenal or māyic world does not exist as an objective reality. There is neither *jīva* nor *Iśvara* nor *māyā* nor universe other than the Self (XV, 16). It is clear, however, that our author uses the term *ajñāna* or ignorance not as a metaphysical principle, but as contrasted with true knowledge or *tattvajñāna*, and asserts that man can dispel his ignorance through his knowledge of the Self or pure intelligence (*cit*) in which alone the universe manifests itself (II, 7). With pure intelligence (*buddhi* or *vijñāna*) the phenomenal world of name and form (*jagat dvaitam*) disappears (XVIII, 69), and the Self's true nature which is eternal, all-pervading, luminousness is discerned.

Thirdly, Aṣṭāvakra, as we have already remarked, seems to have been the founder of the theory of non-origination of the self (*ajātavāda*) or (*ajātivāda*), later on attributed to Gauḍapāda. This brings him near to Buddhist *yogācāra* idealism. There is no *jīva* nor *iśvara* outside the Self which is one, immutable and indivisible. Nothing can exist outside the Self: nothing can proceed from it either (XX, 4). According to him the Self is '*akiñcana bhava*' or unborn (XIII, 1) and has "neither birth, nor action, nor egoism" (XV, 13).

Fourthly, Aṣṭāvakra, like the seer of the *Bhagavad Gītā*, sometimes calls the eternal Self transcendence and Brahman and sometimes the Lord, Creator, of the Universe or *Bhagavān*, without either compromising the absolute aloneness (*kaivalya*) and unborn character of the Self or evincing any theistic slant or fervour as that of the *Bhagavad Gītā*.

Fifthly, he clarifies the mystical or yogic principles of self-realization and self-transcendence, leaning more on the dialectics of abstract contemplation than on *laya* or dissolution of consciousness. *Laya* or oblivion he simply discards as irrelevant or harmful. It belongs to the relativist sphere of the mind, ego-sense and activity. It is nothing like the serene, subtle and alert self-abidance (*svāsthya*) grounded in the profound sense of unity and indivisibility of the absolute Self and the phenominal world (VI, 1-4). In this respect he reinterprets *Pātañjala-Yoga* for *ātmānubhava* and *sākṣātkāra*. According to him, the acme of meditation is no meditation. He is most original and creative in his conception of instinctual or spontaneous self-abidance (*svāsthya*, *svarūpa*) as the supreme state under all human conditions and circumstances reached through the process of dialectic and *vijñāna*. To him the Self is itself natural *samādhi* which is screened or obstructed by meditation of any kind.

A linguistic affinity between the *Aṣṭāvakra Gītā* and the *Bhagavad Gītā* is no doubt evident from the words and phrases borrowed by the former from the latter. Aṣṭāvakra's first line in III, 5 and XV, 6—(*sarvabhūteṣu cātmānaṁ sarvabhūtāni cātmani*) is the same as the first line of VI, 29 of the *Bhagavad Gītā*. The words *nirmama* and *nirahaṁkāra* are juxtaposed in both texts *Aṣṭāvakra*, XV, 6, XVII, 19, XVIII, 73; the *Gītā*, II, 71, XII, 13). Similarly, '*kurvannapi na lipyate*' occurs in both *Aṣṭāvakra* (XI, 4, XVIII, 64) and the *Gītā* (V, 7, XIII, 31). *Kurvan api na karoti* is found in Aṣṭāvakra (XVII, 19, XVIII, 25, 58) and in the *Gītā*(IV, 20, V, 30). *Paśyan śṛṇvan* etc. occur in both Aṣṭāvakra(XVII, 8, 12, XVIII, 47) and the *Gītā* (V, 8). *Samaloṣṭāśmakāñcana* is also found in both Aṣṭāvakra (XVIII, 88) and the *Gītā* (V, 8, XIV, 24).

The Ethics of the Two Gītās

Ethically and philosophically, the *Aṣṭāvakra Gītā* aud the *Bhagavad Gītā* are, however, poles asunder. The former presents an all-sufficient ontology grounded in the cosmic mysticism of the Self. The latter achieves a profound synthesis of ontology, religion and ethics. The teaching about non-attachment is the same in the two *Gītās*. But unlike the *Bhagavad Gītā*, the *Aṣṭāvakra Gītā* altogteher denies the efficacy of actions; for the self is neither doer nor enjoyer and is ever free and unstained (1, 6). Aṣṭāvakra takes into cognisance only actions resulting from the consequences of actions in previous births (XX, 4). To him duty, like desire, is *saṁsāra* (XVIII, 57). The traditional goals and duties in the Indian scheme of life (*Puruṣārtha*) are rejected by him (X, 17, XVII, 6). Like the words, actions are creations of the mind that come and go, interact with one another and vanish in the undivided and untainted Self, all according to nature (II, 23-25), XV, 7-9, 11). The Self is by nature silent, pure and transcendent and into it worldly relations, actions and experiences merge as into the whole and perfect when ignorance is overcome and the fruits of actions worked out in the succession of births.

Thus alone can man rise beyond his ephemeral egoistic sense of pleasure or pain, good or evil, duty or non-compliance in order to attain his completion and fullness (*pūrṇatva*) and attune his life to eternity and cosmos. A philosophy of *summum* and eternity beyond the limits of space and time rejects human ethics and social adjustment as the ultimate goal. There is neither a here nor there (*deśa*) nor a limited present past and future (*kāla*) in the transcendental wisdom of Aṣṭāvakra (XIX, 3) Accordingly a philosophy of morality and social conduct remains secondary to the primary philosophy of the absolute Self. Man's earthly relations and obligations, like life and death, space, time and eternity, belong to the phenomenal sphere (XIX, 7). And so do the notions of duty and non-compliance, good and evil, and expectation, fear and anxiety (XIX, 4). The deep-ocean stillness of the pure, stainless Self must not be stirred by the breeze of the phenomenal mind, and its ends—*dharma*, *artha*, *kāma* and *mokṣa*—hopes and wishes, duties and achievements all deluding, illusionary experiences.

The *Bhagavadgītā's* grand reconciliation between *jñāna-yoga* and *karma-yoga* through the dedication of all goals and activities of life to the Divine and through the assimilation of activity into *samādhi* in the highest wisdom or *Brahmattva* does not interest Aṣṭāvakra. He is too absorbed in the absolute aloneness and impersonality of the non-dual Self. Any worldly relations and experiences bring the Self from the realm of fullness (*pūrṇattva*) and transcendence (*paramārtha*) to the realm of natural attributes (*guṇas*) and relativity (*vyavahāra*). Yet Aṣṭāvakra's *ātmādvaita* leads man not to negativism and nihilism but to cosmic unity and responsibility.

Ethics beyond Good and Evil

Aṣṭāvakra grounds a transcendent, cosmic ethics, beyond good and evil, beyond duties and goals of life in the firm foundation of ontology (XVI I, 57, 90, XVII,6). In the very first verse of the text he commends the cultivation of such moral virtues as forgiveness, straightforwardness, compassion, contentment and truthfulness (I,2). With him self-abidance means a complete equal-mindedness (*samadarśana* in happiness and misery, prosperity and misfortune, honour and dishonour. Neither harm nor compassion, neither arrogance nor abasement, neither agitation nor wonder, arise in the heart of the wise one in his worldly relations (XVII, 11-16, XVIII, 24). His perfect even-mindedness (*samatā*) is stressed by Aṣṭāvakra through quoting the *Bhagavadgītā's* famous phrase, "to him a clod of earth, a precious stone or a piece of gold is the same" (XVIII, 65, 88). In Aṣṭāvakra's ethics the wise man is purged of the attributes of the *rajas* and *tamas* as in the *Bhagavadgītā* (XVIII, 88). Thus is he disciplined for complete self-knowledge and more enduring self-abidance. H's vision of himself in all creatures and of all creatures in himself becomes so pervasive that he is altogether freed from the sense of right and wrong, good and evil (XVIII, 91). For the same Self abides in all and under all conditions. Accordingly, free from ego-sense he cannot do any wrong (XVIII, 29). In fact even though his activity is inactivity, due to the absence of ego-sense and of desire and taint of attachment and imuprity, it becomes conducive to the happiness and welfare of mankind. As the liberated one becomes '*anara*', reaches beyond humanness to the inexpressible or *alakṣya* (XVIII, 70) and the absolute or *nirañjana* (XX, 1) his action, impregnated with absolute intelligence, becomes participation in the absolute blissful and good or auspicious (*Śiva*), even without his wish. "His nature becomes eternal, immutable, undefinable, unlimited, impersonal and beyond-natural". "He becomes absolute bliss and good ness (*Śivam*) and free from any human taint and limitations" (XX, 1, 5, 12, 1ǐ).

There is moral grandeur behind Aṣṭāvakra's ideal of the true knowledge and emancipation of the Self, rooted in complete indifference (*nirveda*) towards worldy concerns and experiences, and even towards the *summum bonum* of life or *puruṣārtha* (XX, 13). The touch of pessimism, due to the emphasis of the toil and moil, transience and sorrow of worldly life and experiences (X, 6-8) and the relegation of human ethics to an inferior and secondary place are overshadowed by the certitude as regards the infiniteness and immutability of the absolute Self in man, and the optimistic faith and confidence in the realization of this as his natural cosmic commitment (*svabhāva*) and status (*svamahiman*). Fearlessness or *abhayam*, rapture or *paramānandam* and serenity or *śāntam* in the face of misfortune, sorrow and death constitute the very core of self-realization—*ātmānubhava* or *sākṣātkāra*. These overcome the vast human undercurrents of insecurity, frustration and anguish and keep alive a universal spiritual urge and appreciation of the condition of liberation in life or *jīvanmukti* as the supremely blessed state—the crown and destiny of man and life and of cosmos itself. To the *jīvanmukta* there are no worlds, no life and death, no space, time or eternity, no gross nor subtle experience (XIX, 6, 7). All these melt away in the all-pervading, effulgent unity of his *vijñāna-svarūpa*.

The Spiritual Dialectic of Aṣṭāvakra

Aṣṭāvakra and the seer of the *Bhagavadgītā* equally lean on both self-knowledge and direct, mystical intuition (*vijñāna*) for the system of morality in the cosmic setting and use the procedure of the dialectic. In both the dialectic is reinforced by mvstical experience which yields the joy and certitude in respect of the supreme Self, *Īśvara* or Brahman. One may, using the categories of the *Taittirīya Upaniṣad*, say that while the *Bagavadgītā* deals with the spiritual movement in all the dimensions or stages of matter (*anna*), life (*prāṇa*), mind (*manas*), pure intelligence (*vijñāna*) and bliss (*ānanda*), Aṣṭāvakra deals only with the dimensions of pure intelligence (*vijñāna*) and bliss (*ānanda*). In Aṣṭāvakra the Self is ever at the stage of suprarational *vijñāna* or *ānanda* beyond the realm of matter, life and mind and of the dialectic, whether empirical or logical. The *Taittirīya Upaniṣad* says, "Truly the final essence of the Self is the rapture ; for whoever gets this rapture becomes blissful. For who could live, who could breathe if this space (*ākāśa*) was not bliss. This, verily, it is that bestows bliss. For whoever in that invisible, bodiless, unutterable, supportless, finds fearless support, he really becomes fearless. But whoever finds even a slight difference between himself and this Ātman, there is fear for him". (II, 7).

The dialectical opposites of freedom and bondage, life and duty, good and evil, *dhyāna* and self-realisation, the status of *jīva* and *Īśvara*, all belong to the lower dimensions of the mind that can only be encompassed and absorbed by the pure, indivisible, rapturous self. Only transcendence of the absolute-self can rend asunder the familiar cobwebs of thought, meaning and word. All names and appearances are false and ephemeral. "That which has form is unreal, the formless alone is permanent and real" (I, 18). The formless and the nameless Self, unborn and ever free, is the ultimate reality. How similar is this to Lao Tze's assertion : "The reality of the formless, the unreality of that which has form—is known to all". "Verily this is your bondage that you practise *samādhi*" (I, 15). For does not *samādhi* bring back the mind to relativist forms and modes of experience ? Thus freedom is natural and spontaneous—man habitually abiding in the real Self under all conditions and circumstances of life. The summit of moral and spiritual development is measured in India by the ease and naturalness of man's identification with the perfect, the whole and the transcendent. He should realize the real Self by his inherent trend and disposition (*svabhāva*). "Blessed is he who is established in the Self (*svasthaḥ*) by his very nature (XI, 8). To Aṣṭāvakra *svabhāva* (man's nature), *svamahimā* (man's majesty) and *svāsthya* (man's self-abidance) are identical. But such identification is possible only through surmounting values and experiences revealed in certain paradoxes. It is these paradoxical statements which can bring home the hard truth that all definitions and denials are creations of thought involving mind, life and body, and that the Self is beyond the range of form of thought.

The Great Paradoxes of Aṣṭāvakra

Nowhere in any Indian scripture or contemplative text do we find such a string of paradoxes leading up to the relationlessness of the absolute Self, which is undivided and unthinkable, and from which speech and mind come back baffled in their functions. Man taints and screens the pure Self not merely through his desire and attcahment, but also through his goals, ends and duties of life, through his yoga contemplation and experinece and through his metaphysical definitions and conceptualizations. Aṣṭāvakra is profound in his movement away from analytical and discursive reasoning (*vimarśa*) about the ultimate reality and his stress of supra-rational intuition grounded in the dialectical meditation of opposite categories. "The paradox is the highest", says a modern European philosopher. Aṣṭāvakra in his final chapters directs us to the highest through the process of rising above affirmation or denial, definition or negation. In Indian logic *apoha* ('*apohana*' of the *Bhagavadgītā* XV, 15) is negative reasoning. *Ūhāpoha* is the dialectical procedure of reasoning through the formulation of contradictory principles for complete discussion of a philosophical issue according to the Indian logical tradition. Accordingly, all opposite or antinomic categories are mentioned by Aṣṭāvakra as surpassed by the Self which overreaches any postulation and conceptulization. The Self is beyond the opposition of subject (*jīva* and object (Brahman) that are usually posited. Postulating Brahman involves the postulation of *jīva* ; postulating liberation or bliss involves the postulation of bondage or misery. Similarly conceiving non-duality involves the conception of duality ; conceiving non-existence involves the conception of existence. Delusion, action and the cycle of birth and death re-establish themselves with the unending chain of contradicting pairs of opposites rooted in the limiting, differentiating and mutually contending modalities of nature or guṇas in the phenomenal sphere. The *Bhagavadgītā* says, "All beings are born deluded, O Arjuna, overcome by the pairs of opposites which arise from wish and aversion" (VII, 27). Aṣṭāvakra insists that for self-knowledge, freedom from the dualities of philosophical notions is as important as the liberation from the empirical oppostsions of happiness and misery, good and evil, existence and non-existence, birth and death. As long as man's mind contains differentiating and restrictive notions, feelings and experiences, woven of the display and interplay of the *guṇas*, he cannot apprehend the reality of the Self as the pure, non-dual absolute. It is only through the devastating force of the paradox that the logic of the ensnaring web of the speculative mind can be successfully combatted. In the transcendent state the differentiations and polarities that are familiar to thought and subjective human experience are united and infinitely surpassed. Only the shattering logic of the paradox, coupled with mystical illumination, can finally overcome the basetting passion of differentiation of metaphysics. All duality is misery, and self-abidance consists in the realization that the various pairs of opposites, whether empirical or abstract, are illusory entangling beings in the net of *māyā* (II, 16, XVIII, 87). The Self devoid of the fallacious appearance of duality for ever remains absolutely alone, unconditioned and unthinkable. That the Supreme is "above existence and non-existence beginning and end" is mentioned by the *Śvetāśvatara Upaniṣad* (IV, 8) and by the *Bhagavadgītā* (XIII, 12) and as "neither gross nor fine, neither short nor long, without shadow or darkness, without mind, without radiance, without within or without" by the *Bṛhadāraṇyaka Upaniṣad* (III, 8, 8).

The transcendence of the absolute Self (*niṣprapañca*), beyond any empirical determinations (*nirvimarśa*), is elaborately expounded by Aṣṭāvakra through the method of dialectic in XIX and XX. This culminates in the remarkable statement, "What is the knower, the means of knowledge, the object of knowledge and knowledge itself, what is something existent or nothing existent, to me the stainless Self" ? (XX, 8).

The true Self gives up action (XX, 9) particularization (XX, 13) and natural attributes (XX, 5) in order to ascend from relativity (*vyavahāra*) to transcendence (*paramārtha*), from change to immutability (*kūṭastha*), from attachment to aloneness (*kaivalya*) and from division to absolute unity (*nirvibhāga*). The Self is the sovereign unity of existence and is accessible only to supra-rational intuition or *anubhāva.* This rises above the metaphysical dialectic of all possible affirmations or negations of form, appearance and thought, Ultimately the empirical oppositions of both existence and non-existence, unity and duality are also denied and surpassed (XX, 14). Such kind of dialectic one rarely encounters outside the *Aṣṭāvakragītā.*

In the realm of philosophy one is the purveyor of error as long as he accepts any distinctions and rejections. Antinomies or opposites, including relativism and absolutism, duality and non-duality, perpetrate violence against the comprehensive and all-pervasive truth of the Self. By and large philosophy mutilates and attenuates the revealed reality and along with it the real Self. The overwhelming, iconoclastic, '*Sarvam Ātmā*' or 'All is Self' of Aṣṭāvakra that irrevocably discards the cult, the gods, the *dharma*, the way and the *samādhi* of orthodox Brahmanism and rejects even its four-fold goals of life, including liberation, is a call to the Self to rise beyond the Beyond. The *jīvanmukta* (XVIII 13) undertakes in life this colossal redemptive task of liberation (*mokṣa*) with full alertness and invincible 'courage to be'.

The Sovereign Unity of Self in Mystical Ontology

It is clear that spiritual experiences in the *Aṣṭāvakragītā,* rising to profound raptures of vision and insight (*ātmānubhava-ullāsa*) terminate in a pure and sovereign unity of the self which dissolves all dualities, contradictions between the knower, knowledge and the knowing. The Self, the unborn and subsistent simplicity, is its own object in a spiritual intuition which is its very essence, and projects itself by its own nature into the mind and the objective or phenomenal world. The Self is both one and many, the eternal unborn as well as the ever-changing universe—both the unknown tranquil abyss of the ocean and its visible changeful, jostling, playful waves (II, 25). Hardly does any contemplative classic in the world invest the Self of man with such fathomless worth and majesty, rooted in its identity with the absolute and the supreme. Aṣṭāvakra is the beacon-light to mankind's quest and appreciation of Being on the cosmic scale.

In the world of the future, there can be only one religion and that will be an ontological religion. The *Aṣṭāvakragītā* that profoundly and uniquely mingles the spirit of religion with ontology in a most courageous, sincere and appealing manner cannot be ignored. World religion will certainly be enriched by the view of Aṣṭāvakra on the Self or Being on which modern Existentialist philosophy dwells so much, delinking, however, the self or Being from transcendence, and identifying Being and non-Being at the biopsychological dimension. This has seriously aggravated the Western man's loneliness, anguish and despair. To Aṣṭāvakra, the Self is however nothing but transcendence, beyond good and evil, existence and non-existence, knowledge and knowing, unity and duality, form and thought.

It is in the great paradoxes of Aṣṭāvakra that the principal *Upaniṣads* are to some extent harmoniously reconciled and integrated as in the teaching of the *Bhagavadgītā*. Aṣṭāvakra achieves this task, as we have explained, mainly through his central mystical doctrine of the uncreated, all-pervading, formless Self, the ultimate reality. Man's unborn and eternal Self is Brahman or That about which the ancient *Upaniṣads* said '*tat tvaṁ asi*' or thou art Brahman (XV, 7). The sage asserts, Thou art the unborn and the universal Self—the pure intelligence (*cinmātra*) in which the universe exists. To reveal and illumine is thy very nature. Thou art nothing but this. As the universe manifests itself, it is Thou alone who shinest (II, 2).

But truly the universe is mere form, appearance and name, belonging to one's subjective experience. Likewise the mind is form, appearance and name. The Self transcends all pairs of dialectical opposites (*saṁkalpa-vikalpa*), products of the mental process. It is beyond the range of form, name and thought. Lao Tze remarks "The Tao which can be named is not the true Tao". To Aṣṭāvakra, the Self is similarly beyond naming, definition or any other activity of the mind. It is non-definable, non-differentiated and devoid of the attributes of human nature (*nissvabhāva*). It is through silencing altogether contemplation, thought and reasoning i. e. through mystical intuition or *anubhāva* that the Self which is of the nature of pure intelligence (*cinmātra rūpa*) can be revealed. We may recall Patañjali's dictum:"All is through intuitive illumination" (*pratibhād vā sarvam*). The abandonment of reasoning, thought or contemplation, therefore, is again stressed by Aṣṭāvakra as the only way of achieving self-abidance —the aloneness and absoluteness of the Self (X, 5, XIII, 7, XV, 15, 20, XVIII, 16-17) The true mystic, with its consciousness fully vacated, then neither encounters *samādhi*, nor distraction nor oblivion, nor defilement of the luminous Self (XVII, 18, XVIII, 18). Supreme and ineffable bliss, beauty, love and peace convince him of the primordial unity and absoluteness of the Self with which no other spiritual value can compete.

Self-Abidance and Worldly Experience

Aṣṭāvakra's ontological mysticism insists that man and universe must be utterly restored to the undivided, uncreated absolute Self, must in some sense be the Self. This alone can lead to the transcendence of all opposites or contradictions that condition and limit creatures. The sage reduces not only religion and philosophy to ontology, but also yoga and meditation to silence before the ineffable mystery of the Self. At the same time the aloneness and absoluteness of the Self become quite compatible with the human predicament in his ideal of *jīvanmukti*, saturated as it is with the profound serenity, bliss and marvel of the Self. What the *Kaṭhopaniṣad* (II, 7) and the *Bhagavadgītā* (II, 29) mention about the wonder (*āścarya*) of the Ātman becomes, accordingly, the dominant note of the *Aṣṭāvakragītā*. (II, 11-14, 25, XVIII, 17, 93). The supreme marvel of man's self-abidance (*svāsthya*) and self-majesty (*svamahiman*) has never been revealed in any other contemplative classic so richly, so profoundly and yet so poetically. At every step the glory and blessedness of the one liberated in living who excels in complete fearlessness (*abhaya*), ineffable spiritual joy (*ānanda*), immutable peace (*śānti*) and perfect evenness (*samatā*) do not nullify but transmute the human contingency and bondage.

It is the mystical transcendence of the *jīvanmukta* which, indeed, makes the bondage of *saṁsāra* a step towards the accrual of the supreme wisdom of the Self through intellectual understanding and meditation and through the emotional experience of profound delight in the Self (*ātmārāma*) leading to spontaneous detachment and obliteration of the world (*sarvavismaraṇa*, XVI). These achieve the effortless surpassing of the duality of attraction (*pravṛtti*) and aversion (*nivṛtti*), pleasure and pain, good and evil, desire and renunciation, from which all misery in this world springs. It is accordingly not by replacting the society by the wilderness (XVIII, 100) and life by asceticism of the loin-cloth (XIII 1), but by transcendence of all dualities of life and the feeling of evenness, equipoise and sameness (*samatā*, V, 4, XVIII, 65,82,88,98,100) under all human conditions and circumstances that Aṣṭāvakra's supreme goal is attained—the oneness of self-disposition and feeling (*svabhāva*), self-abidance (*svāsthya*) and self-majesty (*svamahiman*).

It is obvious that such a goal combines complete indifference (*nirveda*), detachment (*nirlepa*), dispassion (*vairāgya*) and *naiṣkarmyasiddhi*, stressed by the *Bhagavadgītā* (which our author extols) with unswerving devotion to the absolute Self or Parmātman (instead to the personal God—Kṛṣṇa of the *Bhagavadgītā*) and a new feeling of wonderment at the inexpressible glory and blessedness of the Self. Unalloyed reverence (*śraddhā*) for the absolute Self or *cidrūpa* is of the character of supreme knowledge. This is *Aṣṭāvakra's* unique and profound synthesis (*samanvaya*) following Bādarāyaṇa's principle.

The Miracle of Integral Mysticism

To the *jīvanmukta* who overcomes the dualism of all pairs of opposites through his intuitive knowledge of the absolute and transcendent Self encompassing the universe, and his deep emotional experience of completeness, marvel, bliss and beauty of the Self, the differences between creature and God, unity and duality, liberation and bondage are no longer valid. Liberation-in-life to Aṣṭāvakra is nothing more and nothing less than the life of integral, mystical vision of, and abidance in, the absolute aloneness of the Self and of perennial mystical feeling of wonder that make indifference and detachment effortless and spontaneous and completely annul the binding character of contingency, bondage and activity in the world.

There is, accordingly, no conflict between *bandha* and *mokṣa*, *saṁsāra* and salvation, identity and duality. This is time and again stressed by Aṣṭāvakra. The whole being, life and phenomenal world are so metamorphosed that it is freedom when "one does whatever comes to be done, whether good or evil", and it is bondage when one undertakes yogic exercise, prays and practises *samādhi* (I, 15, XII, 1, 7, XV, 20). In the enjoyment of the goods of life, in the undertaking of the duties of the world or in the practice of *samādhi* his mind remains fixed on the serene, beautiful, blissful, wonderous Self beyond all opposites and relativities (XVI,2). That is freedom (*svātantrya*). Life and death, the world and worldly relations, *samādhi* and annihilation of consciousness, all merge in self-effulgence and self-grandeur (XIX, 7).

The mysticism of the Self here achieves the miracle of blunting the edge of both attachment and detachment, freedom and bondage, life and death, absoluteness and relativity and of transforming the finite and miserable status of man into one of immortality, perennial joy and wonder in our contingent world.

More than the *Upaniṣads*, the *Aṣṭāvakragītā* achieves a magnificent integration of the unity and all-pervasiveness of the Self or metaphysical *ātmādvaita* with the world of experience. How, and to whom one may describe the state of the *jīvanmukta*? Aṣṭāvakra asks (XVIII, 93). He is simply blessed, his life and mind perennially filled with nectar (*amṛta*). What the *Bhagavadgītā* achieves through a superb reconciliation of *Upaniṣadic* metaphysical monism with ardent theism, Aṣṭāvakra does through an all-sufficient, thoroughgoing ontological mysticism that even rejects the most elevated yoga-practice and *samādhi* as involving ego-sense, intention and effort. The *Bhagavadgītā's* synthesis could not do away with the toil and moil (*abhyāsa*) of *dhyāna-yoga*. To Aṣṭāvakra the latter is either harmful or irrelevant for the *jīvanmukta*, easily and spontaneously steeped in the aloneness and profound delight and natural marvel of the Self. This has its perennial lesson for Indian thought; while for the modern West, in contrast particularly with the Existentialist philosophers, Aṣṭāvakra fruitfully assimilates metaphysics into religion and the aesthetic-intuitional experience of mysticism into ontology. The *Aṣṭāvakragītā* has a most important significance for the contemporary metaphysical and spiritual crisis in both East and West.

Chapter I

AṢṬĀVAKRA'S VISION OF THE SELF AS THE ALL-PERVADING WITNESS

The preliminary chapter twice (I, 7,15) repeats the pregnant phrase : "This, indeed, is your bondage"—the mind's identification of itself with the body and its pleasures and pains, with the duties and goals of life, with good and evil, even with the practices of yoga and *samādhi*. The pure, effulgent Self is the unattached, serene, omniscient seer and witness of all—both the happenings of the external world and the phenomena of the mind. It is the one supreme and eternal God, Brahman or the ultimate reality (I,12,16,20). The visible, impermanent world exists in the formless, immutable Self.

The unlimited existence, intelligence and bliss of the Self as well as its indivisibilty should be realized through meditation (I,13). The illusion that, 'I am the reflected self, finite and empirical' should be given up (I,13).

Through this illusion, the non-dual, free, all-pervading Self, which bears and transcends the body, mind and the world, appears as if of the changeful world and becomes completely bound to and absorbed by the latter. Thus man suffers endless misery in the world, the figment of his own imagination.

The true knowledge of the Self should root itself in the combination of reason with vision based on supra-rational intuition or *annbhava* (I,16).

जनक उवाच

कथं ज्ञानमवाप्नोति कथं मुक्तिर्भविष्यति ।
वैराग्यं च कथं प्राप्तमेतद्ब्रूहि मम प्रभो ॥१॥

Janaka uvāca

Kathaṁ jñānamavāpnoti kathaṁ muktirbhaviṣyati l
vairāgyaṁ ca kathaṁ prāptametad brūhi mama prabho ll

1. Janaka said :

O, Lord, teach me how man attains wisdom, how salvation comes and renunciation is achieved.

अष्टावक्र उवाच

मुक्तिमिच्छसि चेत्तात विषयान् विषवत्त्यज ।
क्षमार्जवदयातोषसत्यं पीयूषवद्भज ॥२॥

Aṣṭāvakra uvāca

Muktimicchasi cettāta viṣayān viṣavattyaja l
Kṣamārjavadayātoṣasatyaṁ pīyūṣavadbhaja ll

2. Aṣṭāvakra said

O child, if you desire salvation, avoid the objects of the senses as poison and seek forgiveness, straightforwardness, compassion, contentment, truthfulness, and nectar.

Moral discipline is an essential pre-requisite for the spiritual quest. The list of virtues mentioned here closely follows the *Bhagavadgītā* where forgiveness (X, 4,34, XVI, 3), straightforwardness (XIII, 7, XVI, 1, XVII, 14, XVIII, 42), compassion (XVI, 2) and contentment (III, 17; 5, XII, 14,19) are specially stressed. This is however the only verse where Aṣṭāvakra dwells on moral excellences.

Aṣṭāvakra's general position is that the wise one, firmly established in the Self, is beyond the conflicts of good and evil. Pure in heart and purged of all desires and goals of life as well as of the modalities of nature (*guṇas*), whence emerges the irrepressible duality of opposites in life, he sees himself everywhere and under all conditions. Any desire to harm or any compassion does not arise in his heart at all (XVII, 11-15). To him a clod of earth, a stone and a piece of gold are the same. The knots of his heart are rent asunder and he is freed from the sway of the *guṇas* (XVIII, 88). Guileless and straightforward, there is no wantonness or inhibition in him (XVIII, 92). Abiding in the aloneness and absoluteness of the self, he is beyond humanness (*anara* XVII, 16). In fact he cannot do any wrong since he is entirely free from ego-sense, both physically and mentally

(XVIII, 29). The moral sense belongs to the realm of relativity which the wise one has to transcend (XVIII, 57).

न पृथिवी न जलं नाग्निर्न वायुर्द्यौर्न वा भवान् ।
एषां साक्षिणमात्मानं चिद्रूपं विद्धि मुक्तये ॥३॥

Na pṛthvī na jalaṁ nāgnirna vāyurdyaurna vā bhavān 1
Eṣāṁ sākṣiṇamātmānaṁ cidrūpaṁ viddhi muktaye 11

3. You are neither earth nor water nor fire nor wind nor sky. For the sake of freedom know the Self as the embodiment of pure consciousness and the witness of all these.

This is reminiscent of the *Kaivalya Upaniṣad.* "I do not have earth, water, fire, air, ether. Knowing the nature of the supreme Self, dwelling within the heart, stainless without a second; the witness of all, devoid of the duality of existence and non-existence, he achieves the pure nature of the supreme Self" (23).

यदि देहं पृथक्कृत्य चिति विश्राम्य तिष्ठसि ।
अधुनैव सुखी शान्तो बन्धमुक्तो भविष्यसि ॥४॥

Yadi dehaṁ pṛthakkṛtya citi viśrāmya tiṣṭhasi 1
Adhunaiva sukhī śānto bandhamukto bhaviṣyasi 11

4. If you differentiate yourself from the body and abide in rest in pure intelligence, then (in this existence) you will become happy, serene and free from bondage.

The state of deliverance while living (*jīvanmukti*) is indicated here. See also XVII, 7-20, XVIII, 13-26.

न त्वं विप्रादिको वर्णो नाश्रमी नाक्षगोचरः ।
असङ्गोऽसि निराकारो विश्वसाक्षी सुखी भव ॥५॥

Na tvaṁ viprādiko varṇo nāśramī nākṣagocaraḥ 1
Asaṅgo'si nirākāro viśvasākṣī sukhī bhava 11

5. You are neither a *varṇa*, such as the Brāhmaṇa, nor do you belong to an *āśrama*, nor are you perceived by the

senses. You are non-dual, formless and witness of the universe (Thus contemplating, be happy.

Non-dual. The term '*asaṅga*' is used in the *Gītā* (XV,3).

Witness of the universe. That the Self, God or Brahman is the all-encompassing witness or disinterested on-looker of the phenomenal world, is mentioned in the *Śvetāśvatara Upaniṣad* (VI, 11), the *Maitrī Upaniṣad* (VI,60) and the *Kaivalya Upaniṣad* (18). The Supreme Self is the witness of all in the *Kaivalya Upaniṣad*, 23. *Viśva-sākṣī* and *samasta-sākṣī* are elegant cognate terms for pure unconditioned intelligence *sat*, the non-dual *cit* and *ānanda*, God or Brahman in which the phenomenal world rises and vanishes as a false appearance. As many as five times the terms *sākṣī* and *draṣṭā* are used in this chapter for signifying the eternal and universal witness or seer and universal consciousness itself (I, 3, 5, 7, 12). *Sākṣī puruṣa* occurs also in XIV, 3 where it is juxtaposed with God and *Paramātman* and in XV, 4 where the Self is differentiated from the body and the owner of the body agent or enjoyer. The *Bhagavadgītā* uses the term witness for God only once (IX, 18). The *Sarvasāra Upaniṣad* best explains the concept of *sarva-sākṣī* or *viśva-sākṣī* thus: "He is called the witness of all for he is himself the witness of the rise and disappearance of the knower, the knowing and the knowledge. He is the witness because he is free himself from rise and disappearance and shines by himself" (I).

धर्माधर्मौ सुखं दुःखं मानसानि न ते विभो ।
न कर्त्तासि न भोक्तासि मुक्त एवासि सर्वदा ॥६॥

Dharmādharmau sukhaṁ duḥkhaṁ mānasāni na te vibho I
Na kartāsi na bhoktāsi mukta evāsi sarvadā II

6. Oh all-pervasive one, virtue and sin, happiness and sorrow are attributes of the mind, not of yourself. You are neither the doer, nor the enjoyer. Surely you are ever free.

Man's identification of himself with the mind (*manas*) is the basic spring of the relativities of pleasure and pain, right and wrong that enmesh him in the world.

एको द्रष्टासि सर्वस्य मुक्तप्रायोऽसि सर्वदा ।
अयमेव हि ते बन्धो द्रष्टारं पश्यसीतरम् ॥७॥

Eko draṣṭāsi sarvasya muktaprāyo'si sarvadā l
ayameva hi te bandho draṣṭāraṁ paśyasītaraṁ ll

7. You are the one seer of all and surely ever free. This is indeed your bondage that you apprehend the (non-dual, eternal) seer differently.

Seer. The supreme self is mentioned as the seer in the *Bṛhadāraṇyaka Upaniṣad* (III, 7,23), the *Praśna Upaniṣad* (IV, 9) and the *Bhagavadgitā* (XIII, 22, XIV, 19). The Self is the one, detached eternal and omniscient subject or knower of the phenomenal world which is the object. None knows the Self which is always pure consciousness (*cit*) (*Kaivalya Upaniṣad* 2). In the *Praśna Upaniṣad,* the Self is mentioned as transcending all duality, even the distinction of subject and object. This is the metaphysical principle of unity or *advaita* which is basic in Indian philosophical speculation. Man must realize that he is the only seer (*draṣṭā*) or subject, the entire perceptible universe (*dṛśya*) being the object. The *Yoga-Vāsiṣṭha-Rāmāyaṇa,* which is a veritable encyclopaedia of the philosophy of *Advaita* (dated about 700-800 A.D.), stresses that all bondage is due to the existence of the universe (*dṛśya*) due to the imagination of mind like dream-land or fairy-land. Śaṅkara observes, "Man deluded by *māyā* looks on the universe, while awake or asleep, as composed of manifold entities, joined in relation to each other as cause and effect, owner and owned, teacher and pupil, father and son. My obeisance to Dakṣināmūrti in the form of my teacher who incarnates this truth" (VIII).

अहं कर्त्तेत्यहंमानमहाकृष्णाहिदंशितः ॥
नाहं कर्त्तेति विश्वासामृतं पीत्वा सुखी भव ॥८॥

Ahaṁ kartetyahaṁmānamahākṛṣṇāhidaṁśitaḥ l
Nāhaṁ karteti viśvāsāmṛtaṁ pītvā sukhī bhava ll

8. 'That I am the doer', this egoism bites one like a

big black snake. 'That I am non-doer', drink this faith like nectar and be happy.

एको विशुद्धबुद्धोऽहमिति निश्चयवह्निना ।
प्रज्वाल्याज्ञानगहनं वीतशोकः सुखी भव ॥९॥

Eko viśuddhabuddho'hamiti niścayavahninā I
Prajvālyājñānagahanaṁ vītaśokaḥ sukhī bhava II

9. Burn the forest of ignorance with the fire of certitude that 'I am the non-dual and pure consciousness'; abandoning sorrow, be blissful.

यत्र विश्वमिदं भाति कल्पितं रज्जुसर्पवत् ।
आनन्दपरमानन्दः स बोधस्त्वं सुखं चर ॥१०॥

Yatra viśvamidaṁ bhāti kalpitaṁ rajjusarpavat I
Ānandaparamānandaḥ sa bodhastvaṁ sukhaṁ cara II

10. In that pure, supremely blissful consciousness the universe appears as illusory, like the snake apprehended as the rope. Live in that consciousness.

Supremely blissful i.e., beyond the happiness of the mundane world. The reference is to the *Upaniṣadic* concept of the supreme bliss whence everything is derived. The Self is at once pure existence (*sat*), intelligence (*cit*) and bliss (*ānanda*) according to *Advaita Vedānta.*

मुक्ताभिमानी मुक्तो हि बद्धो बद्धाभिमान्यपि ।
किंवदन्तीह सत्येयं या मतिः सा गतिर्भवेत् ॥११॥

Muktābkimāni mukto hi baddho baddhābhimānyapi I
Kiṁvadantīha satyeyaṁ yā matiḥ sā gatirhbavet II

11. One who fixes mind to freedom is free as one is bound who fixes his mind to bondage. There is the true popular saying, like intention, like becoming.

Popular Saying. The *Bhagavadgītā* says, "Whatever appearance a person thinks of at death when he leaves the body that he reaches, whose desires conform to that particular embodiment" (VIII 6). The *Dhammapada* also observes, "All that we are is the result of what we have thought".

आत्मा साक्षी विभुः पूर्ण एको मुक्तश्चिदक्रियः ।
असङ्गो निःस्पृहः शान्तो भ्रमात्संसारवानिव ॥१२॥

Atmā sākṣī vibhuḥ pūrṇa eko muktaścidakriyaḥ 1
Asaṅgo nispṛhaḥ śānto bhramāt saṁsāravāniva 11

12. The Self is witness, all-pervasive, perfect, non-dual, free, intelligent, action-less, desire-less, unattached and serene. It appears through illusion as if absorbed in the world.

This verse echoes IX, 18 of the *Bhagavadgītā* where the terms *prabhu* and *sākṣī* are also used.

The significant term *sākṣī* or witness occurs in the *Śvetāśvatāra Upaniṣad* (VI, 11), the *Maitrī Upaniṣad* (VI, 16), the *Kaivalya Upaniṣad* (18 and 23) and the *Bhagavadgītā* (IX, 18). *Vibhu* or all-pervading is found in the *Kaṭhopaniṣad* (II, 22), the *Śvetāśvatara Upaniṣad* (III, 21, IV, 4), the *Praśna Upaniṣad* (III, 12) and the *Bhagavadgītā* (V, 15 and X, 12). It denotes the immanence of the Self as stressed in III, 5, VI, 4 and XV, 6.

कूटस्थं बोधमद्वैतमात्मानं परिभावय ।
आभासोऽहं भ्रमं मुक्त्वा भावं बाह्यमथान्तरम् ॥१३॥

Kūṭasthaṁ bodhamadvaitamātmānaṁ paribhāvaya 1
ābhāso'haṁ bhramaṁ muktvā bhāvaṁ bāhyamathāntaram 11

13. Having abandoned the illusion of the reflected self and its internal and external fluctuations, meditate on the Self as immutable, non-dual, pure consciousness.

The *Upaniṣads* and the *Bhagavadgītā* emphasize the need of constant meditation on the Supreme Self unaffected by the changes of the phenomenal world.

This is the only verse in the entire text in which the seer commands meditation on the Self. Otherwise his consistently logical position is that *samādhi* or concentration, belonging as it does to the world of experience with its unquenchable duality of opposites, is a cause of bondage of the Self (I,7,15). The Self, according to him, should perennially abide in its own luminousness and bliss (*svāsthya*). Śaṅkara in his *Aparokṣānubhūti* remarks : "The wise one should constantly meditate with care (i.e. without any distraction) on the entire visible (phenomenal) and the transcendent world as embodying his own pure self-effulgent intelligence" (141).

Pure intelligence is the eternal witness or seer (I,3,7) of both the delusion (*bhrama*) of the phenomenal world and of the finite or reflected self (*ābhāsa*) and the fusion of the latter (i.e. the annihilation of the mind) into non-dual intelligence (*cidātman*). The phenomenal world becomes, then, the projection of the one, transcendent Self and the real and the unreal world coincide. "When the universe appears, it is I that verily shine" (II,8).

Immutable : The same word *kūṭastha* is used in the *Bhagavadgītā* (VI, 8, XII, 3, XV, 16). It means unchanging, adamantine as the mountain-top (kūṭa) or hidden in the mystery of māyā as its resting place (kūṭa = mystery). The same word is used in XX, 12. This embodies the *akṣara* aspect of Brahman or the Absolute in the *Upaniṣads*.

देहाभिमानपाशेन चिरं बद्धोऽसि पुत्रक ।
बोधोऽहं ज्ञानखड्गेन तन्निष्कृत्य सुखी भव ॥१४॥

Dehābhimānapāśena ciraṁ baddho'si putraka I
Bodho'haṁ jñānakhaḍgena tanniṣkṛtya sukhī bhava II

14. O child, you are ever bound by the fetters of the ego-sense. 'I am pure consciousness', with the axe of wisdom, rend asunder the fetters and become happy.

The Axe of Wisdom : Saṁsāra is the eternal process in changing states which is kept on going by the chain of *vāsanā-karma-trivarga*, desire-action-goals of life. To escape from the vicious cycle of bondage through successive births man must get rid of his ego-sense and attachment and realise his immutable, all-pervading Self that projects itself in the universe (I, 13). Such wisdom is the direct apprehension that "the Self abides in all existences and all existences abide in the

Self" (VII, 4). With this wisdom which is always there, the distinctions between bondage and salvation, end and means, knowledge and ignorance fade away, and the *Jīvanmukta* overcomes *saṁsāra* where his action no more binds and the duality of opposites no more clouds his pure intelligence—the witness of the phenomenal world and its continual becoming. The *śuddha jñāna* of Aṣṭāvakra corresponds to the *jñāna-vijñāna-sahitam* of the *Gītā* (VI,8) involving intuitive illumination which occurs as soon as ignorance is dispelled.

निःसंगो निष्क्रियोऽसि त्वं स्वप्रकाशो निरञ्जनः ।
अयमेव हि ते गन्धः समाधिमनुतिष्ठसि ॥१५॥

Niḥsaṅgo niṣkriyo'si tvaṁ svaprakāśo nirañjanaḥ l
Ayameva hi te bandhaḥ samādhimanutiṣṭhasi ll

15. You are non-dual, non-active and Self-effulgent. That you practise meditation, this, indeed, is your bondage.

The Supreme Silence of wisdom transcends any effort of thought or conceptualization. For one who has not obtained self-Knowledge, meditation, however, is essential (vide I, 13 above). That meditation belongs to the realm of relativity is stressed again in XII, 3.

त्वया व्याप्तमिदं विश्वं त्वयि प्रोतं यथार्थतः ।
शुद्धबुद्धस्वरूपस्त्वं मा गमः क्षुद्रचित्तताम् ॥१६॥

Tvayā vyāptamidaṁ viśvaṁ tvayi protaṁ yathārthataḥ l
Śuddhabuddhasvarūapastvaṁ mā gamaḥ kṣudracittatām ll

16. You encompass the universe as the universe enters into you. You are in reality the embodiment of pure consciousness. Do not give way to the pettiness of the (finite) mind.

This is the essence of Patañjali's *yoga*.

The first line of the verse echoes the *Bhagavadgītā's* well-known formulation: "All that exists is strung on Me (*protam*) as rows of gems on a string" (VII, 7). The term 'otam' is also used in the *Muṇḍaka Upaniṣad* : "He in whom the sky, the earth and the atmosphere are woven as also the mind, know him alone the one Self (II, 2, 5). The

Bṛhadāraṇyaka Upaniṣad also speaks of the Self as "that thread by which this world and the other world and all things are tied together" (II, 7. 1,).

निरपेक्षो निर्विकारो निर्भरः शीतलाशयः ।
अगाधबुद्धिरक्षुब्धो भव चिन्मात्रवासनः ॥१७॥

Nirapekṣo nirvikāro nirbharaḥ śītalāśayaḥ l
Agādhabuddhirakṣubdho bhava cinmātravāsanaḥ ll

17. Become unconditioned, changeless, dense, serene, profound in intellect, unperturbed, and absolutely fixed on pure consciousness.

Dense—i. e. compact embodiment of pure intelligence and bliss.

साकारमनृतं विद्धि निराकारं तु निश्चलम् ।
एतत्तत्वोपदेशेन न पुनर्भवसम्भवः ॥१८॥

Sākāramanṛtaṁ viddhi nirākāraṁ tu niścalam l
Etattattvopadeśena na punarbhavasambhavaḥ ll

18. All which have form are false. The formless (Self) is the changeless. Knowing this truth there is cessation of births (freedom).

यथैवादर्शमध्यस्थे रूपेऽन्तः परितस्तु सः ।
तथैवास्मिञ्छरीरेऽन्तः परितः परमेश्वरः ॥१९॥

Yathaivādarśamadhyasthe rūpe'ntaḥ paritastu saḥ l
Tathaivāsmin śarīre'ntaḥ paritaḥ parameśvaraḥ ll

19. Just as a reflection covers both the inside and outside of the mirror, so the Supreme Lord (the Supreme Self) encompasses both the interior or exterior of the body.

Supreme Lord: : The *Gītā* calls the Supreme Self the Lord (*Parmeśvara* or *Maheśvara*) in XIII, 22, 27, 31 and XV, 17. In XV, 8, Aṣṭāvakra uses the word '*Bhagavān*' linked with the Self as knowledge in its essence. This elegant metaphor indicates the all-encompassing nature of Ātman conceived as *Īśvara*.

एकं सर्वगतं व्योम बहिरन्तर्यथा घटे ।
नित्यं निरन्तरं ब्रह्म सर्वभूतगणे तथा ॥२०॥

Ekaṁ sarvagataṁ vyoma bahirantaryathā ghaṭe I
Nityaṁ nirantaraṁ brahma sarvabhūtagaṇe tathā II

20. As the same all-pervading sky enters into the jar, even so does the immutable and all-encompassing Brahman enter into all beings and things (existences).

Here the Supreme Self is identified with Brahman as it is identified with *Īśvara* in the preceding verse.

'*All-pervading*', *sarva-gatam*, is a familiar attribute of the Self, Brahman and Kṛṣṇa in the later *Upaniṣads* and the *Gītā*. The term occurs in the *Śvetāśvatara Upaniṣad* (III, 11 and III, 21) and in the *Bhgavadgītā* (II, 24, III, 15, XIII, 32).

The use of the terms *Parameśvara* in I, 18 and of Brahman in this verse is most significant as identifying Ātman with God or Brahman pervading all beings and things. The *Upaniṣads* reiterate that Ātman is Brahman, all-pervasive and all-penetrative. The *Śvetāśvatara Upaniṣad* says, '*sarvātmānam sarvagatam*' (III, 21) and the *Māṇḍūkya* also says, '*nityaṁ vibhuṁ sarvagatam*' (I, 1, 6). Both the transcendence and immanence of the Self, as of Brahman, are posited in the final verse.

CHAPTER II

JANAKA ON THE MARVEL OF THE INFINITE SELF BEYOND NATURE

The disciple's illumination immediately follows the supreme teaching in respect of the Self. The illusion of the distinction between knowledge, the knower and the knowable vanishes (II, 15). The fusion of this triad within the Self is the *sine qua non* of revelation of the infinite Self or Brahman that transcends Nature and all subjectivism. The Self is then cognised as pure and transcendent consciousness (*cinmātra*), from which emanate the universe, body and mind as waves from the ocean and as cloths from the thread (II, 4, 5, 22). The Self is the first cause. It is infinite, indivisible and supreme (*Paramātman*, II, 3). It is uncreated, neither coming from, nor going anywhere, and bears the universe for all eternity (II, 11).

Man's ignorance and attachment foster the sense of duality, the source of all misery and bondage (II, 16, 8, 20). The Self is neither the body, nor the *jīva* nor the *cit* (II, 10, 22). Its nature is pure, all-encompassing luminousness (*cit* or *bodhamātra*). The Self is all that exists. When the universe manifests itself, verily it is the Self which shines (II, 8). In the infinite ocean, the formless and tranquil Self, the wind of the finite mind generates the playful waves of manifold forms—the phenomena of the universe and empirical selves (*jīvas*). These all return to the ocean of the Self and vanish as illusion is overcome (II, 4, 23-25). The Self is simply marvellous (II, 11- 14, 25).

जनक उवाच

अहो निरञ्जनः शान्तो बोधोऽहं प्रकृतेः परः ।
एतावन्तमहं कालं मोहेनैव विडम्बितः ॥१॥

Janaka uvāca

Aho nirañjanaḥ śānto bodho'haṁ prakṛteḥ paraḥ I
Etāvantamahaṁ kālaṁ mohenaiva viḍambitaḥ II

Janaka said:

1. O, I am devoid of any signs, serene and pure consciousness and beyond nature. So far I have spent my days bewildered by delusion.

The disciple benefits immediately from the words of wisdom of the master and has immediate luminous experience of the Self.

Nature: The *Sāṁkhya* philosophy of the dualism of *Puruṣa* and *Prakṛti* is not acceptable to Aṣṭāvakra who holds that it is not *prakṛti* but the supreme non-dual Self which is the primal cause of the universe. The Self as pure consciousness, *cit* or *bodha* is beyond nature (see also xv, 8). The universe is produced from mere illusion, manifested through manifold names, forms and functions (XVIII, 69). The all-encompassing, indivisible Self, according to our sage, is all that exists. The relation of the modalities of nature or *guṇas* to *prakṛti* which is expounded in the *Gītā* is not developed by him at all. The pure Self transcends *prakṛti* and the phenomenal body, mind and guṇas that are all changeful and inconsequential in their nature.

So far i. e. up to the moment of obtaining wisdom from the master.

यथा प्रकाशयाम्येको देहमेनं तथा जगत् ।
अतो मम जगत्सर्वमथवा न च किञ्चन ॥२॥

Yathā prakāśayāmyeko dehamenaṁ tathā jagat I
Ato mama jagatsarvamathavā na ca kiñcana II

2. Just as I am non-dual and make manifest the world as well as the body, so this entire world is mine or indeed nothing is mine.

That the world is but the reflection of the Self is explained through a brilliant imagery by Śaṅkara. "The universe is like the image of a city reflected in the looking-glass. It emerges from the Self due to illusion. It resembles the external objects that one sees in a dream through the power of *māyā*. On the dawn of understanding one realizes that all that was seen is nothing but one's own indivisible Self.

Salutation to Śrī *Dakṣiṇāmūrti* in the form of my guru" (Hymn to Śrī *Dakṣiṇāmūrti*, I).

In Indian Vedāntic thought the universe is considered as the reflection seen in a mirror. It becomes manifest only because of pure consciousness (*cit*).

सशरीरमहो विश्वं परित्यज्य मयाऽऽधुना ।
कुतश्चित् कौशलादेव परमात्मा विलोक्यते ॥३॥

Saśarīramaho viśvaṁ parityajya mayādhunā I
Kutaścit kauśalādeva paramātmā vilokyate II

3. Now I have abandoned the world along with my body due to the wisdom of some teacher. I see only the Supreme Self.

Wisdom : That is to say, the suprarational knowledge or skill derived from the scriptures or the Guru. In the *Gītā*, *yoga* is considered as skill (*kauśalam*) in the way of Action (II, 50).

Abandoned: This is known in the Vedānta as the cessation of *adhyāsa* or imposition, and *adhyātma*-knowledge.

यथा न तोयतो भिन्नास्तरङ्गाः फेनबुद्बुदाः ।
आत्मनो न तथा भिन्नं विश्वमात्मविनिर्गतम् ॥४॥

Yathā na toyato bhinnāstaraṅgāḥ phenabudbudāḥ I
Ātmano na tathā bhinnaṁ viśvamātmavinirgatam II

4. Just as the waves and the bubbles of foam are not different from the water, even so the universe streaming out of the Self is not different from it.

The all-pervasiveness of the Self is here brought out.

तन्तुमात्रो भवेदेव पटो यद्वद्विचारतः ।
आत्मतन्मात्रमेवेदं तद्वद्विश्वं विचारितम् ॥५॥

Tantumātro bhavedeva paṭo yadvadvicāritaḥ I
Ātmatanmātramevedaṁ tadvadviśvaṁ vicāritam II

5. Just as the cloth when analysed becomes nothing but

thread, even so does the universe become to discriminative understanding nothing but the consciousness of Self.

That the Self is the prime cause of the world-process is here formulated together with its all-pervading nature. Śaṅkara says, "The Self as the cause virtually contains all the *states* belonging to its effects. It is indeed called by many different names, but it is one only. The Self is the *operative* cause because there is no other ruling principle, and the *material* cause because there is no other substance from which the world could originate" (Max Müller (Ed.), *The Sacred Books of the East*; XXXIV, p. 286).

यथैवेक्षुरसक्लृप्ता तेन व्याप्तैव शर्करा ।
तथा विश्वं मयि क्लृप्तं मया व्याप्तं निरन्तरम् ॥६॥

Yathaivekṣurase klṛptā tena vyāptaiva śarkarā I
Tathā viśvaṁ mayi klṛptaṁ mayā vyāptaṁ nirantaram II

6. Just as sugar produced in the juice of sugarcane pervades it, even so I encompass the universe produced in me, inside and outside.

The three verses give an exposition of the all-pervasiveness of Ātman divided into the three categories of indivisible existence, consciousness and bliss respectively. 'I am', and hence the world exists, shines with the illumination of my universal consciousness and is wholly enjoyable due to my blissful nature. The three-fold characterization of the Self and the world is different from the Cartesian affirmation, 'I am, hence the world exists'.

आत्माऽज्ञानाज्जगद्भाति आत्मज्ञानान्न भासते ।
रज्ज्वज्ञानादहिर्भाति तज्ज्ञानाद्भासते न हि ॥७॥

Ātmājñānājjagadbhāti ātmajñānānna bhāsate I
Rajjvajñānādahirbhāti tajjñānād bhāsate na hi II

7. The universe becomes manifest due to ignorance. With self-knowledge, it does not. Due to ignorance the snake (instead of the rope) becomes manifest; while with knowledge it disappears.

The contrast between the reality of the rope and the unreality of the snake is familiar in Vedāntic thought.

प्रकाशो मे निजं रूपं नातिरिक्तोऽस्म्यहं ततः ।
यदा प्रकाशते विश्वं तदाऽऽहं भास एव हि ॥८॥

Prakāśo me nijaṁ rūpaṁ nātirikto'smyahaṁ tataḥ l
Yadā prakāśate viśvaṁ tadāhambhāsa eva hi ll

8. To illumine is my own nature. I am not (manifest) otherwise. When this universe becomes manifest, verily it is I alone who shine.

The Upaniṣadic dictum is that Ātman alone is true and is all that exists, shines and rejoices (*sat, cit, ānanda*). The universe is nothing but the projection of the effulgent Self. The *jīvanmukta Gītā* says, "Just as the sun illumines the whole universe so also does Brahman who dwells in all beings as their selves. He who realizes this is called liberated in life" (IV).

अहो विकल्पितं विश्वमज्ञानान्मयि भासते ।
रूप्यं शुक्तौ फणी रज्जौ वारि सूर्यकरे यथा ॥९॥

Aho vikalpitaṁ viśvamajñānānmayi bhāsate l
Rūpyaṁ śuktau phaṇī rajjau vāri sūryyakare yathā ll

9. Even with the false appearance of the universe in imagination, it exists in me even as the silver does in the sea-shell, the snake in the rope and the water in the solar rays.

मत्तो विनिर्गतं विश्वं मय्येव लयमेष्यति ।
मृदि कुम्भो जले वीचिः कनके कटकं यथा ॥१०॥

Matto vinirgataṁ viśvaṁ mayyeva layameṣyati l
Mṛdi kumbho jale vīciḥ kanake kaṭakaṁ yathā ll

10. From me the universe has streamed forth and in me it will disappear, just as the water-pot dissolves into the earth, the wave into the water and the ornament into the gold.

Śaṅkara observes : "The Self is not to be known as manifold qualified by the universe of effects; you are rather to dissolve by true knowledge the universe of effects which is the mere product of nescience and to know that one Self, which is the general abode, as uniform" (Max Müller (Ed.), *The Sacred Books of the East*, XXXIV, p. 155).

अहो अहं नमो मह्यं विनाशो यस्य नास्ति मे ।
ब्रह्मादिस्तम्बपर्यन्तं जगन्नाशेऽपि तिष्ठतः ॥११॥

Aho ahaṁ namo mahyaṁ vināśo yasya nāsti me ।
Brahmādistambaparyantaṁ jagannāśe'pi tiṣṭhataḥ ॥

11. O marvellous am I. I adore myself as I exist even after the universe comprising everything from the Creator to the grass meets its end. I have no destruction.

The adoration of one's own Self in Similar vein, occurs in the *Varāha Upaniṣad* : "Adoration for you and for me who is infinite; for me and for you who is pure intelligence" (II, 33). It is found in the *Jīvanmukta Gītā*: "I salute the pure intelligence who is ever free and dwells in all beings. He is no other than my particular Self. I salute myself over and over again" (I). The *Yoga Vāsiṣṭha Rāmāyaṇa* repeats the verse of the *Varāha Upaniṣad.*

अहो अहं नमो मह्यमेकोऽहं देहवानपि ।
क्वचिन्न गन्ता नागन्ता व्याप्य विश्वमवस्थितः ॥१२॥

Aho ahaṁ namo mahyameko'haṁ dehavānapi ।
kvacinna gantā nāgantā vyāpya viśvamavasthitaḥ ॥

12. Oh, marvellous am I. I adore myself who though with a body am one. I have neither coming nor going anywhere (outside myself) and encompass the universe. *The Avadhūta Gītā* observes, "One which goes or returns cannot be taintless" (IV, 11).

अहो अहं नमो मह्यं दक्षो नास्तीह मत्समः ।
असंस्पृश्य शरीरेण येन विश्वं चिरं धृतम् ॥१३॥

Aho ahaṁ namo mahyaṁ dakṣo nāstīha matsamaḥ l
Asaṁspṛśya śarīreṇa yena viśvaṁ ciraṁ dhṛtam ll

13. Oh, marvellous am I. Adoration to myself. There is none more competent than myself. Unattached to the body, I hold the universe eternally.

अहो अहं नमो मह्यं यस्य मे नास्ति किञ्चन ।
अथवा यस्य मे सर्वं यद्वाङ्मनसगोचरम् ॥१४॥

Aho ahaṁ namo mahyaṁ yasya me nāstı kiñcana l
Athavā yasyame sarvaṁ yadvāṅmanasagocaram ll

14, Oh, marvellous am I. Adoration to myself. I have nothing in posssession, or the entire world accessible to speech and mind belongs to me.

Nothing—because due to non-dual knowledge every thing merges in the Self.

ज्ञानं ज्ञेयं तथा ज्ञाता त्रितयं नास्ति वा स्तवम् ।
अज्ञानाद्भाति यत्रेदं सोऽहमस्मि निरञ्जनः ॥१५॥

Jñānṁ jñeyaṁ tathā jñātā tritayaṁ nāsti vā stavam l
Ajñānādbhāti yatredaṁ so'hamasmi nirañjanaḥ ll

15. The triple categories of the knower, the knowledge, and the object of knowledge do not exist in reality. It is in myself without attributes where the triad becomes manifest due to ignorance.

The merger of the triple categories in meditation *tripuṭīkaraṇa* is the indispensable prelude to the highest samādhi. In the *Gītā* God is knowledge, the object of knowledge and the goal of knowledge (XIII, 17).

The *Kaivalya Upaniṣad* uses the triple basic aspects of consciousness in a larger context embracing all perception and enjoyment of sense-objects. "In the three states of consciousness whatever appears as the object of enjoyment, the enjoyer and the enjoyment, I am different from them, the witness (thereof), pure intelligence, the eternal, absolute good"

(18). In Śaṅkara's *Ātmabodha* or Self-knowledge we have a verse: "In the supreme Self due to its nature of exceeding, non-dual bliss, the distinction of the knower, knowledge and the object of knowledge vanishes. It alone shines" (41). Aṣṭāvakra refers in this verse to what is called *nirvikalpa* as contrasted with *savikalpa samādhi*. In the former the empirical consciousness abides completely absorbed in the absolute or transcendent Self. In the latter, which comprises a lower stage, the distinction between the triple aspects of consciousness lingers jeopardising boundless bliss and serenity.

In Dattātreya's *Avadhūtagītā* we read: "There is no meditative in your consciousness, nor your absorption in *samādhi*: there is no meditation in your consciousness nor any space outside it; there is no object of meditation in your consciousness and nothing exists in time and space. I am the ambrosial joy of wisdom, the evenness of feeling and like unto the boundless sky" (III, 41).

द्वैतमूलमहो दुःखं नान्यत्तस्यास्ति भेषजम् ।
दृश्यमेतन्मृषा सर्वमेकोऽहं चिद्रसोऽमलः ॥१६॥

Dvaitamūlamaho duḥkhaṁ nānyattasyāsti bheṣajam I
Dṛśyametanmṛṣā sarvam eko'haṁ cidraso'malaḥ II

16. Unhappiness has its roots in duality. I am undefiled, non-dual and pure intelligence. All this visible universe is illusory. There is no other remedy (of unhappiness) than this (knowledge).

बोधमात्रोऽहमज्ञानादुपाधिः कल्पितो मया ।
एवं विमृशतो नित्यं निर्विकल्पे स्थितिर्मम ॥१७॥

Bodhamātro'hamajñānādupādhiḥ kalpito mayā I
Evaṁ vimṛśato nityaṁ nirvikalpe sthitirmama II

17. I am only pure consciousness. It is only through ignorance that external qualities are attributed (to the Self). Having exercised constant discrimination I (now) abide in my Self purged of mental activity.

Nirvikalpa—this most significant yogic term which does not occur in *major Upaniṣads* and in the *Gītā* is used six times in the text. It is used by Gauḍapāda (II, 35, III), 34)

न मे बन्धोऽस्ति मोक्षो वा भ्रान्तिः शान्ता निराश्रया ।
अहो मयि स्थितं विश्वं वस्तुतो न मयि स्थितम् ॥१८॥

Na me bandho'sti mokṣo vā bhrāntiḥ śāntā nirāśrayā l
Aho mayi sthitaṁ viśvaṁ vastuto na mayi sthitaṁ ll

18. There is neither bondage nor salvation for me. Oh, the universe really abides in me. The illusion is now silenced, becoming rootless.

Illusion—i. e. of the reality of the universe.

सशरीरमिदं विश्वं न किञ्चिदिति निश्चितम् ।
शुद्धचिन्मात्र आत्मा च तत्कस्मिन्कल्पनाऽऽधुना ॥१९॥

Saśarīramidaṁ viśvaṁ na kiñciditi niścitam l
Śuddhacinmātra ātmā ca tatkasmin kalpanādhunā ll

19. This universe with the body is unsubstantial. This is certain. The Self is pure and is of the nature of consciousness. Then where is the conception of the world ?

शरीरं स्वर्गनरकौ बन्धमोक्षौ भयं तथा ।
कल्पनामात्रमेवैतत्किं मे कार्यं चिदात्मनः ॥२०॥

Śarīraṁ svarganarakau bandhamokṣau bhayaṁ tathā l
Kalpanāmātramevaitat kiṁ me kāryaṁ cidātmanaḥ ll

20. The body together with (the notions of) heaven and hell, bondage and freedom and anxiety are merely illusory. For me who is pure consciousness what is there to be done ?

अहो जनसमूहेऽपि न द्वैतं पश्यतो मम ।
अरण्यमिव संवृत्तं क्व रतिं करवाण्यहम् ॥२१॥

Aho janasamūhe'pi na dvaitaṁ paśyato mama l
Araṇyamiva saṁvṛttaṁ kva ratiṁ karavāṇyaham ll

21. O, I do not see any duality. The assemblage of

men becomes like a forest. (Hence) what attachment should I have?

See XVIII, 190. The wise one when he is in the crowd or in the forest continues in his complete self-abidance, experiencing the Self in all and all in the Self.

नाहं देहो न मे देहो जीवो नाहमहं हि चित् ।
अयमेव हि मे बंध आसीद्या जीविते स्पृहा ॥२२॥

Nāhaṁ deho na me deho jīvo nāhamahaṁ hi cit ।
Ayameva hi me bandha āsīd yā jīvite spṛhā ॥

22. I am not the body, nor does the body belong to me. I am not a being, I am solely myself. This was my bondage that I eagerly desired to live.

अहो भुवनकल्लोलैर्विचित्रैर्द्राक् समुत्थितम् ।
मय्यनन्तमहाम्भोधौ चित्तवाते समुद्यते ॥२३॥

Aho bhuvanakallolairvicitrairdrāk samutthitam ।
Mayyanantamahāmbhodhau cittavāte samudyate ॥

23. Oh, in the boundless ocean of myself as the winds of mind arise, manifold worlds quickly appear as its waves.

There is no creation. The Self alone exists, unborn and unexpendable. It is the mind, distinguishable from the formless, boundless *cit* or pure intelligence, that creates forms (*rūpa*), names (*nāma*) and functions (*kārya*)—the phenomenal world.

It is remarkable that Aṣṭāvakra's oft-used metaphor of the ocean (of Being) and the waves (phenomenal world) has been used by Aśvaghoṣa (C. 100 A. D.) whose monistic and metaphysical speculation significantly contributed to the rise of Mahāyāna Buddhism. Aśvaghoṣa observes: "The waves are stirred up by the wind, but the water remains the same, when the wind ceases, the motion of the waves subsides but the water remains the same. Likewise, when the mind of all creatures which in its own nature is pure and clean, is stirred up by the wind of ignorance, the waves of mentality make their appearance" (*Discourse on the Awakening of Faith in the Mahāyāna*, pp. 55-57). Both Aṣṭāvakra and Aśvaghoṣa identify the fluctuating mind (waves) with *citta*, and the phenomenal world it produces with ideation or imagination, the cause of ignorance and bondage (VII, 3). But the essence of the Self, eternally pure and luminous remains untouched or unmolested.

मय्यनन्तमहाम्भोधौ चित्तवाते प्रशाम्यति ।
अभाग्याज्जीववणिजो जगत्पोतो विनश्वरः ॥२४॥

Mayyanantamahāmbhohdu cittavāte praśāmyati 1
abhāgyājjīvavaṇijo jagatpoto vinaśvaraḥ 11

24. In the infinite ocean of myself as the winds of mind are stilled, the creature-merchant finds its world-vessel transitory due to the vicissitudes of life.

World-vessel : The human body is the ship on which the finite creature-trader carries on his transactions in the sea of the universe—his deeds in successive births bearing good and bad fruits or profit and loss determining his destiny. Man's body, his universe, his transactions in the continual trade and their consequences of good and evil are all transient products of his mind. As the mind merges in the Self, all vanish.

मय्यनन्तमहाम्भोधावाश्चर्यं जीववीचयः ।
उद्यन्ति घ्नन्ति खेलन्ति प्रविशन्ति स्वभावतः ॥२५॥

Mayyanantamahāmbhodhāvāścaryaṁ jīvavīcayaḥ 1
udyanti ghnanti khelanti praviśanti svabhāvataḥ 11

25. It is a marvel that in the boundless ocean of myself creatures like waves rise, jostle, play with one another and merge spontaneously.

The last three lyrical verses emphasize the appearance and disappearance of worlds and creatutes as ephemeral waves emerging from, and returning to the boundless ocean of Being. Like the waves the creatures are mutually aggressive, destructive or playful and merge in the ocean when their ignorance and *karma*, arising out of the latter, are extinguished. The first verse depicts the genesis of the universe and beings, the second their annihilation and the third transitory interrelations and interactions, all in the matrix of the primordial causative Self. Previously in II, 4-5 the universe is spoken of as constituted of the Self only as the waves emanate from the ocean and the cloth from the thread.

The sense of marvel at, and adoration of, the Self, uncreated, boundless and absolute, stressed in 11 to 14, and 23 to 25 echoes the feeling of wonder at the Self in the *Kaṭha Upaniṣad* and the *Bhagavadgītā*. The *Kaṭha Upaniṣad* observes, "Wondrous is he who can teach (the Self) and skilfull is he who finds (the Self). Wondrous is he who knows, even when instructed by the wise" (I, 2, 7). Similarly, the *Bhagavadgītā* says, "One looks upon This as a marvel, another likewise speaks of This as a marvel; another hears of This as a marvel; and even after hearing no one whatsoever has known This" (II, 29). Aṣṭāvakra, however, gives the most poetic expressiocn to the sense of mystical wonder of the Self as the manifold universe and *jīvas* are realized as springing only from *cit* or pure consciousness.

The brilliant metaphor of Being as the boundless ocean is developed in VI, 2, VII, 1—3 and XV, 7, 11,13. Apparently this is most favourite with the sage. It is deployed by him to expound his basic notion of the Self, transcending time and causation in XV, 11, 13. Being is the shoreless ocean, unborn, immutable and perfect. The waves of the phenomenal worlds constantly arise and vanish in the ocean in conformity to time's cycles of creation and dissolution. But Being remains full, calm and unaffected. "No gain or loss accrues to Being". Unity and duality, existence and transcendence are illusions. Nothing in reality emanates from the ocean. "Thou art verily that" (XV, 7).

Chapter III

AṢṬĀVAKRA ON THE SELF IN ALL AND ALL IN THE SELF

In this universe the Self alone is in its nature indestructible, pure and supremely beautiful (III,1,4). Man's discrimination between the real and illusory, the eternal and the transient and his desirelessness as well as freedom from the conflict of all pairs of opposites can come only from his realization of the non-dual, eternal and absolute Self (*kevala*, III, 9, 14). The wise one discovers the all-encompassing Self in all existences and all existences in the Self (III,5). The *Upaniṣadic* formula, 'That I am', is the great truth (III, 3). Abiding in the supreme non-duality, (paramādvaitaṁ, III,6) man realizes the world as mere illusion and has neither fear of death nor any attachment, greed and passion that tarnish the self.

अष्टावक्र उवाच

अविनाशिनमात्मानमेकं विज्ञाय तत्त्वतः ।
तवात्मज्ञस्य धीरस्य कथमर्थार्जने रतिः ॥१॥

Aṣṭāvakra uvāca

Āvināśinamātmānamekaṁ vijñāya tattvataḥ l
Tavātmajñasya dhīrasya kathamarthārjane ratiḥ ll

Aṣṭāvakra said :

1. Knowing the Self in its true nature as eternal and non-dual, where is the passion for earning wealth of the poised man of wisdom?

The word '*tattva*' meaning the wisdom of the self is frequently used in the Upaniṣads and the *Bhagavadgītā*. In the *Kaṭha* (VI, 12), *Śvetāśvatara* (VI.3) and *Muṇḍaka* (I, 2, 13) *Upaniṣads* and in the *Bhagavadgītā* (III, 16 IV, 34, VI 21, IX, 24, XI, 54, XIII, 11, XVIII, 1), the term occurs in this sense.

आत्माऽज्ञानादहो प्रीतिर्विषयभ्रमगोचरे ।
शुक्तेरज्ञानतो लोभो यथा रजतविभ्रमे ॥२॥

Ātmājñānādaho prītirviṣayabhramagocare 1
Śukterajñānato lobho yathā rajatavibhrame 11

2. O disciple, just as due to ignorance a sea-shell is sought by mistaking it for silver, even so due to the ignorance of the Self, there is attachment towards the illusory world of the senses.

विश्वं स्फुरति यत्रेदं तरङ्गा इव सागरे ।
सोऽहमस्मीति विज्ञाय किं दीन इव धावसि ॥३॥

Viśvaṁ sphurati yatredaṁ taraṅgā iva sāgare 1
So'hamasmīti vijñāya kiṁ dīna iva dhāvasi 11

3. Having realized, 'I am That' whence the universe streams forth like waves from the sea, why do you as a wretched creature run (after the universe)?

'*Sa Ahaṁ* and '*Ahaṁ Asmi*' are familiar *Upaniṣadic* formulae. (Skanda, 11; see also Gītā, IX, 29).

श्रुत्वाऽपि शुद्धचैतन्यमात्मानमतिसुन्दरम् ।
उपस्थेऽत्यन्तसंसक्तो मालिन्यमधिगच्छति ॥४॥

Śrutvāpi śudhacaitanyamātmānamatisundaram 1
Upasthe'tyantas-ṁsakto mālinyamadhigacchati 11

4. Even after hearing that the Self is pure consciousness and is unsurpassedly beautiful, why do you become deeply entangled with sex and get tarnished?

Hearing : The disciple not only listens to the teaching about the Self but also directly apprehends it, and becomes the all-knower.

सर्वभूतेषु चात्मानं सर्वभूतानि चात्मनि ।
मुनेर्जानत आश्चर्यं ममत्वमनुवर्तते ॥५॥

Sarvabhūteṣu cātmānaṁ sarvabhūtāni cātmani ।
Munerjānata āścaryaṁ mamatvamanuvarttate ॥

5. Realizing the Self in all beings and all beings in the Self, it is surprising that the man of wisdom continues being egoistic.

It is the Supreme Knowledge which destroys all ego-attachment and involvement. See XI, 6 where the first line of the verse is repeated and the freedom from egoism and sense of mine-ness is stressed. The first line which is derived from the *Bhagavadgītā*, VI, 29 denotes both the immanence and transcendence of the Self. See also VI, 4, where it is repeated in a modified form.

आस्थितः परमाद्वैतं मोक्षार्थेऽपि व्यवस्थितः ।
आश्चर्यं कामवशगो विकलः केलिशिक्षया ॥६॥

Āsthitaḥ paramādvaitaṁ mokṣārthe'pi vyavasthitaḥ ।
Āścaryaṁ kāmavaśago vikalaḥ keliśikṣayā ॥

6. Having realized the transcendent non-duality and become fixed in the goal of liberation, strange it is that a person yet comes under the sway of lust and is distraught by sexual habits.

Goal of Liberation : That is to say, the Supreme Self.

उद्भूतं ज्ञानदुर्मित्रमवधार्यातिदुर्बलः ।
आश्चर्यं काममाकाङ्क्षेत्कालमन्तमनुश्रितः ॥७॥

Udbhūtaṁ jñānadurmitramavadhāryātidurbalaḥ ।
Āścaryaṁ kāmamākāṅkṣet kālamantamanuśritaḥ ॥

7. Strange it is that knowing the upsurging sex as the great enemy of knowledge, one who is extremely feeble and approaches his end should yet desire sex-gratification.

End : Time is regarded here as swallowing up finite existence. In the *Mahābhārata* we have the classical affirmation by Yudhiṣṭhira of Great Time as swallowing up and digesting all finite beings.

इहामुत्र विरक्तस्य नित्यानित्यविवेकिनः ।
आश्चर्यं मोक्षकामस्य मोक्षादेव बिभीषिका ॥८॥

Ihāmutra viraktasya nityānityaviv kinaḥ 1
Āścaryaṁ mokṣakāmasya mokṣādevavibhīṣikā 11

8. The wise are free from attachment to this world and heaven, discriminate between what is ephemeral and what is eternal and aspires after salvation. Strange it is that even they would dread salvation.

Dread : The dissociation from the body and the objects of the senses causes anxiety. Anxiety and fear of death are particularly stressed by modern Existentialism.

धीरस्तु भोज्यमानोऽपि पीड्यमानोऽपि सर्वदा ।
आत्मानं केवलं पश्यन्न तुष्यति न कुप्यति ॥९॥

Dhīrastu bhojyamāno'pi pīḍyamāno'pi sarvadā 1
Ātmānaṁ kevalaṁ paśyan na tuṣyati na kupyati 11

9. The wise man feted or tormented (by the world) ever sees the absolute Self and is neither happy nor angry.

Absolute Self : The adjective *'kevalam'* is used in the sense of Patañjali with whom the Self obtains "absolute loneliness" when the body, senses, mind and intellect detach themselves from *puruṣa* and return to *prakṛti*. The Self then becomes free from the dominance of *prakṛti*. The autonomous, liberated Self contemplates itself and has no more relation with life and the phenomenal world. The word *'kevala'* in the sense of Patañjali occurs neither in the older *Upaniṣads* nor in the *Bhagavadgītā*, but in the *Śvetāśvatara Upaniṣad* (I, 11, IV, 18, VI, 11).

चेष्टमानं शरीरं स्वं पश्यत्यन्यशरीरवत् ।
संस्तवे चापि निन्दायां कथं क्षुभ्येन्महाशयः ॥१०॥

Ceṣṭamānaṁ śarīraṁ svaṁ paśyatyanyaśarīravat 1
Saṁstave cāpi nindāyāṁ kathaṁ kṣubhyet mahāśayaḥ 11

10. The great man witnesses his own active body as that of another person. How can he be perturbed by praise or blame?

मायामात्रमिदं विश्वं पश्यन् विगतकौतुकः ।
अपि सन्निहिते मृत्यौ कथं त्रस्यति धीरधीः ॥११॥

Māyāmātramidaṁ viśvaṁ paśyan vigatakautukaḥ 1
Api sannihite mṛtyau kathaṁ trasyati dhīradhīḥ ll

11. Having realized this world as illusory and lost all zest, why would the person of poised intelligence be frightened by the nearness of death?

निःस्पृहं मानसं यस्य नैराश्येऽपि महात्मनः ।
तस्यात्मज्ञानतृप्तस्य तुलना केन जायते ॥१२॥

Niḥspṛhaṁ mānasaṁ yasya nairāśye'pi mahātmanaḥ 1
Tasyātmajñānatṛptasya tulanā kena jāyate ll

12. What comparisons can there be with a great person whose mind is free from desire even in frustration, and who experiences delight in his self-knowledge?

Delight in Self-knowledge : This is *Ātma-tṛpti*, *Ātma-rati* and *Ātma-saṁtoṣa* of the *Gītā* (III, 17).

स्वभावादेव जानानो दृश्यमेतन्न किञ्चन ।
इदं ग्राह्यमिदं त्याज्यं स किं पश्यति धीरधीः ॥१३॥

Svabhāvādeva jānāno dṛśyametanna kiñcana 1
Idaṁ grāhyamidaṁ tyājyaṁ sa kiṁ paśyati dhīradhīḥ ll

13. The man of poised intelligence knows that the visible world from its very nature has no substance. He considers nothing acceptable or rejectable.

अन्तस्त्यक्तकषायस्य निर्द्वन्द्वस्य निराशिषः ।
यदृच्छयाऽऽगतो भोगो न दुःखाय न तुष्टये ॥१४॥

Antastyaktakaṣāyasya nirdvandvasya nirāśiṣaḥ I
yadṛcchayāgato bhogo na duḥkhāya na tuṣṭaye II

14. For him who has abandoned the mind's passions, who is above the duality of attributes and is desireless, for him any experience that comes as a matter of course gives neither pleasure nor pain.

CHAPTER IV

JANAKA ON THE KNOWER AND THE NON-KNOWER OF THE SELF

The knower of the self plays the sport of life without desire or aversion, fear or elation. His heart becomes stainless and all-encompassing like the sky untouched by either virtue or vice. The *Upaniṣadic* formula which Aṣṭāvakra adopts is, 'The entire universe is the Self' (IV, 3; XV, 15). The knower of the Self understands the universe as himself without a second and as the lord of the Universe. He lives in perfect freedom, fearlessness and bliss. The non-knower of the Self is like a beast of burden of the world, a victim of its lusts and inhibitions, fears and miseries.

अष्टावक्र उवाच
हन्तात्मज्ञस्य धीरस्य खेलतो भोगलीलया ।
न हि संसारवाहीकैर्मूढैः सह समानता ॥१॥

Aṣṭāvakra uvāca
Hantātmajñasya dhīrasya khelato bhogalīlayā 1
Na hi saṁsāravāhīkairmūḍhaiḥ saha samānatā 11

Aṣṭāvakra said:

1. O marvel, there can be no comparison between an ignorant creature who carries the burden of the world and the knower of the Self who plays the sport of life.

Play : because of non-involvement of the knower of the Self. The Self is infinite and unalloyed bliss that saturates all things, activities and relations.

यत्पदं प्रेप्सवो दीनाः शक्राद्याः सर्वदेवताः ।
अहो तत्र स्थितो योगी न हर्षमुपगच्छति ॥२॥

Yatpadaṁ prepsavo dīnāḥ śakrādyāḥ sarvadevatāḥ 1
Aho tatra sthito yogī na harṣamupagachati 11

2. O marvel, the yogī attains that status which all

gods, beginning with Indra seek but do not achieve and yet does not feel elated.

Elated—The experience of *bhūmānanda, ānanda paramānanda* (I,10) or supreme bliss is unaccompanied by elation since the Self is restored its own nature.

तज्ज्ञस्य पुण्यपापाभ्यां स्पर्शो ह्यन्तर्न जायते ।
न ह्याकाशस्य धूमेन दृश्यमानाऽपि संगतिः ॥३॥

Tajjñasya puṇyapāpābhyāṁ sparśo hyantarna jāyate ।
Na hyākāśasya dhūmena dṛśyamānāpi saṅgatiḥ ॥

3. Comprehending that Self, he is untouched in his inner life by the duality of virtue and sin, just as the sky is untouched by the smoke apparently related to it.

Sky—In the *Bṛhadāraṇyaka Upaniṣad* we read, *ākāśaṁ ātmā* (III, 2, 13).

आत्मैवेदं जगत्सर्वं ज्ञातं येन महात्मना ।
यदृच्छया वर्त्तमानं तं निषेद्धुं क्षमेत कः ॥४॥

Ātmaivedaṁ jagatsarvaṁ jñātaṁ yena mahātmanā ।
Yadṛcchayā varttamānaṁ taṁ niṣeddhuṁ kṣameta kaḥ ॥

4. The wise man who comprehends the entire world as his Self (*ātman*) lives as he likes. Him none can forbid.

Ātman—We read in the *Chāndogya Upaniṣad, Ātmā eva idaṁ sarvam* (VII, 26,1). Aṣṭāvakra obviously adopts this ancient formula.

आब्रह्मस्तम्बपर्यन्ते भूतग्रामे चतुर्विधे ।
विज्ञस्यैव हि सामर्थ्यमिच्छानिच्छाविवर्जने ॥५॥

Ābrahmastambaparyante bhūtagrāme caturvidhe ।
Vijñasyaiva hi sāmarthyamicchānicchāvivarjane ॥

5. Among the four categories of existence from Brahma to the tuft of grass it is the wise one alone who can verily abandon desire and aversion.

Four Categories of Existence—The *Gītā* uses the same term meaning the aggregate of beings that all come into existence and merge again and again in the Supreme (VIII, 19; IX,

8 and XVII, 6). In the *Brahmasūtra* we also read, (There is the same teaching) as the Self is within all, as in the case of the aggregate of the elements (III, 3,35).

आत्मानमद्वयं कश्चिज्जानाति जगदीश्वरम् ।
यद्वेत्ति तत्स कुरुते न भयं तस्य कुत्रचित् ॥६॥

Ātmānamadvayaṁ kaścijjānāti jagadīsvaraṁ ।
Yadvetti tat sa kurute na bhayaṁ tasya kutracit ॥

6. Rare is the individual who knows the non-dual Self as the Lord of the Universe. He does whatever comes to his mind and has no fear from anywhere.

Like the *Gītā* and the later *Upaniṣads* such as the *Śvetāśvatara*, the text here significantly identifies the Supreme, non-dual Self with the Divine and introduces a theistic note into Vedāntic absolutism.

The *Śvetāśvatara Upaniṣad* says : "He is the Supreme Lord of lords, is the highest deity of deities, the supreme master of masters, transcendent, him let us know as god, the lord of the world, the adorable" (VI, 7).

The Self is identified by Aṣṭāvakra with *Īśvara* also in I, 12, XI, 2, XIV, 3 and XV, 8. *Bhagavān* or *Īśvara* is identified with *ātman* in the *Śvetāśvatara Upaniṣad* (III,11).

Chapter V

AṢṬĀVAKRA ON THE STAGES OF DISSOLUTION OF CONSCIOUSNESS

Dissolution (*laya*), according to Aṣṭāvakra, means the obliteration of the body, mind and the phenomenal world in the non-dual Self or Brahman (VI, 2). First, the body and the phenomenal world; then, the mind and desire; and, finally the sense of duality of opposites, such as misery and happiness, hope and despair and life and death, have to be dissolved in pure intelligence or *citsvarūpa*. This is identified with the perfect (*pūrṇa*), the even (*sama*) and the absolute (*kevala*). Here is Aṣṭāvakra's re-interpretation of the '*laya yoga*' of Patañjali. Aṣṭāvakra grounds *laya* in the contemplation and knowledge of the pure and absolute Self. The universe though perceptible is unreal, and has, therefore, to be negated. The Self alone is real, and should not have contact with anything whatever. In the later chapters Aṣṭāvakra stresses that self-abidance transcends both *laya* and *samādhi*.

अष्टावक्र उवाच

न ते सङ्गोऽस्ति केनापि किं शुद्धस्त्यक्तुमिच्छसि ।
संघातविलयं कुर्वन्नेवमेव लयं व्रज ॥१॥

Aṣṭāvakra uvāca

Na te saṅgo'sti kenāpi kim śuddhastyaktumicchasi ।
Saṅghātavilayaṁ kurvannevameva layaṁ vraja ॥

Aṣṭāvakra said:

1. For you there is no contact with anything whatever. Pure as you are, what do you wish to renounce? Having dissolved the body aggregate, thus do you undertake dissolution.

The '*laya yoga*' or method of dissolution of the world and consciousness begins here with the abandonment of body-sense. *Laya* achieves the absolute aloneness of the pure self (*Kaivalya*) or self-abidance (*svāsthya*) through the complete forgetting of the body, mind and phenomenal world. This is called *sarva-vismaraṇa* in XVI. According to the *Yogatattva Upaniṣad*, *laya yoga* consists in bringing about the destruction of the *citta* or mind. It comprises innumerable ways. Walking, sitting, sleeping and eating, one should meditate on God who is the whole and indivisible. This is *laya yoga* (2.24).

उदेति भवतो विश्वं वारिधेरिव बुद्बुदः ।
इति ज्ञात्वैकमात्मानमेवमेव लयं व्रज ॥२॥

Udeti bhavato viśvaṁ vāridheriva budbudaḥ 1
Iti jñātvaikamātmānamevameva layaṁ vraja 11

2. From you the universe emerges as a bubble from the sea. In this manner having known your non-dual Self, practise dissolution.

This comprises according to Aṣṭāvakra the second stage of *layayoga*, where the mind and desire become fused with Ātman. This corresponds to the teaching of the *Gītā* that the yogī should abandon thinking of anything whatsoever after completely establishing the mind in the real Self (VI, 10, 15, 19, 20, 25).

प्रत्यक्षमप्यवस्तुत्वाद्विश्वं नास्त्यमले त्वयि ।
रज्जुसर्प इव व्यक्तमेवमेव लयं व्रज ॥३॥

Pratyakṣamapyavastutvādviśvaṁ nāstyamale tvayi 1
Rajjusarpa iva vyaktamevameva layaṁ vraja 11

3. As the universe, even though visible, is dissolved in your non-dual Self, it no longer exists, being unsubstantial, like the snake vanished in the rope. Undertake the dissolution of consciousness in this manner.

This is the third phase of *laya yoga* in which the world with its duality of opposites like heat and cold, pleasure and pain, hope and frustration vanishes.

समदुःखसुखः पूर्णं आशानैराश्ययोः समः ।
समजीवितमृत्युः सन्नेवमेव लयं व्रज ॥४॥

Samaduḥkhasukhaḥ pūrṇa āśānairāśyayoḥ samaḥ l
Samajīvitamṛtyuḥ sannevameva layaṁ vraja ll

4. Become the perfect and the same, whether in pleasure or pain, hope or disappointment, life or death. Undertake the dissolution of consciousness in this manner.

The same : The *Gītā's* familiar phrase, *sama-duḥkhasukha* (II, 15, XII, 13, XIV, 25) is borrowed here. But equipoise in life and death is an opposite addition.

This is the final stage of extinction of consciousness where the fullness of non-duality of Brahman or Ātman is attained. This is associated with Supreme bliss. This stage is also stressed in the Gīta.

In the *Bhagavadgītā* we have the statement that the yogī who beholds the Self through the Self, rejoices in the Self and experiences transcendent bliss beyond the reach of the senses (VI, 20, 21, 28).

The *Bhagavadgītā* calls it *ātma-yoga* or the yoga of the higher Self. The *laya* is definitely mentioned by the *Gītā* by the injunction that the yogī establishing the mind in the Self by the intellect (*buddhi*) regulated by concentration should not think of any thing whatsoever (VI, 25). As in the *Gītā*, so in Aṣṭāvakra the vacation of consciousness is, therefore, not emptying it, but completely filling it with the Self, Brahman or God as the abiding Witness of the fluctuations of the body, consciousness and the phenomenal world (*sākṣī*, IX, 18).

Aṣṭāvakra, like the author of *Gītā*, leans on the contemplative methods of eliminating the instability of mind rather than on the regulation of breath (*prāṇāyāma*) of Pātañjala yoga which has also its following through the centuries (*Yogavāsiṣṭha*, VI, 1, 69, 52 and *Uttaragītā*, I, 10, for instance). This will be more evident in the later chapters (XII, 7; XVIII, I6).

Like Aṣṭāvakra, Gauḍapāda who follows the great master commends in his *Māṇḍūkya Kārikā* the practice of *laya* and complete withdrawal of the mind from the objects of the senses through the contemplative procedure in almost similar phrases (III,4-46). Śaṅkara's *Aparokṣānubhūti* similarly depicts three stages of *laya* by means of contemplation, viz. first, dissociation from the body and the world; second, the identification with the fullness of Brahman or Ātman; and third the forgetting even of the knowledge of Brahman or Ātman in transcendence (124). Elsewhere he says, "Once the mind of the *yogī* merges in cidātman, let not the mind he moved again, rather abide in the still and complete fullness of knowledge, resembling the full and still ocean" (*Pañcīkaraṇam*, 52).

Chapter VI

ON THE IRRELEVANCE OF THE DISSOLUTION OF CONSCIOUSNESS

Laya or dissolution of the world and consciousness is not all relevant, but even harmful for self-knowledge, belonging as it does to the relativist realm of body and mind, ego-sense and action. The pure Self is like the stainless and boundless sky. The phenomenal world is enclosing a part of the sky like the pot. This is true knowledge (VI, 1). When the non-duality and indivisibility of the sky-like Self are realized neither acceptance, nor rejection nor dissolution of the phenomenal world can hold good.

The Self dwells in all beings as all beings dwell in the Self. Aṣṭāvakra stresses both the transcendence and immanence of the Self or rather the identity between the Self and all existences or phenomena. Such non-duality of the Self cannot brook with the notion of either accepting or negating anything which is no other than the Self; besides any such notion involves ego-sense. The non-dual Self is simply the Beyond, Prakṛteḥ Paraḥ)II, 1, XV, 8)

अष्टावक्र उवाच

आकाशवदनन्तोऽहं घटवत्प्राकृतं जगत् ।
इति ज्ञानं तथैतस्य न त्यागो न ग्रहो लयः ॥१॥

Aṣṭāvakra uvāca

Ākāśavadananto'haṁ ghaṭavat prākṛtaṁ jagat 1
Iti jñānaṁ tathaitasya na tyāgo na graho layaḥ 11

Aṣṭāvakra said:

1. I am infinite as the sky. The world of nature is like the (limited) pot. This is true knowledge. Thus neither rejection nor acceptance nor dissolution is possible.

Sky—The *Bṛhadāraṇyka Upaniṣad* says: *ākāśaṁ ātmā*

(III, 2, 13). The *Taittirīya Upaniṣad* also observes *ākāśa ātmā* (I, 7, 1; II, 2, 1). The *Chāndogya Upaniṣad* repeats this (III, 14, 2) and adds *ākāśa brahma* (III, 18). The *Amṛtavindu Upaniṣad* observes: "Space is enclosed by the pot. Just as space is not carried along with the pot as the latter is removed from one place to another, so the Self (when contained in the body) like infinite space remains unmoved and untainted (13). Gauḍapāda's *Māṇḍūkya Kārikā* reiterates, *ātmā ākāśavat* and *jīva ghaṭavat.* Here the metaphor of the Self as sky and of the *jīva* as enclosed sky with forms, attributes and functions is fully developed (III, 3-9). It embodies the notion that subtle, boundless and all-encompassing Self appears in many forms of separate jīvas with various names and activities. The *Mukti Upaniṣad* also says that the Self is like *ghaṭākāśa* freed of all *upādhis* or limitations (2).

Neither Rejection nor Acceptance—Gauḍapāda's celebrated *Māṇḍūkya Kārikā* that was written much later (c. 650) develops the same principle that the Self neither accepts nor rejects anything and uses the same words. "In the Ātman which is free from all acts of mind there is neither any acceptance nor rejection," *no grahas tatra notsargacintā yatra na vidyate,* (*Kārikā,* III, 38). It is noteworthy that in the important chapter where he develops the doctrine of non-origination of the self Gauḍapāda uses at the outset Aṣṭāvakra's metaphor of the Self and the sky, the finite self being compared to the sky enclosed in the pot on the destruction of which the latter merges in the former (*Kārikā,* III, 3-7).

Dissolution—As the self attains fullness or completion, any mental activity such as involved even in extinction of consciousness becomes impossible. This is the crux of immediate intuitive experience (*anubhava*) in which the Self is not required to dialectically deny any opposite category or principle. Ātman or Brahman in the *Gītā* and the *Upaniṣads* is beyond the affirmation and negation of dialectical thought (sat and asat).

According to the *Vedāntasāra,* the contemplative's mind should not lapse into unconsciousness, mistaking this melting or *laya* for that of the mergence in the Self. "Deep sleep supervenes when the spontaneous activity of the introverted mind (*citta-vṛtti*) fails to grasp and hold to the changeless total one" (215).

It may be conceived from the metaphor of the sky confined to the pot that the boundless self somehow undergoes division or restriction. Hence the next verse.

महोदधिरिवाहं स प्रपञ्चो वीचिसन्निभः ।
इति ज्ञानं तथैतस्य न त्यागो न ग्रहो लयः ॥२॥

Mahodadhirivāhaṁ sa prapañco vīcisannibhaḥ l
Iti jñānaṁ tathaitasya na tyāgo na graho layaḥ ll

2. I am like the ocean, and this phenomenal world is like its waves. With such an understanding (for the knower of the Self), there is neither renunciation nor acceptance for dissolution.

Here the possibility of thinking that the infinite Self undergoes modification is not excluded. Hence the next verse. This verse should be read with XV, 11.

अहं स शुक्तिसङ्काशो रूप्यवद्विश्वकल्पना ।
इति ज्ञानं तथैतस्य न त्यागो न ग्रहो लयः ॥३॥

Ahaṁ sa śuktisaṅkāśo rūpyavadviśvakalpanā l
Iti jñānaṁ tathaitasya na tyāgo na graho layaḥ ll

3. I am like the sea-shell. The world sense is (false) like the identification of the sea-shell with the silver. With such an understanding, there is neither rejection nor acceptance nor dissolution for the Self.

It is ignorance which takes the sea-shell to be silver or the world including the body and mind to be the Self. As the Self overcomes this ignorance, there is no need of any contemplation.

अहं वा सर्वभूतेषु सर्वभूतान्यथो मयि ।
इति ज्ञानं तथैतस्य न त्यागो न ग्रहो लयः ॥४॥

Ahaṁ vā sarvabhūteṣu sarvabhūtānyatho mayi I
Iti jñānaṁ tathaitasya na tyāgo na graho layaḥ II

4. I am in all beings and all beings are in me. This is true knowledge. Thus there is neither any renunciation nor acceptance nor dissolution.

This closely follows verse VI, 29 of the *Bhagavadgītā* "He whose Self is integrated by yoga sees the Self abiding in all beings and all beings in the Self; everywhere he sees the same". Only such a dual vision that abolishes the distinction between the inner and the outer can destroy the sense of the separate, finite phenomenal self. It is impersonal mysticism with its profound unity of all beings and things in the One Self without a second which can completely transcend the whole stream of life and consciousness with their contrasted concrete contents of acceptance, rejection and dissolution. The first line of this verse reappears in another form in XIV, 6, where the non-dual experience is associated with freedom from the ego-sense and bliss.

The illustration of the difference between the sea-shell and the silver did not exclude possibility that Self and the world might yet be different and discontinuous entities. Vedāntic non-duality is based on direct experience. It is absolute and continuous identity comprehending both the inner and the outer. The Self is one, continuous, comprehensive whole, fusing the external and the internal. The non-dual, all-encompassing, pure consciousness brooks no activity of thought such as involved in acceptance or denial or lapse but rather assimilates there into itself. Pure consciousness is simply omniscient and perenially luminous (*sadā-ujjvala*). This is the celebrated 'I shine' of the *Upaniṣads*. Ātman is simply self-subsistent and indefinable. The metaphors of the sky, the ocean and the mother-of-pearl with which the Self is compared can give but limited glimpses of the ultimate reality. These are at once true and false.

In spiritual contemplation four major hindrances to the maturation of *samādhi* are recognised: (1) dissolution (*laya*); (2) distraction (*vikṣepa*); (3) void (*kaṣāya*); and (4) delight of realization (*rasasvāda*). Vidyāraṇya identifies *laya* with sleep and *kaṣāya*) with void resulting in perturbation. When all the above hindrances are overcome, the mind neither lapses into the torpor of sleep (*laya*), nor experiences ecstasy or trance (*rasāsvāda*), but achieves a serene, blissful, all-encompassing consciousness without break or unstability. This is the *nirvikalpa* or *asamprajñāta* phase of Pātañjala *yoga* and *asparśa-yoga* of Gauḍapāda—the *yoga* of transcendence whereby the self rises above all relativities of the phenomenal world. The *Bhagavadgīta* first uses the term *mātrāsparśa* or contact with the sense-organs and hence objects of sense-perception, freedom from which is associated with yoga serenity (II, 14). Gauḍapāda obviously derives the term *asparśa yoga* from the *Bhagavadgītā* and elaborates its description from this (*Kārikā*, III, 42-47). He observes, "When the mind neither passes into dissolution (*laya*) nor into distraction (*vikṣepa*); when there is no sign, no appearance it verily becomes Brahman" (*Kārikā*, III, 46). By denying lapse, acceptance and rejection, it was however, Aṣṭāvakra who first reached the profound conception that the self, serene perfect and boundless, and the phenomena of the universe, changeful, limited and imperfect, are not different. The Self knows that contacts, relations or phenomena come and go in its unlimited bosom and abide there. These are the same as itself just as the sky and the pot, the ocean and the waves are identical (II, 4).

It is clear that just as acceptance *graha*, (*grahaṇa*) or rejection (*tyāga*), which is a mode of mental activity, has to be eschewed, so has dissolution or oblivion (*laya*) that is also a mental mode, viz., sleep, torpor or inertia, also to be rejected. The self is perfect and perennial awareness itself—*sakṛtvibhātaṁ sarvajñam ajaṁ ekam avyayam*, "at once self-luminous, all-knowing, unborn, non-dual and immutable" (*Kārikā*, III, 3, 6). Gauḍapāda rightly observes : "The state of dissolution (*laya*) is as harmful as desire" (III, 42). Śaṅkara comments on this : "The mind should be withdrawn from the state of dissolution or oblivion as it should be withdrawn from the objects of enjoyment."

Aṣṭāvakra was the earliest thinker to expound and clarify that *laya yoga* is inconsistent with unflagging and perennial self-awareness svabhāva or svāsthya). Narahari in his *Bodhasāra* (third quarter of the 18th century) observes: "If the oblivion of the world leads to emancipation, why does not man obtain it through mere deep slumber, trance or death ? The *turīya* is the highest condition of *samādhi* (associated with *ātmā-sākṣātkāra*). While there is no dissolution of consciousness here, the experience of the all-pervasive, effulgent self and the sense of unreality of the phenomenal world abide even after waking up from *samādhi* (XXXIV, 20, 24). In a brilliant chapter on *laya yoga* the same author assimilates the ordinary events of life yielding the opposites of either pleasure or pain, happiness or grief, into self-realization or *ātmānubhava* (31). He accordingly reinterprets laya from the viewpoint of *Advaita Vedānta*. "Effort is supreme worship, for every effort manifests pure intelligence. Non-effort is the supreme worship because the complete silence of the mind is recommended by the scriptures" (XXXI, 20). Again, "the *yoga* of action is the supreme worship because action is dedicated to the Self or Brahman. The yoga of devotion is the supreme worship because the devotee is the favourite of Self or Brahman. The *yoga* of knowledge is the supreme worship because it leads to the aloneness of the Self. The *yoga* of transcendence (*turīya*) is the supreme worship because it is the direct experience of the Self or Brahman" (XXXI, 32-33).

Chapter VII

JANAKA ON THE TRANQUIL AND BOUNDLESS OCEAN OF THE SEIF

Even without the contemplative mind's state of dissolution or oblivion (*laya*) consciousness can be self-subsistent and self-effulgent and unaffected by the perturbations of the world and of mind. Not the *laya yoga* or dissolution of the world or consciousness, but genuine self-knowledge (*vijñāna*) or pure intelligence (*citsvarūpa*) is, therefore, essential. Man must constantly abide in the unborn, formless and boundless self, whence the phenomenal world emerges of itself like a magic show, due to the working of the finite mind (II, 23, VII, 2, 5, XV, 11). The creation and the dissolution of the world are mere *māyā* or illusion (XVIII, 73). The self is immutable and silent and transcends the relativist realm of time and possession. To it there can be neither acceptance nor rejection nor dissolution of the mind and the phenomenal world.

जनक उवाच

मय्यनन्तमहाम्भोधौ विश्वपोत इतस्ततः ।
भ्रमति स्वान्तवातेन न ममास्त्यसहिष्णुता ॥१॥

Janaka Uvāca

Mayyanantamahāmbhodhau viśvapota itastataḥ 1
Bhramati svāntavātena na mamāstyasahiṣṇutā 11

Janaka said:

1. In me, the infinite ocean, the ship of the universe moves here and there, driven by the wind of the mind. I do not have any impatience.

The Self is unperturbed by the fluctuations of the mind and the phenomenal world caused by laws inherent in their nature. "The mind is derived from the Self".—(*ātmatomanaḥ*)—says the Upaniṣad.

Wind—Mind is compared to the wind which the ship of

the universe drives hither and thither. The wind blows as it listeth and moves the ship, not the ocean.

मय्यनन्तमहाम्भोधौ जगद्वीचिः स्वभावतः ।
उदेतु वास्तमायातु न मे वृद्धिर्न च क्षतिः ॥२॥

Mayyanantamahāmbhodhau jagadvīciḥ svabhāvataḥ l
Udetu vāstamāyātu na me vṛddhirna ca kṣatiḥ ll

2. In me, the boundless ocean, the waves corresponding to the worlds spontaneously rise and vanish. I experience neither gain nor loss on this account.

The Self is complete and unexpendable by itself. The changes of phenomena do not affect it.

Spontaneously—The same word *svabhāva* is repeated in XV, 11. The Self is the changeless and complete reality. In spite of the superimposition of name, form and function by the empirical or finite consciousness, the phenomenal world remains ever the self, just as the wave is ever the water of the ocean. Creation or becoming is the result of the spontaneous sport of the Self that does not affect it at all, neither adds anything to, nor substracts anything from it. Aṣṭāvakra generally uses the words *ajñāna*, *avidyā* *bhrama* or ignorance of the self from which arises this illusionary perception. Only twice he uses the term māyā (XVIII, 72). With him *māyā* is not philosophical principle at all.

जनक उवाच

मय्यनन्तमहाम्भोधौ विश्वं नाम विकल्पना ।
अतिशान्तो निराकार एतदेवाहमास्थितः ॥३॥

Janaka uvāca

Mayyanantamahāmbhodhau viśvaṁ nāma vikalpanā l
Atiśānto nirākāra etadevāhamāsthitaḥ ll

3. In me, the limitless ocean, rests the familiar illusion of the world. In this knowledge, I, profound serene and formless, abide.

This verse is intended to stress the formlessness (*nirākāra*) of the Self. The phenomenal world is manifold in its names, forms and functions. But the Self in which it moves and abides is formless and perfect. In I, 80 it is emphasized that all that has form is unreal and the formless is immutable.

The notion of the transformation of the Self that may be suggested by the metaphor of the wave and the ocean in the previous verse is counteracted by this verse.

नात्मा भावेषु नो भावस्तत्रानन्ते निरञ्जने ।
इत्यशक्तोऽस्पृहः शान्त एतदेवाहमास्थितः ॥४॥

Nātmā bhāveṣu no bhāvastatrānante nirañjane I
Ityaśakto' spṛhaḥ śānta etadevāhamāsthitaḥ II

The Self is not in any object, nor is any object in the Self which is infinite and signless. Hence I am free from attachment and desire. Serene in this (knowledge) alone I abide.

अहो चिन्मात्रमेवाहमिन्द्रजालोपमं जगत् ।
अतो मम कथं कुत्र हेयोपादेयकल्पना ॥५॥

Aho cinmātramevāhamindrajālopamaṁ jagat I
Aho mama kathaṁ kutra heyopādeyakalpanā II

5. O, I am surely pure consciousness. The world is like the show of the magician. Hence how and where can there be any notion of acceptance or rejection of mine?

Show of Magician—In X, 2 the world is similarly called a dream or a juggler's show. In XVIII, 72 it is observed that the world before the dawning of pure intelligence is nothing but mere illusion (*māyā*).

Acceptance or Rejection—The pair of opposites is also eschewed in III, 13.

CHAPTER VIII

ASTĀVAKRA ON BONDAGE AND FREEDOM

Bondage is the consequence of the mind (*citta*) attaching itself to the sense-organs (instead of merging in the Self, the real and the absolute). Mind then perceives the phenomenal world for its happiness or anger, acceptance or rejection. Liberation is achieved when the mind neither desires nor grieves, neither accepts nor rejects. Mind and I (ego-sense) are bondage. Extinction of mind and I is freedom.

अष्टावक्र उवाच

तदा बन्धो यदा चित्तं किञ्चिद्वाञ्छति शोचति ।
किञ्चिन्मुञ्चति गृह्णाति किञ्चद्धृष्यति कुप्यति ॥१॥

Aṣṭāvakra uvāca

Tadā bandho yadā cittaṁ kiñcidvāñchati śocati l
Kiñcinmuñcati gṛhṇāti kiñciddhṛṣyati kupyati ll

Aṣṭāvakra said

1. Bondage is there when the mind desires or grieves over anything, rejects or accepts anything, feels delight or anger with anything.

तदा मुक्तिर्यदा चित्तं न वाञ्छति न शोचति ।
न मुञ्चति न गृह्णाति न हृष्यति न कुप्यति ॥२॥

Tadā muktiryadā cittaṁ na vāñchati na śocati l
Na muñcati na gṛhṇāti na hṛṣyati na kupyati ll

2. There is freedom when the mind does not desire nor grieve, when it neither accepts nor rejects anything, neither eels happy nor is angry with anything.

तदा बन्धो यदाचित्तं सक्तं स कास्वपि दृष्टिषु ।
तदा मोक्षो यदा चित्तमसक्तं सर्वदृष्टिषु ॥३॥

Tadā bandho yadā cittaṁ saktaṁ kāsvapi dṛṣṭiṣu l
Tadā mokṣo yadā cittamasaktaṁ sarvadṛṣṭiṣu ll

3. There is bondage when the mind is attached to any of the (sensory) perceptions. There is freedom when the mind is unattached to any perception.

Attached—The *Gītā* forcefully stresses non-attachment (*anāsakti*).

Perception—All the five avenues of the senses are covered though only sight is particularized.

यदा नाहं तदा मोक्षो यदाहं बन्धनं तदा ।
मत्वेति हेलया किञ्चिन्मा गृहाण विमुञ्च मा ॥४॥

Yadā nāhaṁ tadā mokṣo yadāhaṁ bandhanaṁ tadā 1
Matveti helayā kiñcit mā gṛhāṇa vimuñca mā 11

4. When there is no ego there is freedom; when there is ego there is bondage. Reflecting on this, refrain from acceptance or rejection of anything with ease.

CHAPTER IX

AṢṬĀVAKRA ON INDIFFERENCE

Nirveda or indifference, equal-mindedness (*samatā*) to all beings and things and ontological reason or *yukti* (springing from contemplation of the Upaniṣadic utterences) are here considered as the triple ways to the attainment of *svarūpa* (IX, 6). Indifference or *nirveda* leads to renunciation and dispassion for life, enjoyment and learning. Man through indifference can get beyond the sense of duty, what should be and should not be done. He overcomes all pairs of opposites and escapes to three-fold misery of the transient valueless world (IX, 3). Thus does he become free from bondage to the phenomenal world, comprising nothing but transformations of the five basic elements of nature, and abide in his true Self (IX, 7). Desire is verily saṁsāra. Indifference is the only road to liberation (IX, 8).

अष्टावक्र उवाच

कृताकृते च द्वन्द्वानि कदा शान्तानि कस्य वा ।
एवं ज्ञात्वेह निर्वेदाद्भव त्यागपरोऽव्रती ॥१॥

Aṣṭāvakra uvāca

Kṛtākṛte ca dvandvāni kadā śāntāni kasya vā l
Evaṁ jñātveha nirvedādbhava tyāgaparo'vratī ll

Aṣṭāvakra said:

1. To whom belong the conflicts relating to what should and should not be done ? When do these cease and for whom either ? Knowing this, practise renunciation and passionlessness through the cultivation of indifference.

Conflicts—The phenomenal body and mind are beset with chronic conflicts and contradictions of various pairs of opposites, such as pleasure and pain, attraction and aversion, happiness and misery, success and failure, good and evil, life and death. These arise due to the interplay of the contending modalities of nature or guṇas. According to Aṣṭāvakra, the opposition between what is done and what is not done in ethics is the basic subjective human experience that must be surpassed (see also XVIII, 12). Unless man releases himself from the pairs of opposites and eradicates his sense of duty through the realization of the transitoriness and unreality of the goals of life, the Self cannot rise from the phenomenal to the unqualified (beyond the guṇas) realm. In the transcendent realm the very frame and content of differentiation and contradictions familiar in human thought and experience vanishes.

Indifference—The *Bhagavadgītā* uses the term *'nirveda'* only once in the sense of indifference towards the fruits of righteous deeds, such as the gain of heaven and enjoyment of kingdom and of the good things of the earth. *Nirveda* is essential for the *buddhiyoga* of the *Gītā* and takes the contemplative beyond the range of the *Vedas* and *Upaniṣads* (II, 52). The *Muṇḍaka Upaniṣad* uses the term *'nirveda'* in the sense of non-attachment to the world and its works as the first step of acquisition of the supreme knowledge (I, 2, 12).

कस्यापि तात धन्यस्य लोकचेष्टावलोकनात् ।
जीवितेच्छा बुभुक्षा च बुभुत्सोपशमं गताः ॥२॥

Kasyāpi tāta dhanyasya lokaceṣṭāvalokanāt 1
Jīvitecchā bubhukṣā ca bubhutsopaśamaṁ gatāḥ 11

2. My son, rare is the blessed person whose passion for living, enjoyment and learning is extinguished through observing the vicissitudes of worldly men.

अनित्यं सर्वमेवेदं तापत्रितयदूषितम् ।
असारं निन्दितं हेयमिति निश्चित्य शाम्यति ॥३॥

Anityaṁ sarvamevedaṁ tāpatritayadūṣitam 1
Asāraṁ ninditaṁ heyamiti niścitya śāmyati 11

3. A man of wisdom becomes serene through the realization that all this world is ephemeral, tainted by the threefold misery, worthless, contemptible and worthy of rejection.

Threefold Misery—viz., those that are related to the

organism, those that are caused by living and non-living objects and those that are due to cosmic accidents.

Transient and Worthless—Prahlāda says in the *Viṣṇu Purāṇa*: "I verily say the truth that I find no contentment in the worthless world with all its fluctuations".

कोऽसौ कालो वयः किं वा यत्र द्वन्द्वानि नो नृणाम् ।
तान्युपेक्ष्य यथा प्राप्तवर्त्ती सिद्धिमवाप्नुयात् ॥४॥

Ko'sau kālo vayaḥ kiṁ vā yatra dvandvāni no nṛṇām 1
Tānyupekṣya yathā prāptavartī siddhimavāpnuyāt 11

4. Realizing that the duality of opposites does not exist for man, where is time and where is age for him? By abjuring these, one who is content with what comes of itself reaches perfection.

Opposites—Such as the duality of desire and non-attachment, pleasure aud pain, good and evil, duty and wish. The *Bhagavadgītā* persistently stresses the need of freedom from the delusion brought about by the pairs of opposites, such as heat and cold, pleasure and pain, love and hatred. Ultimately it is the gross dualism between God and the world that is the basis of man's anguish and creatureliness (IV,22; VII, 27, 28; XV, 5).

नाना मतं महर्षीणां साधूनां योगिनां तथा ।
दृष्ट्वा निर्वेदमापन्नः को न शाम्यति मानवः ॥५॥

Nānā mataṁ maharṣīṇāṁ sādhūnāṁ yogināṁ tathā 1
Dṛṣṭvā nirvedamāpannaḥ ko na śāmyati mānavaḥ 11

5. Observing the diversity of opinion among the great seers, sages and yogīs, what person is there who does not accept indifference and attain tranquility?

Indifference, Nirveda—Aṣṭāvakra here definitely places the quest of the supreme, non-dual Self above the philosophical doctrines, the injunctions of saints and the practices of yogīs. Such is the supremacy attached to ontological vision. The *Gītā* synthesizes ontology, religion and ethics. Aṣṭāvakra, on the other hand, stands for pure and undiluted ontological insight (*Ātmādvaita*) grounded in immediate intuition.

कृत्वा मूर्त्तिपरिज्ञानं चैतन्यस्य न किं गुरुः ।
निर्वेदसमतायुक्त्या यस्तारयति संसृतेः ॥६॥

Kṛtvā mūrtiparijñānaṁ caitanyasya na kiṁ guruḥ l
Nirvedasamatāyuktyā yastārayati saṁsṛteḥ ll

6. He who gains complete knowledge of the true nature of pure consciousness through indifference to the world, equal-mindedness and (ontological) reason, saves himself from the succession of births. He has no other spiritual master except himself.

The threefold ways of ontological vision are summarized here : Indifference to the world, sameness to all beings and intellectual insight of the *Advaita Vedānta*. These lead up to immediate experience of the Self (*ātmānubhava*) as pure existence, consciousness and bliss. Neither seers nor good men nor yogis can be true spiritual guides. The Self is its own guide "Be ye lamps unto yourselves", says the Buddha.

पश्य भूतविकारांस्त्वं भूतमात्रान् यथार्थतः ।
तत्क्षणाद्बन्धनिर्मुक्तः स्वरूपस्थो भविष्यसि ॥७॥

Paśya bhūtavikārāṅstvaṁ bhūtamātrān yathārthataḥ l
Tatkṣaṇādbandhanirmuktaḥ svarūpastho bhaviṣyasi ll

7. Discern the changes of the elements as nothing in reality but the primary elements, and yourself at once as free from their bondage. Thus will you abide in your essential nature.

The Buddhist reasoning about the '*skandhas*' for obtaining insight into truth is reflected here. The undefiled Self is the sole witness of the modifications of the elements of nature, mind and body. The major aim is establishment in *svarūpa*—the stainless and eternal witness of the phenomenal world.

वासना एव संसार इति सर्वा विमुञ्च ताः ।
तत्त्यागो वासनात्यागात् स्थितिरद्य यथा तथा ॥८॥

Vāsanā eva saṁsāra iti sarvā vimuñca tāḥ I
Tattyāgo vāsanātyāgāt sthitiradya yathā tathā II

8. The desire surely is the world. Renounce all desires. The renunciation of the world comes from the renunciation of desire. Now you can remain wherever you are (destined).

CHAPTER X

AṢṬĀVAKRA ON DISPASSION

The pleasures and fortunes of the world are transient. Contentment can come only from non-attachment to desires and the traditional goals of man's life—passion, wealth and piety (*trivarga*). The pure and undivided Self is alone real; the universe is false like a juggler's show. Ignorance does not exist; and likewise the exacting routine of duties undertaken by body, mind and speech from birth to birth for the fulfilment of human goals is unreal. All desires, the three-fold goals of life, even the aspirations for higher knowledge have to be extinguished through absolute *vairāgya*. The true, non-dual pure intelligence can alone dispel the ignorance, toil and moil and misery of innumerable births, and give lasting joy and peace.

अष्टावक्र उवाच

विहाय वैरिणं काममर्थं चानर्थसंकुलम् ।
धर्ममप्येतयोर्हेतुं सर्वत्रानादरं कुरु ॥१॥

Aṣṭāvakra uvāca

Vihāya vairiṇaṁ kāmamarthaṁ cānarthasaṅkulam l
Dharmamapyetayorhetuṁ sarvatrānādaraṁ kuru ll

Aṣṭāvakra said:

1. Having given up desire as the enemy, wealth as associated with mischief and also piety as leading to both desire and wealth, practise neglect (of the goals of life).

Mokṣa or freedom as the final goal in the Indian scheme of life cannot be reached without abandoning the three cognate goals viz., *kāma* (desire), *artha* (wealth) and *dharma* (piety) that are usually stressed together in Indian ethics. The quest of the Supreme Self is based here on complete indifference (*nirveda*) and renunciation (*vairāgya*), even the abandonment of *dharma*. The stress of dispassion (*vairāgya*) comes from the *Bhagavadgītā* (VI, 36, XIII, 8, XVIII, 52) and *Pātañjala yoga*. For the control of the mind, the *Gītā* insists upon the combination of constant practice (*abhyāsa*) and dispassion or *vairāgya* (VI, 35). Patañjali in his *Yoga Sūtra* also commends both practice and dispassion (I, 12).

स्वप्नेन्द्रजालवत्पश्य दिनानि त्रीणि पञ्च वा ।
मित्रक्षेत्रधनागारदारदायादिसम्पदः ॥२॥

Svapnendrajālavat paśya dināni trīṇi pañca vā ।
Mitrakṣetradhanāgāradāradāyādisampadaḥ ॥

2. Look upon friend, land, wealth, house, wife and other objects of fortune as a dream or a magician's show, lasting (only) for three or five days.

यत्र यत्र भवेत्तृष्णा संसारं विद्धि तत्र वै ।
प्रौढवैराग्यमाश्रित्य वीततृष्णः सुखी भव ॥३॥

Yatra yatra bhavettṛṣṇā saṁsāraṁ viddhi tatra vai ।
Prauḍhavairāgyamāśritya vītatṛṣṇaḥ sukhī bhava ॥

3. Know that as the world wherever there is desire. Cultivating strong dispassion, free yourself from desire and be contented.

तृष्णामात्रात्मको बन्धस्तन्नाशो मोक्ष उच्यते ।
भवासंसक्तिमात्रेण प्राप्तितुष्टिर्मुहुर्मुहुः ॥४॥

Tṛṣṇāmātrātmako bandhastannāśo mokṣa uccyate ।
Bhavāsaṁsaktimātreṇa prāptituṣṭirmuhurmuhuḥ ॥

4. Desire alone is the soul of bondage. Its annihilation is said to be salvation. Through non-attachment to the world alone one attains constant bliss of realization (of the Self).

Non-attachment—Aṣṭāvakra uses the word *asaṁsakti* meaning literally absolute exclusion of all contacts.

त्वमेकश्चेतनः शुद्धो जडं विश्वमसत्तथा ।
अविद्यापि न किञ्चित्सा का बुभुत्सा तथापि ते ॥५॥

Tvamekaścetanaḥ śuddho jaḍaṁ viśvamasattathā 1
Avidyāpi na kiñcitsā kā bubhutsā tathāpi te 11

5. You are the one, pure intelligence. The universe is material and unreal (devoid of intelligence). Ignorance is also non-existent. Then what wish to know can be there for you?

In the system of the Vedānta, Ātman or Brahman alone is consciousness. The world is material and unconscious.

राज्यं सुताः कलत्राणि शरीराणि सुखानि च ।
संसक्तस्यापि नष्टानि तव जन्मनि जन्मनि ॥६॥

Rājyaṁ sutāḥ kalatrāṇi śarīrāṇi sukhāni ca 1
Saṁsaktasyāpi naṣṭāni tava janmani janmani 11

6. From birth to birth, kingdoms, sons, wives, bodies and pleasures to which you were attached have been lost.

अलमर्थेन कामेन सुकृतेनापि कर्मणा ।
एभ्यः संसारकान्तारे न विश्रान्तमभून्मनः ॥७॥

Alamarthena kāmena sukṛtenāpi karmaṇā 1
Ebhyaḥ saṁsārakāntāre na viśrāntamabhūnmanaḥ 11

7. Enough of wealth, desire and piety in the wilderness of the world. The mind cannot find peace in these.

Aṣṭāvakra again denies even *dharma*, along with desire and wealth, reiterating X, 1.

कृतं न कति जन्मानि कायेन मनसा गिरा ।
दुःखमायासदं कर्म तदद्याप्युपरम्यताम् ॥८॥

Kṛtaṁ na kati janmāni kāyena manasā girā I
Duḥkhamāyāsadaṁ karma tadadyāpyuparamyatām II

8. For innumerable births have you undertaken work, painful and exacting, with your body, mind and speech. Hence find rest at least now.

Chapter XI

AṢṬĀVAKRA ON THE SELF AS PURE AND RADIANT INTELLIGENCE

This chapter delineates the supreme experience of the Self as pure intelligence or *bodha* (XI, 6, 8), freedom from intention and discursive reasoning or *nirvikalpa* (XI, 7) and absolute aloneness or *kaivalya* (XI, 6), (as recommended by Patañjali). The Self lives in the body but has lost the body-sense. It lives in time but has realized that it shares in the omnipresence and immortality of God and Creator of the Cosmos (XI, 2). The manifold and marvellous cosmos manifests itself as the embodiment of pure, unconditioned intelligence (*sphūrtimātra*, XI, 8). The Self identifies itself with everything and every being, "from Brahma down to the tuft of grass", sets the desires at rest and becomes happy and serene since nothing exists for and outside it.

From the viewpoint of Patañjali's dialectic of liberation, this is the yogī's state of *asamprajñāta samādhi* leading to his *kaivalya* or absolute aloneness.

From the viewpoint of Aṣṭāvakra this is his supreme and natural state of self-abidance or *svāsthya*, All-Being (*Īśvara*) or pure intelligence (*cit*) where he senses this phenomenal world as himself that shines (II, 8, XI, 8). This makes him ever desireless, pure and serene (XI, 1, 7, 8).

From the viewpoint of ethics, the pure self completely rids itself of all desires and goals of life and becomes perfectly tranquil and non-active. As man coincides with the absolute and supreme Self, his deeds do not involve him (XI, 4). Unlike the seer of the *Bhagvadgītā* who bridges ontology and ethics through the dedication of work to God or Brahman, Aṣṭāvakra denies ethics altogether. The ontic Self and the world, according to him, are the same and continuous. The self gets its final release from all the unquenchable dualities of desire and renunciation, good and evil, aspiration and attainment and cares not for what is done or what is not done (XI, 5, 7). The world shines in the full purity and grandeur of the Self (*cidrūpa*) enjoying absolute aloneness, freedom and serenity. 'I am *bodha*, *cit* or That, is the supreme realization.

अष्टावक्र उवाच
भावाभावविकारश्च स्वभावादिति निश्चयी ।
निर्विकारो गतक्लेशः सुखेनैवोपशाम्यति ॥१॥

Aṣṭāvakra uvāca
Bhāvābhāvavikāraśca svabhāvāditi niścayī l
Nirvikāro gatakleśaḥ sukhenaivopaśāmyati ll

Aṣṭāvakra said :

1. One who understands with certitude that existence, destruction and change are inherent in things becomes unaffected and free from pain. It is he who can easily find peace.

ईश्वरः सर्वनिर्माता नेहान्य इति निश्चयी ।
अन्तर्गलितसर्वाशः शान्तः क्वापि न सज्जते ॥२॥

Īśvaraḥ sarvanirmātā nehānya iti niścayī l
Antargalitasarvāśaḥ śāntaḥ kvāpi na sajjate ll

2. God (the Self) is the creator of all, there is none else in the universe. Knowing this for certain, one finds desire melted away and becomes serene. He becomes attached to nothing.

The term *Īśvara* or God is used here and in other verses for Ātman following the *Bhagavadgītā*.

आपदः सम्पदः काले दैवादेवेति निश्चयी ।
तृप्तः स्वस्थेन्द्रियो नित्यं न वाञ्छति न शोचति ॥३॥

Āpadaḥ sampadaḥ kāle daivādeveti niscayī l
Tṛptaḥ svasthendriyo nityaṁ na vāñchati na śocati ll

3. Knowing for certain that in the course of time

fortune and misfortune visit one through destiny, he becomes ever contented and constantly holds the senses in check. He neither desires nor grieves.

Senses—The sense-organs and the mind are through meditation fixed on the Self. This is the way of control of desires. See the *Bhagavadgītā*, VI, 25.

सुखदुःखे जन्ममृत्यू दैवादेवेति निश्चयी ।
साध्यादर्शी निरायासः कुर्वन्नपि न लिप्यते ॥४॥

Sukhaduḥkhe janmamṛtyū daivādeveti niścayī 1
Sādhyādarśī nirāyāsaḥ kurvannapi na lipyate 11

4. Knowing for certain that happiness and sorrow, birth and death surely come of themselves through fate, one does not seek after the goals of life and becomes non-active. His deeds do not involve him.

Do not involve him—This phrase '*kurvan api na lipyate*' is borrowed *verbatim* from the *Gītā* (V, 7) and repeated in XVII, 19. Aṣṭāvakra utilizes the *Gītā's* famous doctrine of inaction in action (IV, 14; V, 7, 10; XIII, 31; XVIII, 17). In XVIII, 25, again, Aṣṭāvakra has '*yaḥ kurvan api karoti na.*' In the *Gītā* XIII, 31 we read, '*na karoti na lipyate.*'

चिन्तया जायते दुःखं नान्यथेहेति निश्चयी ।
तया हीनः सुखी शान्तः सर्वत्र गलितस्पृहः ॥५॥

Cintayā jāyate duḥkhaṁ nānyatheheti niścayī 1
Tayā hīnaḥ sukhī śāntaḥ sarvatra galitaspṛhaḥ 11

5. Knowing for certain that in the world sorrow is caused through anxiety and not otherwise, a person free from this becomes happy and peaceful with his desires melted away.

नाहं देहो न मे देहो बोधोऽहमिति निश्चयी ।
कैवल्यमिव संप्राप्तो न स्मरत्यकृतं कृतम् ॥६॥

Nāhaṁ deho na me deho bodho'hamiti niścayī 1
Kaivalyamiva saṁprāpto na smaratyakṛtaṁ kṛtam 11

6. Knowing for certain that 'I am not the body nor the body belongs to me, and I am intelligence itself', one attains the absolute aloneness of the self. He does not remember what he has done and what has been left undone.

Aloneness of the Self—The *Bhagavadgītā* does not use at all the term *kaivalya* (aloneness or absoluteness of the self) of the system of Patañjali. The notion of *kaivalya*, derived from *Pātañjala yoga*, is much elaborated by Aṣṭāvakra. (III, 9, XI, 3, 6, XVII, 18, XVIII, 87, XX, 4)

आब्रह्मस्तम्बपर्यन्तमहमेवेति निश्चयी ।
निर्विकल्पः शुचिः शान्तः प्राप्ताप्राप्तविनिर्वृतः ॥७॥

Ābrahmastambaparyantamahameveti niścayī l
Nirvikalpaḥ śuci śāntaḥ prāptāprāptavinirvṛtah ll

7. Knowing for certain that it is verily I who am from Brahma to the clump of grass, one becomes free from the fluctuations of thought or reasoning; pure and serene he withdraws himself from what is to be attained and not attained.

Nirvikalpa is a yogic term used by Aṣṭāvakra as many as seven times. According to him, the changeful mind is neither the self nor belongs to it. Every mental activity is a limitation of the self which is of the nature of pure intelligence or *cinmātra* (II, 17). Thus the mind's vacuity is self-abidance in freedom and non-duality. *Nirvikalpa* as applied to *samādhi* is defined by Bhartṛhari as an exclusive concentration upon the one entity without distinct and separate consciousness of the knower, the known and the knowing, and without even self-consciousness. The term is not used at all by the principal *Upaniṣads* and the *Bhagavadgītā*.

Pure—due to the absence of contact of the self, the senses and sense-organs.

नानाश्चर्यमिदं विश्वं न किञ्चिदिति निश्चयी ।
निर्वासनः स्फूर्तिमात्रो न किञ्चदिव शाम्यति ॥८॥

Nānāścaryamidaṁ viśvaṁ na kiñciditi niścayī l
Nirvāsanaḥ sphūrtimātro na kiñcidiva śāmyati ll

8. Knowing for certain that this manifold, marvellous world is non-existent, one becomes desireless and pure intelligence. He becomes, serene, since nothing exists (for him).

The sense of all-pervasiveness of the pure Self and the ontological insight that nothing exists except the unborn, witnessing Self embody the acme of wisdom, according to Aṣṭāvakra. The illusion of the world disappears as the all-encompassing intelligence transforms it from inert or *jaḍa* to living or *cetana*. From this follow complete desirelessness, serenity and freedom. The uprooting of all desires, feelings and thoughts, and even of the time-honoured four goals of life, viz., *dharma, artha, kāma* and *mokṣa* is grounded in the Self's attainment of the state of absolute aloneness or *kaivalya* (XI, 3). With Aṣṭāvakra, there is even no striving for liberation or *mokṣa*. The liberation or bondage is the same to a person abiding in his unborn, indivisible life (XX. 12).

Chapter XII

JANAKA ON THE ASCENT OF CONTEMPLATION

This chapter deals with the stages of elevated contemplation that should neither be disturbed by yogic exercise and recitation of Upaniṣadic formula nor stained by any thought or experience whatever. Any kind of effort, physical, mental or spiritual, takes the self away from its indivisible essence. Man must ever be established in the unborn, immutable self (*svasthaḥ, svarūpa*). The verses gradually lead up to the state of *svasthaḥ* through withdrawal first from yogic exercise and prayer, and then from contemplation (XII, 1) together with the rejection of all routine activities and duties of life causing conflicts of opposites (XII, 4, 5).

The pure Self, finally, should get rid of *samādhi* itself. Establishment in the non-dual Self is not possible unless the *dhyāna* of Ātman or Brahman itself is eschewed (XI, 7). The latter is a mode of mind (*vṛtti*) at the relativist dimension (XI, 7) and has to be extinguished through fusion with Ātman or *Brahma-vṛtti*. Self-abidance follows man's essential disposition. '*Svasthaḥ*' and '*svabhāva*' are identical (XII, 8).

The whole chapter, as it delineates the ascent of meditation, stresses the need of complete vacation of consciousness in meditation forfinal intuitive realization of the unknowable Self as *cinmātra*. *Niṣkriya* or *nirvyāpāra* (cessation of physical activity) (XII, 3, XX,9) and *nirvikalpa* (cessation of mental activity) (II, 17, XI, 2, 7, XV, 5, XVIII, 76) must go together for reaching the blessed state.

जनक उवाच

कायकृत्यासहः पूर्वं ततो वाग्विस्तरासहः ।
अथ चिन्तासहस्तस्मादेवमेवाहमास्थितः ॥१॥

Janaka uvāca

Kāyakṛtyāsahaḥ pūrvaṁ tato vāgvistarāsahaḥ I
Atha cintāsahastasmādevamevāhamāsthitaḥ II

Janaka said:

1. At first I could not stand physical exercise (yogic), then expansion of the word (*mantra*) and then meditation. Thus verily do I therefore abide (in myself).

The contemplative has gradually to give up all activity, beginning with yogic physical exercise and prayer or silent recital of *mantra* (*Japa*) and then to refrain even from contemplation itself. Thus can he rise to his pure self beyond word, meaning and action, beyond all relativity.

Thus—Here the contemplative reaches the state of complete *physical* poise or impassivity.

प्रीत्यभावेन शब्दादेरदृश्यत्वेन चात्मनः ।
विक्षेपैकाग्रहृदय एवमेवाहमास्थितः ॥२॥

Prītyabhāvena śabdāderadṛśyatvena cātmanaḥ 1
Vikṣepaikāgrahṛdaya evamevāhamāsthitaḥ 11

2. Due to lack of interest in any verbal formula and the invisibility of Self I have my mind free from any distraction and single-pointed (to the Self). Thus do I verily abide (in myself).

Formula—The repetition of the sounds of the *mantra* which at the outset leads to concentration is rejected here on the contemplative's way of ascent to the absolute Self.

Invisibility—The Self is not an object of perception and is inaccessible. It can be reached only by intuition. Invisibility here means incomprehensibility. Aṣṭāvakra repeatedly emphasises that the Self is not an object of perception but is absolute transcendence. It is beyond any positive or negative formulations (XX).

Thus—Here the contemplative reaches the state of complete *mental* poise or non-distraction.

समाध्यासादिविक्षिप्तौ व्यवहारः समाधये ।
एवं विलोक्य नियममेवमेवाहमास्थितः ॥३॥

Samādhyāsādivikṣiptau vyavahāraḥ samādhaye 1
Evaṁ vilokya niyamamevamevāhamāsthitaḥ 11

3. (A man's) effort becomes necessary for the purpose of concentration only when the mind is thoroughly distracted due to superimposition and other falsehoods. Discerning this as the rule, thus verily do I abide (in myself).

In this verse even *samādhi* is given up in order that the pure and absolute Self can shine by itself. *Samādhi* is here regarded as activity belonging to the relativist dimension required as long as any superimposition, such as doership and enjoyership, according to the *Vedānta*, persists. The Self is alone the doer and enjoyer. On its complete silence it rids itself of *samādhi*.

Thoroughly—Same here means thoroughly or completely.

Thus—Here the contemplative withdraws himself from any effort of concentration or samādhi. Aṣṭāvakra insists in I, 15 that the practice of *samādhi* is itself bondage.

हेयोपादेयविरहादेवं हर्षविषादयोः ।
अभावादद्य हे ब्रह्मन्नेवमेवाहमास्थितः ॥४॥

Heyopādeyavirahādevaṁ harṣaviṣādayoḥ I
Abhāvādadya he brahmannevamevāhamāsthitaḥ II

4. Due to the absence of both the rejectable (evil) and the acceptable (good) and of any happiness and sorrow, O Brahman, thus verily do I abide in myself.

Brahman, i.e. the Self or *guru.*

Thus—Here the contemplative transcends the duality of all opposites such as joy and sorrow, good and evil, preference and aversion.

आश्रमानाश्रमं ध्यानं चित्तस्वीकृतवर्जनम् ।
विकल्पं मम वीक्ष्यैतैरेवमेवाहमास्थितः ॥५॥

Āśramānāśramaṁ dhyānaṁ cittasvīkṛtavarjanam I
Vikalpaṁ mama vīkṣyaitairevamevāhamāsthitaḥ II

5. A stage of life or its negation, meditation and withdrawal from the objects which the mind desires—discerning these as causing distraction, thus verily do I abide (in myself).

Stage—This refers to one of the four stages in the Indian scheme of Life. The contemplative transcends the stage of *Saṁnyāsa*. He is, therefore, called an *avadhūta* or *atyāśramī*.

Thus—Here the contemplative transcends not only the life of the senses, mind and desires but also the goal and pattern of living enjoined by society.

कर्माऽनुष्ठानमज्ञानाद्यथैवोपरमस्तथा ।
बुद्ध्वा सम्यगिदं तत्त्वमेवमेवाहमास्थितः ॥६॥

Karmānuṣṭhānamajñānādyathaivoparamastathā I
Buddhvā samyagidaṁ tattvamevamevāhamāsthitaḥ II

6. Understanding fully that it is from ignorance that both the undertaking and cessation of action take place thus verily do I abide (in myself).

Thus—Here the contemplative transcends any activity or inactivity.

अचिन्त्यं चिन्त्यमानोऽपि चिन्तारूपं भजत्यसौ ।
त्यक्त्वा तद्भावनं तस्मादेवमेवाहमास्थितः ॥७॥

Acintyaṁ cintyamāno'pi cintārūpaṁ bhajatyasau I
Tyaktvā tadbhāvanaṁ tasmādevamevāhamāsthitaḥ I

7. A man who meditates on the unthinkable (reality) resorts only to a form of (his) thought. Hence abandoning that meditation, thus verily do I abide (in myself).

That meditation—viz., the meditation of the incomprehensible Ātman or Brahman, which is "too subtle to be known" (*Bhagavadgītā*, XIII, 15) and "transcends knowledge, the knower and the knowable" (XII, 15, XX, 8).

Form of thought—hence belonging to the phenomenal world and unreal. In the *Yoga-Vāsiṣṭha Rāmāyaṇa* we read, "The truth flashed past one like lightning in between the gaps created by the absence of thought".

Thus—The contemplative here takes the final leap beyond word and meaning, beyond thought. The highest *samādhi* which is depicted as unpenetrated by word (*śabda*) and meaning (*artha*), is that where the contemplative becomes Brahman itself (*brahmabhāvanā* of the *Gītā*).

In Śaṅkara's *Aparokṣānubhūti* we have the following brief definition of *samādhi* : "Withdraw the mind from the objects of the senses, then fill it with Self or Brahman and finally completely forget the mind itself, that is *samādhi* which is of the nature of absolute knowledge". Here the self-luminous Ātman or Brahman reveals of itself with the disappearance of the knower, the knowing and the object of knowledge or the phenomenal world.

Compare the following from Narahari's *Bodhasāra* : "Contemplation is the means of emancipation, observe all the scriptures. My opinion is the reverse. It is through the meditation of nothing that the Supreme reality shines by itself. When the self-effulgent One is revealed, immediately become one with it" (LXVII, 86). The *Avadhūta Gītā* says, "For me there is neither the apprehender nor the apprehended, neither cause nor effect; neither the thinkable nor the unthinkable can be spoken of me. I am the embodiment of annihilation and am taintless" (IV, 10).

एवमेव कृतं येन स कृतार्थो भवेदसौ ।
एवमेव स्वभावो यः सः कृतार्थो भवेदसौ ॥८॥

Evameva kṛtaṁ yena sa kṛtārtho bhavedasau ।
Evameva svabhāvo yaḥ saḥ kṛtārtho bhavedasau ॥

8. Blessed is the man who has accomplished these. Blessed indeed, is he who thus fulfils himself by his nature.

Thus—Here the highest stage is predicated of a man who does not achieve through effort but realizes the Self or Brahman by his inherent disposition. He has no *sādhanā* neither *dhyāna*, nor *samādhi*. He transcends all actions physical, mental and spiritual. He envisions the Self, effulgent, unborn and absolute, instinctually in all conditions. No more can be said about him.

Chapter XII

JANAKA ON THE TRANSCENDENT BLISS

The supreme bliss comes only to one who abides in the Self, giving up all activities of the body, mind and speech. For him there is neither action nor inaction, neither good nor evil, neither acceptance nor renunciation (XIII, 2-4). Self-abidance or *svāsthya* is absolute happiness in all possible human condition. It certainly represents a higher spiritual stage than the renunciation of the ascetic with the loin-cloth who does not rise above all physical and mental opposites and relativities such as action and inaction, acceptance and rejection, good and evil (XIII, 1, 4, 7).

From this suprarational ontological insight *vijñāna*, III, 1, 3, XIV, 2, 3) emerges the doctrine of non-origination and primordial singleness of the Self(*ajātavāda*, or *ajātivāda* XIII, 1). The Self is unborn and all-pervading and confers supreme peace and tranquility (Śivaṁ Śāntam).

जनक उवाच

अकिञ्चनभवं स्वास्थ्यं कौपीनत्वेऽपि दुर्लभम् ।
त्यागादाने विहायास्मादहमासे यथासुखम् ॥१॥

Janaka uvāca

Akiñcanabhavaṁ svāsthyaṁ kaupīnatve'pi durlabham I
Tyāgādāne vihāyāsmādahamāse yathāsukham II

Janaka said:

1. Abidance with the Self which does not spring from anything (unborn) cannot be obtained even in the state of renunciation with only a loin-cloth. Hence abandoning renunciation and acceptance I live in true happiness.

Self-abidance—The word *svāsthya* has suffered a serious semantic decline meaning now physical health or well-being. Throughout the text svāsthya means establishment in the (real) Self and is used often. Several cognate words having the same denotation are used: *svasthaḥ*, *svarūpasthaḥ*, *svapāda* and *svarūpa*. It is noteworthy that in the *Bhagavadgītā* the term *svasthaḥ* comes but only once, meaning one who dwells in the Self (XIV, 24). In Gauḍapāda we have *svastha* in III, 47 and *ātmasaṁstha* in III, 34.

Does not spring from anything—Aṣṭāvakra is the real originator of the doctrine of non-origination of the Self which was later on elaborated by Gauḍapāda in his famous *Kārikās* (c. 600 A. D.). The latter uses very similar words: "There does not exist any cause which can produce jīva" The highest truth, according to the *Kārikā* is that nothing originates (III, 2, 48 IV, 5, 71) *sambhavo asya na vidyate* (*Kārikā* III, 48). This notion indeed goes back to the *Bṛhadāraṇyaka Upaniṣad* which observes: "When born, he is not born again; who indeed can generate him? (III, 9, 28) The "*Ātmatattva*", aptly says Śaṅkara, "is unborn (*aja*) and non-dual (*advaya*). It has no internal distinctions, nor are these things outside it. This is certain" (Śaṅkara on Gauḍapāda's *Kārikā*, III, 27).

Akiñcana means 'without anything outside the self'. The Self cannot be produced (*bhava*), because the cause which can produce it is non-existent; everything comprises the immutable, indivisible all-encompassing Self. *Akiñcanabhava* means, therefore, unborn or uncreated. That the Self has no birth is indicated in several other passages (II, 12, XV, 9, 13, 16, XX, 14).

'The self is all that exists', or *sarvaṁ ātmā* (XV, 15), *ātmā eva idaṁ jagat sarvam* (IV, 4) is Aṣṭāvakra's version of the famous formulation *imāni bhūtāni, idaṁ sarvaṁ, yad ayaṁ* ātmā of the *Bṛhadāraṇyaka Upaniṣad* (IV, 5, 7) *ātmā eva idaṁ sarvaṁ* of the *Chāndogya Upaniṣad* (VII, 26, 1), *ayaṁ ātmā brahma* of the *Bṛhadāraṇyaka Upaniṣad* (I, IV, 8) and the *Māṇḍūkya Upaniṣad* (7) and of *Vāsudevaḥ sarvam* of the *Bhagavadgītā* (VII, 19).

कुत्रापि खेदः कायस्य जिह्वा कुत्रापि खिद्यते ।
मनः कुत्रापि तत्त्यक्त्वा पुरुषार्थे स्थितः सुखम् ॥२॥

Kutrāpi khedaḥ kāyasya jihvā kutrāpi khidyate ।
Manaḥ kutrāpi tattyaktvā puruṣārthe sthitaḥ sukham ॥

2. There is distress of the body. There is distress of the mind. Forsaking all these I abide in the supreme goal of life (establishment in the Self).

Body—Yogic exercise is painful.

Speech—Recitation of *mantra* causes distress.

Mind—Effort of concentration also causes distress.

The establishment in the Self involves neither effort nor pain. Hence '*svāsthya*' or abidance in the Self denotes perfect ease.

कृतं किमपि नैव स्यादिति सञ्चिन्त्य तत्त्वतः ।
यदा यत्कर्तुमायाति तत्कृत्वाऽऽसे यथासुखम् ॥३॥

Kṛtaṁ kimapi naiva syāditi sañcintya tattvataḥ l
Yadā yatkartumāyāti tatkṛtvāse yathāsukham ll

3. Fully understanding that nothing in reality is done (by the Self), I only do whatever comes of itself. Hence I live in true happiness.

Do whatever comes of itself—What the Gītā calls action for the maintenance of physical life (*śarīrayātrā*) is binding by its nature (III, 8).

Hence—Because of the absence of egoism.

कर्मनैष्कर्म्यनिर्बन्धभावा देहस्थयोगिनः ।
संयोगायोगविरहादहमासे यथासुखम् ॥४॥

Karmanaiṣkarmyanirbandhabhāvā dehasthayoginaḥ l
Saṁyogāyogavirahādahamāse yathāsukham l

4. The yogīs who are attached to the body show insistence on action or inaction. Due to my abandonment of the sense of association or disassociation (with the body) I live in true happiness.

This verse deprecates the body-sense that lingers in the yogī. With self-abidance, *yoga-abhyāsa* becomes meaningless and a cause of bondage. In XVII, 1, however, Aṣṭāvakra refers to the combination of *yogābhyāsa* or yogic practice with the Vedantic discipline of discrimination and self-knowledge and in XVIII, 9 to the silence of the yogī who realizes that the Self is all that exists.

Inaction—Naiṣkarmya is celebrated in the *Bhagavadgītā* which enjoins inaction in action and action in inaction(III, 4; XVIII, 49). Aṣṭāvakra conforms to this principle grounding it in the realization of the true Self.

अर्थानर्थौ न मे स्थित्या गत्या वा शयनेन वा ।
तिष्ठन् गच्छन् स्वपंस्तस्मादहमासे यथासुखम् ॥५॥

Arthānarthau na me sthityā gatyā na śayanena vā ।
Tiṣṭhan gacchan svapan tasmādahamāse yathāsukham ॥

5. Neither any good nor any evil is associated with my stability, movement or repose. Hence I live in true happiness whether I am at rest, move about or sleep.

स्वपतो नास्ति मे हानिः सिद्धिर्यत्नवतो न वा ।
नाशोल्लासौ विहायास्मादहमासे यथासुखम् ॥६॥

Svapato nāsti me hāniḥ siddhiryatnavato na vā ।
Nāśollāsau vihāyāsmādahamāse yathāsukham ॥

6. There is neither any lapse of mine in rest nor in effort. Hence abandoning the sense of deprivation and delight, I live in true happiness.

सुखादिरूपानियमं भावेष्वालोक्य भूरिशः ।
शुभाशुभे विहायास्मादहमासे यथासुखम् ॥७॥

Sukhādirūpāniyamaṁ bhāveṣvālokya bhūriśaḥ ।
Śubhāśubhe vihāyāsmādahamāse yathāsukham ॥

7. Finding repeatedly the fluctuations of pleasure etc. under different circumstances, I have given up good and evil and live in true happiness.

The repetition of 'living in true happiness or *yathā-sukham*' from the first to the last verse of the chapter underlines man's self-abidance or *svāsthya* as the only source of true happiness in the world.

Chapter XIV

JANAKA ON THE NATURAL DISSOLUTION OF THE MIND

The wise one who knows the supreme Self as the eternal Witness and Lord of the world has no care in either bondage or liberation. His desires melt away and he becomes void-minded (*śūnyacitta*). He has no thoughts within, and lives and moves at his pleasure. Asleep in his waking state, he can be understood only by one like him.

जनक उवाच

प्रकृत्या शून्यचित्तो यः प्रमादाद्भावभावनः ।
निद्रितो बोधित इव क्षीणसंस्मरणो हि सः ॥१॥

Janaka uvāca

Prakṛtyā śūnyacitto yaḥ pramādādbhāvabhāvanaḥ /
Nidrito bodhita iva kṣīṇasaṁsmaraṇo hi saḥ ll

Janaka said:

1. The wise one who is void-minded by nature perceives objects through inadvertence and is seen as awake though physically asleep. Verily his memories (of the world) are extinguished.

Void-minded—This is repeated in XVIII, 24.

क्व धनानि क्व मित्राणि क्व मे विषयदस्यवः ।
क्व शास्त्रं क्व च विज्ञानं यदा मे गलिता स्पृहा ॥२॥

Kva dhanāni kva mitrāṇi kva me viṣayavpsyavaḥ 1
Kva śāstraṁ kva ca vijñānaṁ yadā me galitā spṛhā ll

2. As my desires melt away, where can be my riches, my friends, my thieves taking the forms of sense-objects, where can be the scripture and where the wisdom?

Scripture—According to the *Gītā* 'as is the use of a pond in an over-flooded place, so is that of all the scriptures for a Brāhmin of wisdom' (II, 96).

The *Mahābhārata* also says "just as one who obtains water from the river does not care for a well, so the wise do not attach any importance to ritual action" (*Śāntiparva*, 240, 10).

Wisdom—For the man of wisdom even the formula, '*ahaṁ brahmāsmi*', is unnecessary.

विज्ञाते साक्षिपुरुषे परमात्मनि चेश्वरे ।
नैराश्ये बन्धमोक्षे च न चिन्तामुक्तये मम ॥३॥

Vijñāte sākṣipuruṣe paramātmani ceśvare ।
Nairāśye bandhamokṣe ca na cintāmuktaye mama ॥

3. As I have known the Supreme Self who is the eternal Person as the Witness and who is the Lord, I have no desire for bondage and liberation, nor care for salvation.

Aṣṭāvakra follows the *Bhagavadgītā's* identification of the Supreme Self (*Paramātman*) with the eternal Witness of all that exists (*Viśva-Sākṣī*, I, 5) and with *Īśvara* and Brahman.

Witness—The *Gītā* speaks of God as the Lord and the Witness in similar combination (IX, 18). Aṣṭāvakra's reference to *Puruṣa* in this context echoes the constant usage of the term in the major *Upaniṣads* and the *Bhagavadgītā*. But this is the only occasion where the term is used in this text and with the same transcendent meaning with reference to the Self.

No desire—That self-abidance (*svāsthya*) extinguishes the body-sense, and together with it the consciousness of bondage and freedom is stressed throughout the text.

अन्तर्विकल्पशून्यस्य बहिः स्वच्छन्दचारिणः ।
भ्रान्तस्येव दशास्तास्तास्तादृशा एव जानते ॥४॥

Antarvikalpaśūnyasya bahiḥ svacchandacāriṇaḥ ।
Bhrāntasyeva daśāstāstāstādṛśā eva jānate ॥

4. Devoid of any thoughts within, and moving about at his pleasure like a deluded person without, the wise man's different conditions can only be understood by similar (wise) one.

The *jīvanmukta* does not permit any competing *vṛttis* to emerge in his mind, saturated as the latter is with ātman-bliss and peace. Thus is he spoken of as one who is void-minded by nature. He has no anxiety even for liberation. Self-abidance is void-mindedness, not by effort but by instinct and disposition. In XVIII, 23-24 the voidness of mind is further explained. The intellectual climate of the age in which Aṣṭāvakra wrote was full of speculations relating to the void among the Buddhists, Ājīvikas and other denominations.

Chapter XV

AṢṬĀVAKRA ON THE SELF OR BRAHMAN

In this most important chapter Aṣṭāvakra emphasises that there is one ultimate Reality—the Self. The Self is supreme wisdom, God, Brahman or That (XV, 7, 8). It is immutable, indivisible and silent. It neither comes nor goes (XV, 9). It has no birth, nor action nor egoism (XV, 11). As the waves of the worlds emanate from the ocean-like uncreated, boundless and tranquil Self, there is neither gain nor loss to it (XV, 11). "The Self is in all existences and all existences are in it" (XV, 6). The last is repeated from III, **5** and derived from the *Bhagavadgītā* (VI, 29). It implies here both the absolute aloneness and non-origination of the Self and its identity with all that belongs to the mind's frame of causation. Have faithfulness for the Self. This is repeated (XV, 8). The absolute Self is as much an object of reverence and worship as God (*Īśvara*, *Bhagavān*).

अष्टावक्र उवाच

यथातथोपदेशेन कृतार्थः सत्त्वबुद्धिमान् ।
आजीवमपि जिज्ञासुः परस्तत्र विमुह्यति ॥१॥

Aṣṭāvakra uvāca

Yathātathopadeśena kṛtārthaḥ sattvabuddhimān l
Ājīvamapi jijñāsuḥ parastatra vimuhyati ll

Aṣṭāvakra said:

1. A person of pure intelligence obtains his supreme goal even by being taught casually. Another person is confused in this even after enquiring throughout life.

Intelligence—The contrast here is between the man of *sattva guṇa* and the man dominated by the attributes of rajas and *tamas*. Self-knowledge is possible only for a man of sāttvic disposition. He hardly requires instruction. The well-known instance is that of Virocana who fails to obtain the supreme knowledge from Brahmā himself.

मोक्षो विषयवैरस्यं बन्धो वैषयिको रसः ।
एतावदेव विज्ञानं यथेच्छसि तथा कुरु ॥२॥

Mokṣo viṣayavairasyaṁ bandho Vaiṣayiko rasaḥ 1
Etāvadeva vijñānaṁ yathecchasi tathā kuru 11

2. Detachment from sense-objects is salvation; passion for sense-objects is bondage. Knowing this do as you please.

The teaching in X, 4 is repeated here in a different context.

वाग्मिप्राज्ञमहोद्योगं जनं मूकजडालसम् ।
करोति तत्त्वबोधोऽयमतस्त्यक्तो बुभुक्षुभिः ॥३॥

Vāgmiprājñamahodyogaṁ janaṁ mūkajaḍālasam 1
Karoti tattvabodho'yamatastyakto bubhukṣubhiḥ 11

3. This knowledge of the truth (of Ātman) makes a person who is eloquent, wise and vigorous, mute, inert and inactive. Hence it is shunned by those who wish to enjoy (the world).

The *Māṇḍūkya Upaniṣad*, while expounding the Self in the realm of sounds as '*aum*', identifies the highest state or portion of the Self as silence (*turīya*). The Buddha's silence, expressive of the highest, is famous.

न त्वं देहो न ते देहो भोक्ता कर्ता न वा भवान् ।
चिद्रूपोऽसि सदा साक्षी निरपेक्षः सुखं चर ॥४॥

Na tvaṁ deho na te deho bhoktā kartā na vā bhavān
Cidrūpo'si sadā sākṣī nirapekṣaḥ sukhaṁ cara 11

4. You are not the body, nor is the body yours; you are neither the enjoyer nor the doer. You are pure intelligence itself, the eternal witness and the indifferent onlooker. Move about happily.

रागद्वेषौ मनोधर्मौ न मनस्ते कदाचन ।
निर्विकल्पोऽसि बोधात्मा निर्विकारः सुखं चर ॥५॥

Rāgadveṣau manodharmau na manaste kadācana l
Nirvikalpo'si bodhātmā nirvikāraḥ sukhaṁ cara ll

5. Passion and aversion are qualities of mind (not of yours). The mind is never yours. (Hence) you are free from desires and thoughts. You are intelligence itself and free from fluctuations. Move about happily.

सर्वभूतेषु चात्मानं सर्वभूतानि चात्मनि ।
विज्ञाय निरहंकारो निर्ममस्त्वं सुखी भव ॥६॥

Sarvabhuteṣu cātmānaṁ sarvabhūtāni cātmani l
Vijñāya nirahaṁkāro nirmamastvaṁ sukhī bhava ll

6. Realizing the Self in all beings and all beings in the Self, be free from ego-sense and possessiveness and make yourself happy.

The first line of this verse, repeated from III, 5, is borrowed verbatim from the *Gītā* (VI, 29). Aṣṭāvakra has another version of the same in VI, 4. Like the *Gītā*, Aṣṭāvakra stresses both the transcendence and the immanence of the Self. The intuitive comprehension of the Self as the essence of all beings and things (immanence) and of all things and beings abiding in the Self (transcendence) is the core of ontological experience. The Self must rise above the fluctuations of the mind, above ego-sense and possessiveness, above all relativities, before it can enjoy the supreme bliss of the non-dual immutable Self. The Self is the whole, the perfect and the eternal and shines in all parts, imperfections and transiences. This may be further described as the unborn, all-encompassing Brahman or That (XV, 7). With absorption in That or the absolute, unborn and indivisible Self, the sense of existence or non-existence, unity or duality melts away (XX, 14)

विश्वं स्फुरति यत्रेदं तरङ्गा इव सागरे ।
तत्त्वमेव न सन्देहश्चिन्मूर्ते विज्वरो भव ॥७॥

Viśvaṁ sphurati yatredaṁ taraṅgā iva ,sāgare I
Tattvameva na sandehaścinmūrte vijvaro bhava II

7. It is from you whence the world springs as the waves from the ocean. That (intelligence) verily you are. O you, pure intelligence, be free from the fever of the world.

World—The Supreme Self is the matrix (*adhiṣṭhāna*) of the universe. All finite things, beings and experiences are but waves of this infinite ocean of pure intelligence.

श्रद्धत्स्व तात श्रद्धत्स्व नात्र मोहं कुरुष्व भोः ।
ज्ञानस्वरूपो भगवानात्मा त्वं प्रकृतेः परः ॥८॥

Śraddhasva tāta śraddhasva nātra mohaṁ kuruṣva bhoḥ I
Jñānasvarūpo bhagavānātmā tvaṁ prakṛteḥ paraḥ II

8. Have faithfulness, my child, have faithfulness. Have no delusion about this. You are the essence of supreme wisdom, transcending nature. You are the Lord, you are the (supreme) Self.

Faithfulness—Aṣṭāvakra here enjoins the reverence of the self for the Self as fundamental for self-knowledge and self-transcendence. *Upaniṣadic* thought teaches reverence as indispensable for the quest of ultimate reality. The *Chāndogya Upaniṣad* places it on a par side by side with right knowledge or *vidyā* and meditative insight (I, 1, 10). The *Taittirīya Upaniṣad* speaks of reverence as constituting the head of the supreme transcendent Person (II, 4, 1). The *Gītā* stresses *śraddhā* or faithfulness particularly in VII, 21-22, XVII, 1-6.

Faithfulness, the word used by the modern French philosopher Gabriel Marcel, is basic for the quest of the true Self or Being. It is not acceptance of belief or dogma but an inner apprehension of reality or the true Self which harnesses all the powers of the mind—intelligence, intuition and imagination – for self-realization. Both the *Gītā* and the *Bhāgavata* say that the fruit of man's worship follows his faithfulness or *śraddhā*.

Transcends—The self, like Brahman, encompasses as well as *transcends* nature. *Paraḥ* or transcendent is most frequently used as the adjective for Brahman and Ātman by the *Upaniṣads* and the *Gītā*. The *Kaṭha Upaniṣad* says: *buddherātmā mahān paraḥ* (III, 10). The *Gītā* uses the term para (superior or greater, the other or another) as many as twenty-eight times.

Lord—Īśvara or *Bhagavān* is the transcendent That (*tat*) of the *Upaniṣads*, while Ātman is yourself (*tvam*).

The *Aṣṭāvakra Gītā*, like the *Śvetāśvatara Upaniṣad*, was composed in a mystical milieu and its conception of *Ātman-Brahman* comprises elements of genuine mystical experience. The *Śvetāśvatara Upaniṣad* similarly identifies the omnipresent or immanent Brahman as *Bhagavān* (III, 11)

Supreme Wisdom—The *Sarvasāra Upaniṣad* thus identifies wisdom with pure consciousness, "What does wisdom, *jñāna* mean ? The consciousness, *caitanya* which is devoid of birth and destruction and which is enduring is called wisdom, *jñāna*" (70). Unlike the *Gītā*, Āṣṭāvakra shows little theistic slant or fervour, associating it as he does with the self's delusion. The sage stands for absolute Vedāntic idealism with its inevitable corollary of ajātavāda, as pointed out by Śaṅkara—the doctrine of the all-encompassing Self, beginningless and endless, with no creation.

In the major *Upaniṣads* the Self is in its essence all-encompassing wisdom itself. *cit-svarūpa*, *ātmajyotiḥ* or vijñānam beyond name, form and function.

गुणैः संवेष्टितो देहस्तिष्ठत्यायाति याति च ।
आत्मा न गन्ता नागन्ता किमेनमनुशोचसि ॥६॥

Guṇaiḥ saṁveṣṭhito dehastiṣṭhatyāyāti yāti ca l
Ātmā na gantā nāgantā kimenamanu Śocasi ll

9. The human body, saturated by attributes (of the senses), comes, stays and goes. (But the Self neither comes nor goes. Why do you lament over this?

Lament—The *Gītā* also says that the wise one is nor perplexed by changes in the body through childhood, youth and age nor by death (II.11,13,16,18).

देहस्तिष्ठतु कल्पान्तं गच्छत्वद्यैव वा पुनः ।
क्व वृद्धिः क्व च वा हानिस्तव चिन्मात्ररूपिणः ॥१०॥

Dehastiṣṭhatu kalpāntaṁ gacchatvadyaiva vā punaḥ l
Kva vṛddhiḥ kva ca vā hānistava cinmātrarūpiṇaḥ ll

10. Let the body remain to the end of the cycle of eras or vanish even today. Is there any increase or decrease of yourself who are pure intelligence?

No activity or movement can be associated with the Self, subsistent eternal and immutable.

त्वय्यनन्तमहाम्भोधौ विश्ववीचिः स्वभावतः ।
उदेतु वास्तमायातु न ते वृद्धिर्न वा क्षतिः ।।११।।

Tyayyanantamahāmbhodhau viśvavīciḥ svabhāvataḥ l
Udetu vāstamāyātu na te vṛddhirna vā kṣatiḥ ll

11. The waves representing the universe spontaneously rise and disappear in you, the infinite ocean (of consciousness). There is no gain or loss of yours.

This verse is virtually a repetition of VII, 2, and could easily have been omitted. The still and self-existent ocean of Self is beyond the cycle of time and manifestation. In a previous similar verse, VI, 2, the Self and the phenomenal world are compared to the ocean and the wave, respectively implying their essential identity of substance.

तात चिन्मात्ररूपोऽसि न ते भिन्नमिदं जगत् ।
अतः कस्य कथं कुत्र हेयोपादेयकल्पना ।।१२।।

Tāta cinmātrarūpo'si na te bhinnamidaṁ jagat l
Ataḥ kasya kathaṁ kutra heyopādeyakalpanā ll

12. O child, you are pure intelligence itself. This visible universe is not different from you. Hence how, where and whose can there be any thought of (its) acceptance or rejection?

It is the identity of the Self with the universe which alone can enable one to rise above all opposites, such as pleasure and pain, good and evil, acceptance or rejection. That identity, again, springs from the consciousness of the one as pure, all-pervading intelligence.

एकस्मिन्नव्यये शान्ते चिदाकाशेऽमले त्वयि ।
कुतो जन्म कुतः कर्म कुतोऽहंकार एव च ॥१३॥

Ekasminnavyaye śānte cidākāśe'male tyayi l
Kuto janma kutaḥ karma kuto'haṁkāra eva ca ll

13. From you who are indivisible, changeless, serene and stainless, all-pervasive consciousness, how can there be birth, activity and egoism?

All-pervasive Consciousness—This is the unconditioned, all-encompassing, pure-consciousness, *cinmātra*. '*Avikalpo hi ayaṁ ātmā cidrūpaḥ*', says the Upaniṣad. Aṣṭāvakra again suggests here the non-origination of the Self beyond birth, action or movement.

यत्त्वं पश्यसि तत्रैकस्त्वमेव प्रतिभाससे ।
किं पृथग्भासते स्वर्णात्कटकांगदनूपुरम् ॥१४॥

Yattvaṁ paśyasi tatraikastvameva pratibhāsase l
Kiṁ pṛthak bhāsate svarṇāt kaṭakāṅgadanūpuram ll

14. You alone are manifest in whatever you see. Do the bracelets, armlets and anklets appear different from the gold.

Not the ornaments, but the gold shines. Not the universe but I alone shine. Name, form and function cannot belie the Self that is all that exists. See II, 8 and XV,7.

The *Upaniṣadic* formula, *Kāraṇarūpa ātmā eva sarvam*, is expounded here. The Self as the single prime cause appears in all names, forms and functions of the universe—its effects. The transcendent Self is all that exists.

अयं सोऽहमयं नाहं विभागमिति सन्त्यज ।
सर्वमात्मेति निश्चित्य निःसंकल्पः सुखी भव ॥१५॥

Ayaṁ so'hamayaṁ nāhaṁ vibhāgamiti santyaja l
Sarvamātmeti niścitya niḥsaṅkalpaḥ sukhī bhava ll

15. Abandon all such distinctions as 'I am that', 'I am

this', and 'I am neither this nor that'. Knowing for certain that the Self is all, be free from any reasoning whatever and be happy.

That—This is the *Upaniṣadic* transcendent reality which cannot be expressed in words. This verse expounds the ancient formulae, *ātmā eva idaṁ sarvam*, *ātmā eva brahma*, *brahma eva ātmā*. Any deviation from the sense of the oneness of Ātman is the root of all misery.

तवैवाज्ञानतो विश्वं त्वमेकः परमार्थतः ।
त्वत्तोऽन्यो नास्ति संसारी नासंसारी च कश्चन ॥१६॥

Tavaivājñānato viśvaṁ tvamekaḥ paramārthataḥ I
Tvatto'nyo nāsti saṁsārī nāsaṁsārī ca kaścana II

16. The universe verily exists due to your ignorance. In reality you alone exist, (Hence) there is no God or creature other than yourself.

The distinctions between God and man, between the mundane world of birth, death and transmigration and emancipation fade away in the indivisibility and immutability of the unborn, non-dual Self.

भ्रान्तिमात्रमिदं विश्वं न किञ्चिदिति निश्चयी ।
निर्वासनः स्फूर्तिमात्रो न किञ्चिदिव शाम्यति ॥१७॥

Bhrāntimātramidaṁ viśvaṁ na kiñciditi niścayī I
nirvāsanaḥ sphūrtimātro na kiñcidiva śāmyati II

17. This world it only an illusion and is nothing. Knowing this for certain, one becomes desireless and pure intelligence and finds serenity because (for him) nothing exists.

This verse virtually repeats XI, 8. That the transcendent Self is pure intelligence unrelated to the phenomenal world is the object of emphasis. In different verses different phrases are used such as *cit-rūpa*, (I,3), *cinmātra* (I,13), *cinmaya* (XV,19), *sphūrti-mātra* (XI, 8; XV, 17), *bodha-ātma* (XV, 5) *bhāsa* (II, [illegible]) and *sva-prakāśa* (I, 15), all denoting eternal effulgence consciousness. The radiance which is the very nature of the Self itself is contrasted in the verse with the illusion that is the phenomenal world.

एक एव भवाम्भोधावासीदस्ति भविष्यति ।
न ते बन्धोऽस्ति मोक्षो वा कृतकृत्यः सुखं चर ॥१८॥

Eka eva bhavāmbhodhāvāsīdasti bhaviṣyati l
Na te bandho'sti mokṣo vā kṛtakṛtyaḥ sukhaṁ cara ll

18. In the ocean of existence the one (the pure Self) only was, is and will be. There is neither bondage nor salvation for you. Fulfil yourself and move about happily.

The juxtaposition of time, covering the past, the present and the future in the Self, points to the non-origination of the Self (*ajātavāda*).

मा संकल्पविकल्पाभ्यां चित्तं क्षोभय चिन्मय ।
उपशाम्य सुखं तिष्ठ स्वात्मन्यानन्दविग्रहे ॥१९॥

Mā saṅkalpavikalpābhyāṁ cittaṁ kṣobhaya cinmaya l
Upaśāmya sukhaṁ tiṣṭha svātmanyānandavigrahe ll

19. O pure intelligence, do not agitate your mind with (the thoughts of) affirmation and denial. Silencing these abide happily in your own Self—the embodiment of bliss itself.

Pure Intelligence—This verse clinches the instruction of XV, 12 where the universe is identified with *cinmātra svarūpa* meaning the same as *cinmaya* here.

Affirmation and Denial—In the yoga-system of Patañjali, the fluctuations of the mind, characterised by the opposites of acceptance and rejection, affirmation and negation, are dialectically transcended, and then the mind discovers its essential nature viz., unalloyed, everlasting bliss.

त्यजैव ध्यानं सर्वत्र मा किञ्चिद्धृदि धारय ।
आत्मा त्वम्मुक्त एवासि किंविमृश्य करिष्यसि ॥२०॥

Tyajaiva dhyānaṁ sarvatra mā kiñciddhṛdi dhāraya ।
Ātmā tvaṁ mukta evāsi kiṁ vimṛśya kariṣyasi ॥

20. Forsake in every way even contemplation. Hold nothing in your consciousness. You are the Self and surely ever free. Why do you ponder (over the Self) for nothing?

Contemplation—This and the preceding verse, like a few more verses of the text, have been used by Indian contemplatives through the centuries for the vacation of consciousness and filling it entirely with the thought of the Self or Brahman as the unborn, eternal and unknowable Witness of the universe. With complete silence, when the effort at silence is itself abjured, the Self easily and spontaneously abides in the absolute. The highest meditation is, paradoxically speaking, the cessation of meditation. The perturbations of meditation only screen the Self's essential free, immutable and luminous nature. The Self, in other words, is itself *samādhi* which is blocked by *manana* or *dhyāna*. This is stressed also in XII, 3,7, XVI, 2 and XVIII, 16, 17.

In XVIII, 1 Aṣṭāvakra says that the supreme goal is achieved through the combination of wisdom (*jñāna*) and the practice of yoga (*yogābhyāsa*). His conception of *samādhi* through intuitive illumination or *vijñāna* is, however, far different from *samādhi* in the yoga system, leaning as the latter does on *laya*, dissolution or oblivion—a state in which the contemplative cannot achieve perfect awareness of the nature of his Self, what comes from a thorough and persistent intellectual discrimination between the real and the unreal. 'Unborn and non-dual, I alone am' (XV, 16), 'I neither come nor go' (XV, 9), 'I have neither birth, nor ego-sense nor action' comprise a state of self-sameness or *samatā* (V, 4, VI,4, XV, 6; *Gītā*, VI, 29-32) and self-abidance (*svāsthya*) for which the yoga method can serve only a temporary and auxilliary end. The finite consciousness can move into, and abide in the unborn, silent, effulgent Self in perfect silence and clarity only through the true knowledge of Self which is awareness of awareness.

Aṣṭāvakra briefly summarises in this chapter his practical instruction relating to mystical realization of the self (*ātmasākṣātkāra* or *anubhava*). This chapter is, therefore, one of the finest and most significant in the whole text. We give below the main principles at the risk of some repetition or overlapping. The sage more than once observes that the Self is neither a *jīva,* nor an object nor a mental mode to be apprehended (II, 22, VII, 4), but rather the all-encompassing eternal and omniscent seer and witness of all. It is the Self which 'illumines' the phenomenal world, including the body, the senses and the mind. It cannot be discerned by the finite mind with its desires and attachments, its discursive reasoning and its duality of pairs of opposites. Rather the mind should shun its passion for sense-objects which is its bondage. Man's empirical consciousness should be silenced and freed from the conflict of all opposites, including the final opposites of affirmation and denial *nirvikalpa,* XV 5). Even the meditation of the Ātman or Brahman should be given up completely for the realization of the supreme freedom, silence and bliss of the unborn Self (XV, 20).

The true knowledge of the Self (*tattvabodha* XV, 3) is to be carefully distinguished from the false knowledge of the I with its contents of body-sense, governed by the modalities of nature or guṇas that is fleeting (VIII, 4, XV, 9) and of ego-sense and possessiveness (XV, 6), attachment and aversion (XV, 5). Neither the *jīva* nor the body nor the mind (*manas*) is the Self (II, 22, XV,5).

True self-knowledge proceeds from the I not at the *dimensions* of matter (*anna*), life (*prāṇa*) and (*manas*), but at the dimension of pure intelligence,. impersonal and unlimited (*vijñāna*). Neither materialism, nor biologism nor psychologism but ontology holds therefore the key to *ātmavijñāna* or direct apprehension of the Self (XV, 2, XVIII, 36). Cit is the focus of the true knowledge of the Self. The latter is identical with cit, and not with *manas,* nor with *prāṇa* nor with *anna.* Says Aṣṭāvakra, "to illumine is the very nature of the Self" (II, 8). The manifestation of the phenomenal world is the shining of pure intelligence (*cit*).

The light of pure intelligence (*cidrūpa*), stainless,

unattached and boundless in its own nature, is the ultimate Reality—the Self or Ātman. The Ātman is self-luminous, the sole eternal *draṣṭā* or *sākṣī* (I, 7, XV, 4) of the phenomenal world, both gross and subtle (XIX, 6). The phenomenal world, including the body, senses, mind and understanding, is *dṛśya* or objects of consciousness. All this is briefly set forth or restated in XV. The non-dual self as pure intelligence (cit) is directly intuited (I, 13, XII, 1-8). Aṣṭāvakra's ideal of self-abidance or *svāsthya* postulates, to be sure, immediate supra-rational intuition of the Self. This is stressed throughout the text. *Śraddhā* or unswerving faithfulness to the Self, *vijñāna* or intuitional insight and *yoga-abhyāsa* or constant practice of yoga are the major means of realization of the unborn, taintless Self (XVIII, 1) beyond empirical and relativist conditions including *ātma-dhyāna* and *samādhi*. Giving up *japa*, *manana* and *samādhi* and yet firmly and naturally resting in the Self or Brahman, i.e. becoming Ātman or Brahman itself, is considered the highest condition (XII, 7, XV, 19, XVIII, 16-17). Even in *samādhi* one still yearns fondly for that which is the source of serenity and bliss (XVI 2). It is clear that this cannot be reached except by direct intuition. *Vijñāna* or suprarational mystical insight into the Self is emphasized by the conjunction of the terms '*Bhagavān*' or the Lord and '*prakṛteḥ paraḥ*' or transcending nature with Ātman (XV, 8). This, no doubt, is disturbed by the effort of *dhyāna* or that at this level becomes distraction, and has to be transcended. Intuitive illumination is bliss or freedom itself (XV, 19,20).

To clarify and establish the supreme reality of the principle of pure intelligence (*bodha* ātmā, XV, 5), Aṣṭāvakrs adapts in this chapter several Upaniṣadic formulae or Vedāntic *mahāvākyas* and phrases : 'Thou art That' (XV, 7); 'the Self or Ātman is all that exists' (XV, 15); 'the Self is the eternal witness or *sākṣi* and pure intelligence or *chidrūpa* (XV, 4), *cinmātra* (XV, 6), *cinmātra-svarūpa* (XV.12), *sphūrtimātra* (XV, 17), and *cinmaya* (XV,19); 'the Self is the supreme knowledge itself (*jñāna svarūpa*) and God or Brahman and transcends nature or *prakṛti*' (XV,8); 'the Self is unborn and neither comes nor goes' (XV,9); nor finally, 'the Self alone is', there being no empirical self of *jīva* nor God or *Īśvara* (XV, 16).

A clear and comprehensive knowledge of the Self or Brahman marked by unwavering certitude and profound bliss and serenity, is accordingly derived from direct and immediate apprehension, aided by the above Vedāntic sentences or phrases. Such *knowledge* of Self or Brahman is itself Self or Brahman i.e. supreme *awareness of all awareness*. Once the Self as pure, stainless and uncreated intelligence is thus revealed in *anubhava* or *sākṣātkāra*, the I becomes serene and free and abides happily in the Self which is supreme bliss itself (XV, 19,20). In this state the Self becomes the absolute to which such names as the essence of wisdom, God and transcendence are equally applicable (XV, 8). That is supreme realization (*kṛtakṛtya*, XV, 18). Truly, the Self has neither bondage nor salvation (XV, 18). This is reiterated in the final chapter (XX,12). The waves of the phenomenal world spring from and merge in the still, formless and boundless ocean of the Self. There is no fluctuation in the Self (XV, 11). That is the blessed realization of the *jīvanmukta* about whom Aṣṭāvakra speaks so often. The *jīvanmukta's* way of life and behaviour are entirely changed as described in the later chapters (XVII, 7-20, XVIII, 13,26).

It may be pointed out that the mystical experience of the Self cannot be reached by stray introspection and analytical and discursive reasoning about the ego. It is an integral vision, based on a true understanding of the nature of the universe, mind and Self, constant pondering over the Upaniṣadic formulae and yogic practices that most fully reveal the universal and eternal nature of the Self, devoid of all relations and modes and surpassing the categories of distinction of knower, known and the act of knowing. Such non-dual vision of the Self is far different from many visions and ecstasies recorded by various schools of Vaiṣṇava, Tāntrika, Sūfī or Christian mystics through the centuries. These largely spring from the soil of subjectivity, and are moulded and shaped by relativist and contingent socio-religious factors and circumstances. No wonder that Rudolf Otto erroneously considers that *ontological* mysticism is no mysticism. Yet the mystical tradition of India has valued most through the ages the supra-rational ontological vision of the Self or Brahman, beyond all relativities, yielding *sapientia experimentalis*. Aṣṭāvakra's teaching in this chapter regarding the mystical non-dual intuition or *anubhava* of the self is at once profound and practical and has few parallels even in India.

Chapter XVI

AṢṬĀVAKRA ON SELF-ABIDANCE THROUGH OBLITERATION OF THE WORLD

Mind and the phenomenal world go together. As the mind completely establishes itself in the Self, and there is nothing but the cognition of the Self everywhere, the world vanishes. Here is neither deep slumber, nor *laya*, nor ecstasy, but full and all-pervasive self-awareness. Self-abidance (*svāsthya*) is the supreme truth or *tattva*. This alone can lead to the complete oblivion of the world and of the goals and duties of life, and the final uprooting of ignorance and duality of various pairs of opposites (*dvandva*)—happiness and misery, acceptance and rejection, attachment and aversion, duty and lapse—making up the world (XVI, 5-8).

The pure Self and the phenomenal world are indivisible and continuous. Beyond enjoyment, duty of life and *samādhi* is the call of the Self ever radiant, serene and blissful (XVI, 2). Profound joy makes the wise one spontaneously oblivious of the world and of the ego-feeling towards liberation or bondage (XVI, 10). Effortlessness is his characteristic; he is the head idler (XVI, 4). On the other hand, without his instinctual obliteration of the world his self-abidance is not possible in spite of habitual study of the scriptures and instruction from the highest (XIV, 1, XVI, 1, 11).

अष्टावक्र उवाच

आचक्ष्व शृणु वा तात नानाशास्त्राण्यनेकशः ।
तथापि न तव स्वास्थ्यं सर्वविस्मरणादृते ॥१॥

Aṣṭāvakra uvāca

Ācakṣva śṛṇu vā tāta nānāśāstrāṇyanekaśaḥ I
Tathāpi na tava svāsthyaṁ sarvavismaraṇādṛte II

Aṣṭāvakra said:

1. O, child, you may expound the diverse scriptures

or listen to them time and again. Yet you cannot have self-abidance without complete obliteration of the world.

Besides the waking state there are, according to Indian ontic psychology three other states of consciousness: dream, slumber and ecstasy. In both dream and slumber the vestiges of the sensory world still linger. In ecstasy also the world does not completely vanish since ignorance is not altogether destroyed. Only *svāsthya* or radiance of the Self in its purity and non-duality can completely annihilate ignorance which creates the manifold universe.

भोगं कर्मसमाधिं वा कुरु विज्ञ तथापि ते ।
चित्तं निरस्तसर्वाशमत्यर्थं रोचयिष्यति ॥२॥

Bhogaṁ karmasamādhiṁ vā kuru vijña tathāpi te l
Cittaṁ nirastasarvāśamatyarthaṁ rocayiṣyati ll

2. O wise one, you may enjoy the (world), undertake the duties or practise *samādhi*. Yet your mind will fondly yearn for that which transcends all goals of life (the essential Self), and in which all desires find their extinction.

Duties of Life—The *puruṣārthas* or goals of life are forsaken. See XVI, 5.

Extinction of Desires—because of the obliteration of the world.

Yearn—Because the Self is the embodiment of unfathomable bliss. It is the latter which makes the *jīvanmukta's* life in the world completely effortless and autonomous. He has neither *samādhi* nor activity nor enjoyment of his own (XVIII, 18).

आयासात्सकलो दुःखी नैनं जानाति कश्चन ।
अनेनैवोपदेशेन धन्यः प्राप्नोति निर्वृतिम् ॥३॥

Āyāsāt sakalo duḥkhī nainaṁ jānāti kaścana l
Anenaivopadeśena dhanyaḥ prāpnoti nirvṛtim ll

3. All are unhappy because of effort. But none appreciates this. Through this teaching alone the blessed one obtains liberation.

Effort—The wise one is without any striving or effort because of extinction of his desires and goals of life; and forgetfulness of the world.

व्यापारे खिद्यते यस्तु निमेषोन्मेषयोरपि ।
तस्यालस्यधुरीणस्य सुखं नान्यस्य कस्यचित् ॥४॥

Vyāpāre khidyate yastu nimeṣonmeṣayorapi 1
Tasyālasyadhurīṇasys sukhaṁ nānyasya kasyacit 11

4. Happiness is for him, that head idler, who feels distressed even at the effort of opening and closing the eyelids. It belongs to none else.

It is only the complete extinction of bodily consciousness or ego-sense that guarantees the supreme happiness of self-realization. The true yogī is, in this sense, the chief idler. Even reflex movements cannot bind him to the body. Such is his detachment from the body and the ego-feeling.

The Self is the *samādhi*, undisturbed by any activities of body and mind. Abandonment of all activity (*sarvavyāpāra*) includes the eschewing of *manana* or *dhyāna* as stressed in XV, 19-20 as well as of the slightest bodily sense. Thus does "the chief idler" abide in the absolute aloneness of the Ātman or Brahman.

इदं कृतमिदं नेति द्वन्द्वैर्मुक्तं यदा मनः ।
धर्मार्थकाममोक्षेषु निरपेक्षं तदा भवेत् ॥५॥

Idaṁ kṛtaṁ idaṁ neti dvandvairmuktaṁ yadā manaḥ 1
Dharmārthakāmamokṣesu nirapekṣaṁ tadā bhavet 11

5. When the mind becomes free from such duality of opposites as 'this is done' and 'this is left undone', it attains indifference towards righteousness, wealth, desire and liberation (the four-fold goals of life).

The man who is liberated in life leaves behind his care and effort for the four-fold human ends in the Indian scheme of life.

विरक्तो विषयद्वेष्टा रागी विषयलोलुपः ।
ग्रहमोक्षविहीनस्तु न विरक्तो न रागवान् ॥६॥

Virakto viṣayadveṣṭā rāgī viṣayalolupaḥ I
Grahamokṣavihīnastu na virakto na rāgavān II

6. One who has aversion for sense-objects is (called) non-attached. One who hankers after them is called sensual. But he who does not accept or reject is neither non-attached nor sensual.

The man of wisdom has to rise above the acceptance of, or withdrawal from the objects of the senses and the phenomenal world.

हेयोपादेयता तावत्संसारविटपाङ्कुराः ।
स्पृहा जीवति यावद्वै निर्विचारदशास्पदम् ॥७॥

Heyopādeyatā tāvat saṁsāraviṭapāṅkurāḥ I
Spṛhā jīvati yāvadvai nirvicāradaśāspadam II

7. As long as any desire which is the seat of non-discrimination lingers, there will persist the sense of acceptance and aversion, which is, indeed, the root and branch (of the tree) of *saṁsāra.*

प्रवृत्तौ जायते रागो निर्वृत्तौ द्वेष एव हि ।
निर्द्वन्द्वो बालवद्धीमानेवमेव व्यवस्थितः ॥८॥

Pravṛttau jāyate rāgo nirvṛttau dveṣa eva hi I
Nirdvandvo bālavaddhīmānevameva vyavasthitaḥ II

8. From impulse arises the feeling of attachment. From withdrawal arises the feeling of aversion. The wise man is like a child free from the duality of opposites and is verily well established (in his Self).

हातुमिच्छति संसारं रागी दुःखजिहासया ।
वीतरागो हि निर्दुःखस्तस्मिन्नपि न खिद्यति ॥९॥

Hātumicchati saṁsāraṁ rāgī duḥkhajihāsayā l
Vītarāgo hi nirduḥkhastasminnapi na khidyati ll

9. A person, attached to the world, wants to escape from misery and to renounce the world. The unattached one is free from misery and does not suffer.

The *jīvanmukta's* absolute non-attachment as well as his profound serenity and bliss in self-abidance enable him to live and move happily in the world that he does not renounce like the ascetic yogi. Aṣṭāvakra prefers the condition of the *jīvanmukta* to that of the yogi. This will also be evident from the next verse.

यस्याभिमानो मोक्षेऽपि देहेऽपि ममता तथा ।
न च ज्ञानी न वा योगी केवलं दुःखभागसौ ॥१०॥

Yasyābhimāno mokṣe'pi dehe'pi mamatā tathā l
Na ca jñānī na vā yogī kevalaṁ duḥkhabhāgasau ll

10. One who has an ego-sense in respect even of emancipation, and also attachment to his body is neither a wise man nor a yogī. He simply suffers misery.

हरो यद्युपदेष्टा ते हरिः कमलजोऽपि वा ।
तथापि न तव स्वास्थ्यं सर्वविस्मरणादृते ॥११॥

Haro yadyupadeṣṭā te Hariḥ kamalajo'pi vā l
Tathāpi na tava svāsthyaṁ sarvavismaraṇādṛte ll

11. Even if Śiva, Hari or Brahmā becomes your preceptor yet without complete obliteration of the world, you cannot achieve self-abidance.

Self-obliviousness, self-knowledge and self-abidance are linked with one another, all grounded in the attainment of the all-encompassing, non-dual, pure intelligence (cit). The preliminary step is withdrawal from, or effacement of the world. In *Pātañjala yoga* this is described as *pratyāhāra* or restraining of, and emancipation of the sense-organs and activities from the domination of the external objects of the phenomenal world. According to Bhoja, the senses instead of directing themselves towards external objects "abide within themselves". It is then that the wisdom of the yogī "knows all things as they are". *Pratyāhāra* through the suppression of the psycho-physical states (*cittavṛttinirodha*) leads to the final obliteration of the phenomenal world. Aṣṭāvakra, like the seer of the *Gītā* , builds up this on the basis of establishment of the mind in the real self, God or Brahman rather than on the subjugation or suppression of the mind through psycho-physical processes as in *Pātañjala yoga*. The difference between Aṣṭāvakra's and Patañjali's methods for obliteration of the world can be best brought out by Śaṅkara's redefinition of *pratyāhāra* in the light of *Kevala-advaita*. "The complete merger of the mind in the Self through discerning pure intelligence in all external objects is *pratyāhāra*. It is this kind of *pratyāhāra* which the seekers of self-knowledge should practise" (*Aparokṣānubhūti*, 121).

Chapter XVII

AṢṬĀVAKRA ON THE ABSOLUTE ALONENESS OF THE SELF

This chapter extols the supreme state of aloneness of the self. The self is solitary, filling alone the whole constellation of the universes and enjoying supreme delight in itself. All desires and goals of life, even those of liberation are extinguished (XVII, 6). Mind and its activities, viz. delusion, imagination and inertia and the dualities of happiness and sorrow, man and woman, good and evil, life and death, disappear (XVII, 15). Even the body and senses cease to operate (XVII, 9). The mind alone is liberated. For him nothing exists or he exists everywhere (XVII, 11), With his void mind and transcendence of contemplation and no contemplation, and of good and evil, he abides in the state of absolute aloneness or *kaivalya* (XVII,18) which verily is his true nature.

अष्टावक्र उवाच

तेन ज्ञानफलं प्राप्तं योगाभ्यासफलं तथा।
तृप्तः स्वच्छेन्द्रियो नित्यमेकाकी रमते तु यः ॥१॥

Aṣṭāvakra uvāca

Tena jñānaphalaṁ prāptaṁ yogābhyāsaphalaṁ tathā l
Tṛptaḥ svacchendriyo nityamekākī ramate tu yaḥ ll

Aṣṭāvakra said :

1. He has obtained the fruit of wisdom as well as of the practice of *yoga* who, self-contended and purified in senses, constantly moves about in his aloneness.

Aloneness—The yogī finds his own Self in all and all in his own Self. His senses becoming non-attached from the phenomenal world achieve their naturalness. Aṣṭāvakra's concept of absolute aloneness of the Self, grounded in supra-sensible ontological insight that yields perfect detachment, omniscience and beatitude, is very different from that of Patañjali who relies for this state on psychophysical exercises.

न कदाचिज्जगत्यस्मिंस्तत्त्वज्ञो हन्त खिद्यति ।
यत एकेन तेनेदं पूर्णं ब्रह्माण्डमण्डलम् ॥२॥

Na kadācijjagatyasmiṁstattvajño hanta khidyati I
Yataḥ ekena tenedaṁ pūrṇaṁ brahmāṇḍamaṇḍalam II

2. O, the wise man never suffers misery in this world. For he alone fills the whole constellation of the universe.

Alone—Non-duality is the only method of overcoming misery and obtaining perfect detachment and isolation, on one side, and omniscience and beatitude, on the other.

न जातु विषयाः केऽपि स्वारामं हर्षयन्त्यमी ।
सल्लकीपल्लवप्रीतमिवेभं निम्बपल्लवाः ॥३॥

Na jātu viṣayāḥ ke'pi svārāmaṁ harṣayantyamī I
Sallakīpallavaprītamivebhaṁ nimbapallavāḥ II

3. Just as the elephant, which delights in the leaves of the *sallakī* tree, dislikes the leaves of *nimba*, so is he contented in the Self, ever displeased with any sense-objects.

Contentment in Self: *Svārāma* echoes the ātmakrīḍā and ātma-rati of the *Muṇḍaka Upaniṣad* (III, 1,4) and the *ātmaprīti* and *ātma-rati* of the *Bhagavadgītā* (III, 17).

यस्तु भोगेषु भुक्तेषु न भवत्यधिवासितः ।
अभुक्तेषु निराकाङ्क्षी तादृशो भवदुर्लभः ॥४॥

Yastu bhogeṣu bhukteṣu na bhavatyadhivāsitaḥ I
Abhukteṣu nirākāṅkṣī tādṛśo bhavadurlabhaḥ II

4. Such a person is rare in the world who does not hanker after the enjoyment of things enjoyed by him, or after things not enjoyed.

बुभुक्षुरिह संसारे मुमुक्षुरपि दृश्यते ।
भोगमोक्षनिराकांक्षी विरलो हि महाशयः ॥५॥

Bubhukṣuriha saṁsāre mumukṣurapi dṛśyate l
Bhogamokṣanirākāṅkṣī viralo hi mahāśayaḥ ll

5. Men who seek enjoyment and men who seek emancipation are both found in this world. Rare is the noble-minded one who desires neither enjoyment nor emancipation.

धर्मार्थकाममोक्षेषु जीविते मरणे तथा ।
कस्याप्युदारचित्तस्य हेयोपादेयता न हि ॥६॥

Dharmārthakāmamokṣeṣu jīvite maraṇe Tathā l
Kasyāpyudāracittasya heyopādeyatā na hi ll

6. It is only a few broad-minded persons who have no sense of either attraction for, or rejection of righteousness, wealth, desire and emancipation as well as of life and death.

The *kevála* rises above the traditional four goals of life (*caturvarga*) due to his absolute knowledge.

वाञ्छा न विश्वविलये न द्वेषस्तस्य च स्थितौ ।
यथा जीविकया तस्माद्धन्य आस्ते यथासुखम् ॥७॥

Vāñchā na viśvavilaye na dveṣastasya ca sthitau l
Yathā jīvikayā tasmāddhanya āste yathāsukham ll

7. For the man of wisdom there is neither longing for the dissolution of the universe nor aversion for its existence. Hence he is blessed as he lives contentedly with whatever kind of living comes to his lot.

कृतार्थोऽनेन ज्ञानेनेत्येवं गलितधीः कृती ।
पश्यञ्छृण्वन्स्पृशञ्जिघ्रन्नश्नन्नास्ते यथासुखम् ॥८॥

Kṛtārtho'nena jñānenetyevaṁ galitadhīḥ kṛtī l
Paśyan śṛṇvan spṛśan jighrannaśnannāste yathāsukham ll

8. Fulfilled by this wisdom (of the Self), with his mind merged and contented (in the Self), he lives happily, seeing, hearing, touching, smelling and assimilating (the objects of senses).

Seeing etc.—Because his ego-sense is eliminated.

शून्या दृष्टिर्वृथा चेष्टा विकलानीन्द्रियाणि च ।
न स्पृहा न विरक्तिर्वा क्षीणसंसारसागरे ॥९॥

Śūnyā dṛṣṭirvṛthā ceṣṭā vikalānīndriyāṇi ca l
Na spṛhā na viraktirvā kṣīṇasaṁsārasāgare ll

9. For him the sense of reality of the world is annihilated and he has neither attachment nor aversion for it. His gaze becomes vacant, his bodily action purposeless, and his senses inoperative.

This is reminiscent of the passage in the *Gītā* which relates that what is night for all creatures is the time for working for the disciplined *yogī*; and what is the time of waking for all beings is night for the sage of true vision (II,69).

न जागर्ति न निद्राति नोन्मीलति न मीलति ।
अहो परदशा क्वापि वर्तते मुक्तचेतसः ॥१०॥

Na jāgarti na nidrāti nonmīlati na mīlati l
Aho paradaśā kvāpi vartate muktacetasaḥ ll

10. The wise man is neither waked-up nor asleep, he neither opens nor closes his eyes. Oh, the liberated soul everywhere experiences the supreme condition.

सर्वत्र दृश्यते स्वस्थः सर्वत्र विमलाशयः ।
समस्तवासनामुक्तो मुक्तः सर्वत्र राजते ॥११॥

Sarvatra dṛśyate svasthaḥ sarvatra vimalāśayaḥ l
Samastavāsanāmukto muktaḥ sarvatra rājate ll

11. The wise man abides in himself everywhere, is undefiled in his desires everywhere. Released from all passions he shines like the free being everywhere.

This noble verse with the repetition of the term *sarvatra* or everywhere is reminiscent of many passages of the

Upaniṣads and the *Gītā* which stress the omnipresence and sameness of the Self under all human conditions and circumstances (*Chāndogya*, 4, 1, 1; *Śvetāśvatara*, III, 16; *Gītā*, VI, 29, 30,32, XII, 4, XIII, 38, XVIII, 49). The *Avadhūtagītā* has the following verse :

"The Self is everywhere, always and in all, enduring and abiding. Know me as the all, void as well as non-void. This is certain" (33).

पश्यञ्शृण्वन् स्पृशञ्जिघ्रन्नश्नन् गृह्णन् वदन् व्रजन् ।
ईहितानीहितैर्मुक्तो मुक्त एव महाशयः ॥१२॥

Paśyan śṛṇvan spṛśan jighrannaśnan gṛhṇan vadan vrajan l
Īhitānīhitairmukto mukta eva mahāśayaḥ ll

12. The emancipated person, the noble-minded one as he sees, hears, touches, smells, eats, accepts, speaks and moves is free, indeed, from attachment or aversion.

न निन्दति न च स्तौति न हृष्यति न कुप्यति ।
न ददाति न गृह्णाति मुक्तः सर्वत्र नीरसः ॥१३॥

Na nindati na ca stauti na hṛṣyati na kupyati l
Na dadāti na gṛhṇāti muktaḥ sarvatra nīrasaḥ ll

13. He neither abuses nor praises, neither rejoices nor is angry. He neither gives nor receives. He is bereft of flavours in respect of all things.

सानुरागां स्त्रियं दृष्ट्वा मृत्युं वा समुपस्थितम् ।
अविह्वलमनाः स्वस्थो मुक्त एव महाशयः ॥१४॥

Sānurāgāṁ striyaṁ dṛṣṭvā mṛtyuṁ vā samupasthitam l
Avihvalamanāḥ svastho mukta eva mahāśayaḥ ll

14. The noble-minded one remains unperturbed and self-poised at the sight of a woman full of passion and at the approach of death. Verily is he emancipated.

सुखे दुःखे नरे नार्यां संपत्सु च विपत्सु च ।
विशेषो नैव धीरस्य सर्वत्र समदर्शिनः ॥१५॥

Sukhe duḥkhe nare nāryāṁ sampatsu ca vipatsu ca l
Viśeṣo naiva dhīrasya sarvatra samadarśinaḥ ll

15. The wise one, who sees the same everywhere, finds no difference between happiness and misery, man and woman, fortune and misfortune.

न हिंसा नैव कारुण्यं नौद्धत्यं न च दीनता ।
नाश्चर्यं नैव च क्षोभः क्षीणसंसरणे नरे ॥१६॥

Na hiṁsā naiva kāruṇyaṁ naudhatyaṁ na ca dīnatā l
Nāścaryaṁ naiva ca kṣobhaḥ kṣīṇasaṁsaraṇe nare ll

16. In the wise man whose mundane life has waned, and who transcends humanness, there is neither violence nor compassion, neither pride nor humility, neither surprise nor agitation.

न मुक्तो विषयद्वेष्टा न वा विषयलोलुपः ।
असंसक्तमनाः नित्यं प्राप्ताप्राप्तमुपाश्नुते ॥१७॥

Na mukto viṣayadveṣṭā na vā viṣayalolupaḥ l
Asaṁsaktamanā nityaṁ prāptāprāptamupāśnute ll

17. The emancipated one has neither aversion nor craving for the objects of the senses. With his detached mind he enjoys (equally) what is attained and what is not attained.

समाधानासमाधानहिताहितविकल्पनाः ।
शून्यचित्तो न जानाति कैवल्यमिव संस्थितः॥१८॥

Samādhānāsamādhānahitāhitavikalpanāḥ l
Śūnyacitto na jānāti kaivalyamiva saṁsthitaḥ ll

18. The wise man with an empty mind does not know the mental alternatives of contemplation and non-contemplation

ion and of good and evil. He abides as if in the state of absolute aloneness.

Kaivalya denotes not only the supreme loneliness, non-attachment and purity of the Self (II, 9, XI, 6) but also its perfection, omniscience and bliss (XVII, 2,3,18, XVIII,87).

निर्ममो निरहङ्कारो न किञ्चिदिति निश्चितः ।
अन्तर्गलितसर्वाशः कुर्वन्नपि करोति न ॥१९॥

Nirmamo nirahaṅkāro na kiñciditi niścitaḥ 1
Antargalitasarvāśaḥ kurvannapi karoti na 11

19. He is devoid of ego-sense and ego-feeling. He knows for certain that nothing is. With all desires melted away in the inner life, he has no action though he acts.

The last phrase, inaction in action, is borrowed from the *Gītā*.

मनःप्रकाशसंमोहस्वप्नजाड्यविवर्जितः ।
दशां कामपि संप्राप्तो भवेद्गलितमानसः ॥२०॥

Manaḥprakāśasammohasvapnajāḍyavivarjitaḥ 1
Daśām kāmapi samprāpto bhavedgalitamānasaḥ 11

20. A supreme state is attained by the man of wisdom who with his mind melted away is denuded of the expressions of the mind, delusion, imagination and inertia.

The sense of perfect fulness and all-pervasiveness of the Self, (pūrṇa, XVII, 2) absolute delight in the Self (ātmārāma, XVIII,3), freedom from desires and goals of life (XVIII,4-9), even-mindedness in all possible human conditions (XVII, 11-15) and the melting away of the mind are essential phases of the Self's attainment of *kaivalya*. Mind becomes vacant and surpasses the duality of attachment and non-attachment, freedom and liberation, contemplation and non-contemplation (XVII, 16-19). *Kaivalya* means man's isolation from the senses and the world and his solitary enjoyment of the Self as the all or Brahman. It, therefore, integrates the notions of non-duality, completeness, even-mindedness and aloneness.

This is a condition of complete transcendence or beyond-humanness (*anara*, XVII, 16) and release from all earthly conditions—man's supreme state (*paramaṁ padam*) according to the *Yogatattva Upaniṣad*. The *Tejobindu Upaniṣad* says, Brahman is the all and the alone, '*sarvaṁ brahmaiva kevalam* (VI, 65). In XVIII, 87, the *kevala* whose doubts are finally rent asunder, who transcends all pairs of opposites is the same in all things and moves about freely in the world, is glorified.

The Pātañjala terms and concepts of *kevala* and *kaivalya* do not occur at all, as we have already noted, in the *Bhagavadgītā*. Only in the *Śvetāśvatara Upaniṣad* (I and VI) the *Kaivalya Upaniṣad* (25), the *Amṛtabindu Upaniṣad* (29) and the *Mukti Upaniṣad* (1. 18, 26, 31) we encounter the terms *kevala*, *kaivalya* or *kaivalya-mukti*. The philosophy and religion of Jainism use the term *Kevalin* for denoting the Jain Saint or *Tīrthaṁkara*, the finally emancipated, omniscient and perfect being who ascends in complete aloneness to the summit of creation. Aṣṭāvakra uses this ancient Pātañjala *yoga* term in several places : III, 9, XI, 6, XVII, 18, XVIII, 87 and XX, 4.

Samādhi leads to the discovery of an ontological modality inaccessible to man, ordinarily speaking—the omnipresence and aloneness of the Self. It is, however, only the later *Upaniṣads*, such as the *Śvetāśvatara* which use the word *kevala* in the sense of supreme aloneness or absoluteness (1, 11, IV, 18 and VI, 11). The *Kaivalya Upaniṣad* identifies the oneness of the Self with the supreme Brahman and release from the wheel of time and change in the phenomenal world as the state of *kaivalya* or absolute aloneness (25). The *Yogatattva Upaniṣad* defines *kaivalya* thus : "*Kaivalya* is the very nature of the self, the supreme state (*paramaṁ padam*). It is without parts and is stainless. It is the direct intuition of the Real—existence, intelligence and bliss. It is devoid of birth, existence, destruction, recognition and experience. This is called knowledge" (16-18).

Aṣṭāvakra's conception of *kaivalya* requires careful analysis. It is a supreme state where human consciousness is completely obliterated, i.e. it no longer functions. Body-sense, egoism and action (together with their dualities and opposites) that are the constituents of consciousness are reabsorbed into the primordial Self. Man ultimately becomes *anara*, i.e. transcends himself. This is the real destiny of one's self and (*matsvarūpa*) : to become stainless (*nirañjana*), undifferentiated (*nirviśeṣa*), devoid of limitations (*nirupādhi*), actionless (*niṣkriya*) and free from natural attributes or limitations of human nature (*niḥsvabhāva*) as mentioned in XX, 1,4,5,8,12). Man, gaining the fruits of knowledge and the practice of yoga, then revels being alone in the Self (XVII,1).

In XI, 6, the *kevala* Self is mentioned as having transcended the body-sense, possessiveness and memory of action. In XVII, 18, the state of *kaivalya* is associated with the vacation of mind and transcendence of the opposites, contemplation and non-contemplation, good and evil. Freedom from any attachment, doubt and duality of opposites is also mentioned as features of *kaivalya* in XVIII, 87. Mādhava observes, "*Nirodha* (final arrest of all mental activity) must not be imagined as a non-existence, but rather as the support of a particular condition of the Spirit". The *kevala* Self neither perceives nor experiences anything, for the relation between the consciousness and life or the world terminates. But there is the unveiling or revelation of pure consciousness. Thus the Self says, I am pure intelligence itself (XI, 6). Only the *kevala* Self can assert this, and abide perennially in the state of absoluteness (*svāsthya*). Aṣṭāvakra reaches the climax as he observes that the pure Self denies *videha-kaivalya* itself, i.e. aloneness-at-death along with *jīvanmukti* or liberation-in-life (XX, 4). The *kevala* who denies both life as well as liberation finds the Vedantic ideal of *jīvanmukti* as itself a product of ignorance and delusion. *Kaivalya*, *svāsthya* or self-abidance and pure intelligence, bliss, serenity and majesty of the Self (*svamahimā*) are identical in the Aṣṭāvakragītā. Man's primordial nature (*svabhāva*) is *kaivalya* itself. Blessed is the man who achieves *kaivalya*—perennial abidance in the Self, Brahman or *Īśvara* (*svāsthya*). Blessed is he who is *kevala* by nature or *svabhāva*, and is absorbed in natural *samādhi* in the supreme isolation, and beatitude of the Self (XII, 8, XVIII, 67).

CHAPTER XVIII

AṢṬĀVAKRA ON THE WAY AND GOAL OF NATURAL SAMĀDHI

Like the eighteenth or final chapter of the *Bhagavadgītā*, the 18th chapter here briefly and elegantly sums up the previous teaching and also develops a new ontological insight. The *Upaniṣadic* formulae, '*ātman* is Brahman' (XVIII, 8), '*ātman* is *sarvam* or all' (XVIII, 9), 'I am Brahman' (XVIII 28, 37), 'I am beyond the states of waking, dream and slumber' (XVIII, 94) and 'I am *śānta* (serene), *pūrṇa* (full) *śuddha* (pure), *buddha* (intelligent), *priya* (beloved) and *sukha* (bliss) (XVIII, 1,3,85) are fully utilised for indicating the nature of the absolute Self. Aṣṭāvakra, of course, also deploys here several new epithets of the Self, such as *niṣprapañca* (beyond relativity) (XVIII, 35), *nīrasa* (flavourless) (XVIII, 68), *niḥsvabhāva* (devoid of natural attributes) (XVIII, 79) and *nirāyāsa* (effortless) (XVIII, 5). The universe is mere imagination. The Self is Brahman and is unborn, eternal, ever-free and undivided (XVIII, 1,5-9). There is neither distraction nor samādhi nor involvement for the Self which is effortless and is always there. For the wise one to abide in the non-dual Self is instinctual, easy and spontaneous. With self-abidance, the knots of his heart are rent asunder, his doubts removed and his activities destroyed (XVIII, 77,87, 88); *Māṇḍūkya Upaniṣad* II, 28). He is purged of *rajas* and *tamas* guṇas (XVIII, 88; *Bhagavadgītā* XII, 31, XIV, 23-26). For him there is neither liberation nor bondage in life The Self is the one perfect and absolute—formless, immutable, untainted, blissful, beloved and spontaneous (XVIII, 35,57).

The chapter ends with a series of paradoxical statements about the life and experience of the liberated one, perennially established in the Self that resolve all pairs of dualities or opposites springing from the mutually contending guṇas and preferences in the phenomenal world (XVIII, 78-100). As a matter of fact he surpasses the human condition (*anara*,

XVIII, 16). He is beyond both happiness and sorrow, good and evil, wonder and mental perturbation. Shining as the infinite, all-encompassing intelligence and not perceiving the relative existence (XVIII,72), he remains in pure self-effulgence (XVIII, 71), absolute aloneness (XVIII,87), perfect autonomy (XVIII, 50) and continual boundless happiness (XVIII, 59). Thus does he abide constantly in natural (*akṛtrima*) samādhi in the ineffable and the unconditioned (XVIII, 67,70). He exists, as it were, without his body, sense-organs and intellect in this world (XVIII, 22,25), suffusing it with his pure intelligence as the supreme Brahman or the absolute itself (XVIII,28,40,71,72). Glory to him who attains natural samādhi in the infinite bliss which is the Self's own nature (*pūrṇa-svarasa-vigraha*).

अष्टावक्र उवाच

यस्य बोधोदये तावत्स्वप्नवद्भवति भ्रमः ।
तस्मै सुखैकरूपाय नमः शान्ताय तेजसे ॥१॥

Aṣṭāvakra uvāca

Yasya bodhodaye tāvat svapnavadbhavati bhramaḥ l
Tasmai sukhaikarūpāya namaḥ śāntāya tejase ll

Aṣṭāvakra said :

1. Adoration to the one, the embodiment of bliss, serenity and effulgence, with the dawning of knowledge of which one's delusion (of the world) becomes like a dream.

Dream—With the replacement of superimposition of the world (*adhyāsa*) by the truth of the pure all-encompassing Self, the delusion itself becomes as trivial as a dream.

Effulgent—Self-illumination is denoted here. *Ātmā jyotiḥ* is a familiar *Upaniṣadic* concept, stressing that the Self though unknowable can be cognized only by itself. The *Kaivalya Upaniṣad* says : "I know (all). I am devoid of form. None knows me. I am always pure consciousness" (21).

अर्जयित्वाऽखिलानर्थान् भोगानाप्नोति पुष्कलान् ।
न हि सर्वपरित्यागमन्तरेण सुखी भवेत् ॥२॥

Arjayitvā'khilānarthān bhogānāpnoti puṣkalān I
Na hi sarvaparityāgamantareṇa sukhī bhavet II

2. Having acquired manifold objects of the senses and enjoyed them, surely one cannot be happy without renouncing all.

कर्तव्यदुःखमार्तण्डज्वालादग्धान्तरात्मनः ।
कुतः प्रशमपीयूषधारासारमृते सुखम् ॥३॥

Karttavyaduḥkhamārtaṇḍajvālādagdhāntarātmanaḥ I
Kutaḥ praśamapīyūṣadhārāsāramṛte sukham II

3. For one, whose inner self is tormented by the scorching heat of the sun of sorrow springing from his deeds, where is (his) happiness without the ambrosial shower of the cessation of desires?

Deeds—The ordinary duties of life produce misery due to their being linked with attachment to the world of senses and desires. Aṣṭāvakra does not envisage, as the *Bhagavadgītā* does, the transformation of work into worship through its dedication to the Self, God or the absolute.

Cessation—Compare Aṣṭāvakra's term '*praśama*' with Gauḍapāda's *prapañcopaśama*'.

भवोऽयं भावनामात्रो न किञ्चित्परमार्थतः ।
नास्त्यभावः स्वभावानां भावाभावविभाविनाम् ॥४॥

Bhavo'yaṁ bhāvanāmātro na kiñcit paramārthataḥ I
Nāstyabhāvaḥ svabhāvānāṁ bhāvābhāvavibhāvinām II

4. This world is merely a mode of thinking. In truth it is nothing. Self-validating beings that apprehend both existence and non-existence never cease to be.

The Buddhist notion of nihilism is here countered by Aṣṭāvakra. Even if the universe springing from man's conceptualization vanishes, the unconditioned Self still exists as the one, all-encompassing, eternal reality. This is *ekajīvavāda*. The reality of Ātman is affirmed, not denied here as by the Buddhist schools. Aṣṭāvakra is certainly more positive than

Buddhist schools. Āṣṭāvakra is certainly more positive than the Buddhist philosophers.

न दूरं न च संकोचाल्लब्धमेवात्मनः पदम् ।
निर्विकल्पं निरायासं निर्विकारं निरञ्जनम् ॥५॥

Na dūraṁ na ca saṅkocāllabdhamevātmanaḥ padam l
Nirvikalpaṁ nirāyāsaṁ nirvikāraṁ nirañjanam ll

5. The essential nature of the Self is unconditioned, serene, changeless and stainless. The Self is neither inaccessible nor attainable because (of being) limited.

Inaccessible—This is reminiscent of the *Bhagavadgītā's* '*dūrastha*', that which is far away (XIII, 15). In the *Vājasaneya Upaniṣad* we also read "He is far as well as near" (V).

व्यामोहमात्रविरतौ स्वरूपादानमात्रतः
वीतशोका विराजन्ते निरावरणदृष्टयः ॥६॥

Vyāmohamātraviratau svarūpādānamātrataḥ l
Vītaśokā virājante nirāvaraṇadṛṣṭayaḥ ll

6. As soon as the essential nature of the Self is apprehended with the illusion dispelled and the vision unscreened, the wise shine free from misery.

समस्तं कल्पनामात्रमात्मा मुक्तः सनातनः ।
इति विज्ञाय धीरो हि किमभ्यस्यति बालवत् ॥७॥

Samastaṁ kalpanāmātramātmā muktaḥ sanātanaḥ l
Iti vijñāya dhīro hi kīmabhyasyati bālavat ll

7. All that exists is mere imagination. The Self is free and eternal. Knowing this does the wise man behave childlike?

Childlike—For the wise one the obliteration of the world does not mean the ignorance and playfulness of the child. Though inactive, he is full, complete and omniscient.

आत्मा ब्रह्मेति निश्चित्य भावाभावौ च कल्पितौ ।
निष्कामः किं विजानाति किं ब्रूते च करोति किम् ॥८॥

Ātmā brahmeti niścitya bhāvābhāvau ca kalpitau ।
Niṣkāmaḥ kiṁ vijānāti kiṁ brūte ca karoti kim ॥

8. Understanding for certain that the Self is Brahman and that existence and non-existence are mere imaginings, one becomes free from desires. What would he know, say or do?

अयं सोऽहमयं नाहमिति क्षीणा विकल्पनाः ।
सर्वमात्मेति निश्चित्य तूष्णीभूतस्य योगिनः ॥९॥

Ayaṁ so'hamayaṁ nāhamiti kṣīṇā vikalpanāḥ ।
Sarvamātmeti niścitya tūṣṇībhūtasya yoginaḥ ॥

9. 'This is That', 'I am That', and 'I am not That', such thoughts are extinguished for the yogī who has become silent and who knows for certain that all is the Self.

This verse which virtually repeats XV, 15 refers to the *Upaniṣadic* formulae '*ātmā eva idaṁ sarvam* (*Chāndogya Upaniṣad*, VII, 25,2, *sarvaṁ ātmānaṁ paśyati* (*Bṛhadāraṇyaka Upaniṣad*, IV, 4, 23) the Self is all that exists.

न विक्षेपो न चैकाग्र्यं नातिबोधो न मूढता ।
न सुखं न च वा दुःखमुपशान्तस्य योगिनः ॥१०॥

Na vikṣepo na caikāgryaṁ nātibodho na mūḍhatā ।
Na sukhaṁ na ca vā duḥkhamupaśāntasya yoginaḥ ॥

10. For the yogī who has achieved serenity, there is neither distraction nor concentration, neither gain nor decrease of knowledge. neither pleasure nor pain.

Gain—One established in the fullness of the Self does not experience any fluctuation of knowledge and feeling.

स्वाराज्ये भैक्ष्यवृत्तौ च लाभालाभे जने वने ।
निर्विकल्पस्वभावस्य न विशेषोऽस्ति योगिनः ॥११॥

Svārājye bhaikṣavṛttau ca lābhālābhe jane vane ।
Nirvikalpasvabhāvasya na viśeṣo'sti yoginaḥ ॥

11. Whether he possesses the kingdom of heaven or adopts mendicancy, whether he gains or loses, whether he is in society or solitude, the yogi whose nature is free from desires finds no difference.

क्व धर्मः क्व च वा कामः क्व चार्थः क्व विवेकिता ।
इदं कृतमिदं नेति द्वन्द्वैर्मुक्तस्य योगिनः ॥१२॥

Kva dharmaḥ kva ca vā kāmaḥ kva cārthaḥ kva vivekitā ।
Idaṁ kṛtamidaṁ neti dvandvairmuktasya yoginaḥ ॥

12. For the yogī who is free from the duality of opposites where are righteousness, desire, wealth and conscience? Where is the difference between what is done and what is not done?

The traditional four-fold goals of life are mentioned here along with the obligatory duties. These all fade away in the yogī's absolute consciousness.

कृत्यं किमपि नैवास्ति न कापि हृदि रञ्जना ।
यथा जीवनमेवेह जीवन्मुक्तस्य योगिनः ॥१३॥

Kṛtyaṁ kimapi naivāsti na kāpi hṛdi rañjanā ।
Yathā jīvanameveha jīvanamuktasya yoginaḥ ॥

13. For the yogī who is liberated while living, there is neither any duty nor passion in the heart. In this world his deeds merely follow the lot of his life.

Lot of his Life—For the man of self-realization the incentives of life drop off; he simply follows the dictates of his *prārabdha*—the consequences of his deeds in his previous births. We first encounter the conception of jīvanamukti in the Mukti upaniṣad (I, 43, II, 33,75,76).

क्व मोहः क्व च वा विश्वं क्व तद्ध्यानं क्व मुक्तता ।
सर्वसंकल्पसीमायां विश्रान्तस्य महात्मनः ॥१४॥

Kva mohaḥ kva ca vā viśvaṁ kva taddhyānaṁ kva muktatā ।
Sarvasaṅkalpasīmāyāṁ viśrāntasya mahātmanaḥ ॥

14. Where is delusion, where is the world, where is the meditation of the Reality, where is liberation for the serene, noble-minded one, who is beyond the boundary of all desires?

येन विश्वमिदं दृष्टं स नास्तीति करोतु वै ।
निर्वासनः किं कुरुते पश्यन्नपि न पश्यति ॥१५॥

Yena viśvmidaṁ dṛṣṭaṁ sa nāstīti karotu vai l
Nirvāsanaḥ kiṁ kurute paśyannapi na paśyati ll

15. One who sees the universe endeavours to obliterate it. What would the desireless one do, who beholds not though he sees (with his eyes)?

Does not see—There is the well-known *yoga* text which says, the yogī stares although he does not see anything, his breath is still without any restraint.

येन दृष्टं परं ब्रह्म सोऽहं ब्रह्मेति चिन्तयेत् ।
किं चिन्तयति निश्चिन्तो द्वितीयं यो न पश्यति ॥१६॥

Yena dṛṣṭaṁ paraṁ brahma so'haṁ brahmeti cintayet l
Kiṁ cintayati niścinto dvitīyaṁ yo na paśyati ll

16. One who sees the supreme Brahman meditates, 'I am Brahman'. What would he meditate who sees no duality and ceases to think?

For the yogī of complete and absolute non-dual experience, true meditation on Ātman or Brahman ceases. When I and Ātman, Brahman or the All become identical, there is neither thought nor any relationship of I with Ātman or Brahman. Such relationship is "the bondage of heart" about which the *Muṇḍaka Upaniṣad* speaks, "Destroyed is the knot of heart, dispelled are all doubts, annihilated are all impulses of action, on seeing Him, Supreme and non-Supreme" (II,28).

Narahari in his *Bodhasāra* beautifully explains that I (*ahaṁ brahmāsmi*), you (*tvaṁ Brahma*) and that (*tat brahma*) all fade away in immediate non-dual experience (*sākṣātkāra*). I-ness, thy-ness and that-ness merge together in the pure, unborn Ātman or Brahman. Then, what is the Ātman or Brahman? he asks. The answer is, "When the wise one's sleep of delusion is over and his mind melts away that which remains beyond it and is inaccessible to mind and word, that is the transcendent Ātman or Brahman" (LXVI, 17-20). This self-effulgent Ātman or Brahman is the eternal Witness (sākṣī) of both delusion and the melting away of the mind. It is directly cognised and appreciated with absolute certitude and bliss through an awareness of pure all encompassing existence, intelligence and bliss, (I alone am, alone I shine; alone I exalt).

दृष्टो येनात्मविक्षेपो निरोधं कुरुते त्वसौ ।
उदारस्तु न विक्षिप्तः साध्याभावात्करोति किम् ॥१७॥

Dṛṣṭo yenātmavikṣepo nirodhaṁ kurute tvasau l
Udārastu na vikṣiptaḥ sādhyābhāvātkaroti kim ll

17. One who experiences distraction (in the Self) undertakes self-control. The equal-minded one is not distracted. Having nothing to achieve what would he do?

Equal-minded one—i.e. one who sees the Self in all and all in the Self. See XV, 6.

Self-control—Consciousness remains dual so long as the sense of I meditating Brahman or the I and Thou or That relation lingers. In complete non-duality, I, Thou or That and meditation or the process of checking distraction vanish altogether. There is neither meditation nor distraction in complete self-abidance.

What would he do—He does nothing, for he transforms himself into the effulgent All. He abides in the All—his true Self. This is Aṣṭāvakra's normal *svāsthya* or *svarūpa.*

धीरो लोकविपर्यस्तो वर्त्तमानोऽपि लोकवत् ।
न समाधिं न विक्षेपं न लेपं स्वस्य पश्यति ॥१८॥

Dhīro lokaviparyasto varttamāno'pi lokavat l
Na samādhiṁ na vikṣepaṁ na lepaṁ svasya paśyati ll

18. The wise man is the reverse of the average man

though living like him. He sees neither absorption nor distraction nor involvement of himself.

भावाभावविहीनो यस्तृप्तो निर्वासनो बुधः ।
नैव किञ्चित् कृतं तेन लोकदृष्टया विकुर्वता ॥१६॥

Bhāvābhāvavihīno yastṛpto nirvāsano budhaḥ I
Naiva kiñcit kṛtaṁ tena lokadṛṣṭyā vikurvatā II

19. The wise one who transcends existence and non-existence, is contented and devoid of desire; he does nothing even though he apparently acts in the eyes of the world.

Existence and non-existence—The contemplative neither accepts nor rejects existence. For him there is neither involvement, nor renunciation nor obliteration. See chapter VI.

प्रवृत्तौ वा निवृत्तौ वा नैव धीरस्य दुर्ग्रहः ।
यदा यत्कर्तुमायाति तत्कृत्वा तिष्ठतः सुखम् ॥२०॥

Pravṛttau vā nivṛttau vā naiva dhīrasya durgrahaḥ I
Yadā yatkartumāyāti tatkṛtvā tiṣṭhataḥ sukham II

20. For the wise one there is no trouble in either action or inaction. What and when comes to him for action, he undertakes and lives happily.

निर्वासनो निरालम्बः स्वच्छन्दो मुक्तबन्धनः ।
क्षिप्तः संस्कारवातेन चेष्टते शुष्कपर्णवत् ॥२१॥

Nirvāsano nirālambaḥ svacchando muktabandhanaḥ I
Kṣiptaḥ saṁskāravātena ceṣṭate śuṣkaparṇavat II

21. Desireless, autonomous, free and emancipated, he moves about like a dry leaf driven by the wind of the *saṁskāras* (inner trends due to past deeds).

असंसारस्य तु क्वापि न हर्षो न विषादिता ।
स शीतलमना नित्यं विदेह इव राजते ॥२२॥

Asaṁsārasya tu kvāpi na harṣo na viṣāditā I
Sa śitalamanā nityaṁ videha iva rājate II

22. He is not of the world and has no happiness or unhappiness. Tranquil in mind he lives as if he has no body.

कुत्रापि न जिहासाऽस्ति नाशो वाऽपि न कुत्रचित् ।
आत्मारामस्य धीरस्य शीतलाच्छतरात्मनः ॥२३॥

Kutrāpi na jihāsāsti nāśo vāpi na kutracit I
Ātmārāmasya dhīrasya śītalācchatarātmanaḥ II

23. For the wise one, delighted in the Self, with his mind serene and pure, there is no desire to renounce or sense of loss anywhere.

प्रकृत्या शून्यचित्तस्य कुर्वतोऽस्य यदृच्छया ।
प्राकृतस्येव धीरस्य न मानो नावमानता ॥२४॥

Prakṛtyā śūnyacittasya kurvato'sya yadṛcchayā I
Prākṛtasyeva dhīrasya na māno nāvamānatā II

24. By nature void in mind and acting according to his wish, he has no feeling of honour or dishonour as that of an ordinary man.

Void—The same phrase is used in XIV.

कृतं देहेन कर्मेदं न मया शुद्धरूपिणा ।
इति चिन्तानुरोधी यः कुर्वन्नपि करोति न ॥२५॥

Kṛtaṁ dehena karmedaṁ na mayā śuddharūpiṇā I
Iti cintānurodhī yaḥ kurvannapi karoti na II

25. He acts in pursuance of such a thought, 'this is done by the body, not by me, the pure Self'.

Though undertaking action, he does not act. The above echoes the teaching of the *Bhagavadgītā* (III, 27-28, IV, 20,21, V, 8-9,13) and is repeated in XVII. 9 and XVIII,58.

अतद्वादीव कुरुते न भवेदपि बालिशः ।
जीवन्मुक्तः सुखी श्रीमान् संसरन्नपि शोभते ॥२६॥

Atadvādīva kurute na bhavedapi bāliśaḥ l
Jīvanmuktaḥ sukhī śrīmān saṁsarannapi śobhate ll

26. A person liberated in life, performs his action but would not say it, although he is not a fool. Though living in the world, he is quite happy and blessed.

Would not say it—The liberated one has no goals for his actions and cannot indicate these if asked. Apparently he behaves like a fool.

नानाविचारसुश्रान्तो धीरो विश्रान्तिमागतः ।
न कल्पते न जानाति न शृणोति न पश्यति ॥२७॥

Nānāvicārasuśrānto dhīro viśrāntimāgataḥ l
Na kalpate na jānāti na śṛṇoti na paśyati ll

27. Withdrawing himself from diverse reasonings (as regards the reality) the wise one attains complete repose. He neither thinks, nor knows, nor hears, nor perceives.

असमाधेरविक्षेपान्न मुमुक्षुर्न चेतरः ।
निश्चित्य कल्पितं पश्यन् ब्रह्मैवास्ते महाशयः ॥२८॥

Asamādheravikṣepānna mumukṣurna cetaraḥ l
Niścitya kalpitaṁ paśyan brahmaivāste mahāśayaḥ ll

28. The wise one being without both concentration and distraction is neither a seeker of liberation nor the reverse. Knowing for certain that this world is a figment of imagination, even though he sees it, he lives as Brahman.

Reverse—i.e. he is not in bondage.

यस्यान्तः स्यादहंकारो न करोति करोति सः ।
निरहंकारधीरेण न किञ्चिदकृतं कृतम् ॥२९॥

Yasyāntaḥ syādahaṅkāro na karoti karoti saḥ l
Nirahaṅkāradhīreṇa na kiñcidakṛtaṁ kṛtam ll

29. One who has egoism in his mind acts even though he is inactive. The wise man, free from egoism, does not commit any wrong deed.

Egoism—The *Gītā's* principle of inaction in action and action in inaction is reproduced here.

Wrong—The liberated in life, free from the ego-sense, can do no wrong. His actions, even without goal and purpose, are for the benefit of mankind, *bahujana hitāya, bahujana sukhāya,* as the Buddha put it.

नोद्विग्नं न च संतुष्टमकर्तृ स्पन्दवर्जितम् ।
निराशं गतसंदेहं चित्तं मुक्तस्य राजते ।।३०।।

Nodvignaṁ na ca santuṣṭamakartṛ spandavarjitam ।
Nirāśaṁ gatasandehaṁ cittaṁ muktasya rājate ।।

30. The mind of the liberated one is without either agitation or action. It is passive, free from fluctuations, desireless and purged of doubts.

निर्ध्यातुं चेष्टितुं वापि यच्चित्तं न प्रवर्त्तते ।
निर्निमित्तमिदं किन्तु निर्ध्यायति विचेष्टते ।।३१।।

Nirdhyātuṁ ceṣṭituṁ vāpi yaccittaṁ na pravarttate ।
Nirnimittamidaṁ kintu nirdhyāyati viceṣṭate ।।

31. The mind of the liberated one does not engage itself in either meditation or activity, but becomes meditative and active without any intention.

तत्त्वं यथार्थमाकर्ण्य मन्दः प्राप्नोति मूढताम् ।
अथवाऽऽयाति सङ्कोचममूढः कोऽपि मूढवत् ।।३२।।

Tattvaṁ yathārthamākarṇya mandaḥ prāpnoti mūḍhatām ।
Athavāyāti saṅkocamamūḍhaḥ ko'pi mūḍhavat ।।

32. The unintelligent one becomes confused on hearing the real truth. Or (rarely) the intelligent one achieves withdrawal (of the senses for samādhi). He behaves like a dullard.

Real truth i.e. truth of the Self. *Tattva* means the philosophy of the identity of *Tat* or That and *Tvam* or you.

Dullard—The liberated man in constant samādhi behaves outwardly like a dullard.

एकाग्रता निरोधो वा मूढैरभ्यस्यते भृशम् ।
धीराः कृत्यं न पश्यन्ति सुप्तवत्स्वपदे स्थिताः ॥३३॥

Ekāgratā nirodho vā mūḍhairabhyasyate bhṛśam 1
Dhīrāḥ kṛtyaṁ na paśyanti suptavat svapade sthitāḥ 11

33. The ignorant one intensely practises fixation and control of the mind. The wise, abiding in the Self, do not find anything to be attained like persons asleep.

Abiding in the Self—svapada, svarūpa, svasti and *svāsthya* are cognate terms denoting establishment in the unborn, non-dual self.

अप्रयत्नात्प्रयत्नाद्वा मूढो नाप्नोति निर्वृतिम् ।
तत्त्वनिश्चयमात्रेण प्राज्ञो भवति निर्वृतः ॥३४॥

Aprayatnāt prayatnādvā mūḍho nāpnoti nirvṛtim 1
Tattvaniścayamātreṇa prājño bhavati nirvṛtaḥ 11

34. Tne ignorant one does not achieve repose either through effort or through inactivity. The wise one becomes tranquil merely by ascertaining the truth of the Self.

Inactivity i.e., control of mind.

Merely i.e., without *japa*, *yoga* and *samādhi*.

शुद्धं बुद्धं प्रियं पूर्णं निष्प्रपञ्चं निरामयम् ।
आत्मानं तं न जानन्ति तत्राभ्यासपरा जनाः ॥३५॥

Śuddhaṁ buddhaṁ priyaṁ pūrṇaṁ nispropañcaṁ nirāmayaṁ 1
Ātmānaṁ taṁ na jānanti tatrābhyāsaparā janāḥ 11

35. In this world men who are habituated to various practices (of yoga) do not know the Self, which is pure, enlightened, beloved, perfect, transcendent and stainless.

Beloved—"The Self is dear, dearer than anything else, and is innermost" (*Bṛhadāraṇyaka Upaniṣad,* I, IV,8). It is because the Self is dear that one loves the dear ones (*Bṛhadāraṇyaka Upaniṣad,* IV, 5,6). The *Gītā* also speaks of the intimacy of God as "a lover to his beloved" (XI, 44).

नाप्नोति कर्मणा मोक्षं विमूढोऽभ्यासरूपिणा ।
धन्यो विज्ञानमात्रेण मुक्तस्तिष्ठत्यविक्रियः ॥३६॥

Nāpnoti karmaṇā mokṣaṁ vimūḍho'bhyāsarūpiṇā I
Dhanyo vijñānamātreṇa muktastiṣṭhatyavikriyaḥ II

36. The ignorant one does not attain liberation through his effort of yoga practice. The blessed one abides emancipated without any effort through mere intuitive enlightenment.

Intuitive enlightenment—This is direct apprehension, not knowledge by description or report. This is the same as *pratyakṣāvagama* of the *Gītā* (IX,2).

मूढो नाप्नोति तद्ब्रह्म यतो भवितुमिच्छति ।
अनिच्छन्नपि धीरो हि परब्रह्मस्वरूपभाक् ॥३७॥

Mūḍho nāpnoti tadbrahma yato bhavitumicchati I
Anicchannapi dhīro hi parabrahmasvarūpabhāk II

37. The ignorant one does not attain Brahman as he wants to become Brahman. The wise one, in spite of his absence of desire for Brahman, enjoys the nature of the Supreme Brahman.

The method of attainment of Brahman or Self is the obliteration of the ego-sense through the realization of the Self in all rather than the repeated practice of mind-control or discursive reasoning. *Vijñāna* is the direct, all-comprehensive apprehension of the Self.

निराधारा ग्रहव्यग्रा मूढाः संसारपोषकाः ।
एतस्यानर्थमूलस्य मूलच्छेदः कृतो बुधैः ॥३८॥

Nirādhārā grahavyagrā mūḍhāḥ saṁsāraposakāḥ I
Etasyānarthamūlasya mūlacchedaḥ kṛto budhaiḥ II

38. The ignorant (merely) sustain the world unsupported (by the supreme knowledge) and feverish for the attainment (of liberation). The wise sunder the very roots of this (world), the source of all suffering.

Unsupported—The self is autonomous and supportless. See XVIII, 21.

Sunder the roots—This is reminiscent of "cutting the roots of the tree of *saṁsāra*" of the *Gītā* (XV,) and is the same as *turīya* or transcendent state of consciousness. Vi like pari and abhi denotes completeness or infinitude of advaita knowledge (*samyak-jñāna*) (IX,6). The *Bhagavadgītā* says : "For the Brahman who has gained the highest knowledge (vijñāna), all the Vedas are of as much use as a reservoir when there is flood everywhere (II, 46).

न शान्तिं लभते मूढो यतः शमितुमिच्छति ।
धीरस्तत्त्वं विनिश्चित्य सर्वदा शान्तमानसः ॥३९॥

Na śāntiṁ labhate mūḍho yataḥ śamitumicchati ।
Dhīrastattvaṁ viniścitya sarvadā śāntamānasaḥ ॥

39. As the ignorant one wants peace, he does not attain it. The wise one is always peaceful in mind by knowing for certain the truth of the Self.

Wants peace—i.e. through the practice of yoga. In Śaṅkara's *Aparokṣānubhūti* or the Immediate Experience of the Self the various psycho-physical exercises of yoga are discounted in favour of Brahman or Ātman. Knowledge and complete freedom from any practices is commended (verses 113-126).

क्वात्मनो दर्शनं तस्य यद्दृष्टमवलम्बते ।
धीरास्तं तं न पश्यन्ति पश्यन्त्यात्मानमव्ययम् ॥४०॥

Kvātmano darśanaṁ tasya yaddṛṣṭamavalambate ।
Dhīrāstaṁ taṁ na paśyanti paśyantyātmānamavyayam ॥

40. Where is the vision (of the Self) of one who takes resort to seeing the visible world? The wise do not see this and that (object) but see (only) the immutable Self.

Immutable—The Self is to be seen as *cidrūpa*, the effulgent, eternal one which illumines every object of the universe. 'This Self is without the fluctuations of the mind, it is pure consciousness' (*avikalpo hi ayaṁ ātmā cidrūpaḥ*), says the *Nṛsiṁhottaratāpanī Upaniṣad*, 8.

क्व निरोधो विमूढस्य यो निर्बन्धं करोति वै ।
स्वारामस्यैव धीरस्य सर्वदाऽसावकृत्रिमः ॥४१॥

Kva nirodho vimūḍhasya yo nirbandhaṁ karoti vai l
Svārāmasyaiva dhīrasya sarvadā'sāvakṛtrimaḥ ll

41. Where is control (of the mind) for the ignorant one who strives for it? For the wise one who delights in the Self such control is perennial and natural.

भावस्य भावकः कश्चिन्न किञ्चिद्भावकोऽपरः ।
उभयाऽभावकः कश्चिदेवमेव निराकुलः ॥४२॥

Bhāvasya bhāvakaḥ kaścinna kiñcidbhāvako'paraḥ l
Ubhayābhāvakaḥ kaścidevameva nirākulaḥ ll

42. Some acknowledge that existence is and others that nothing is. Rare is the individual who acknowledges neither. He is perfectly serene.

Some—i.e. the logicians.

Others that nothing is—This probably refers to the Buddhist Mādhyamika philosophers. See also XVIII, 63 and XX, 1.

Serene—Śaṅkara in his *Aparokṣānubhūti* also uses the words *bhāvatvam* and *śūnyatā* in this manner and commends the meditation not of void but of fullness (129).

शुद्धमद्वयमात्मानं भावयन्ति कुबुद्धयः ।
न तु जानन्ति संमोहाद्यावज्जीवमनिर्वृताः ॥४३॥

Śuddhamadvayamātmānaṁ bhāvayanti kubuddhayaḥ l
Na tu jānanti saṁmohādyāvajjīvamanirvṛtāḥ ll

43. Men of defective intelligence meditate on the pure,

non-dual Self but do not realize it. Due to delusion they remain bereft of happiness throughout life.

Do not realize—The immediate, suprarational intuition (Vijñāna) of the Self rests paradoxically on the complete absence of meditation—relativist process that always seeks Being as object.

Delusion—The delusion consists in the contemplation of the absolute Self as *object*. This prevents the intuition from soaring beyond the realm of relativities.

In XII,7, Aṣṭāvakra mentions that one who reflects on the unthinkable Self resorts only to a certain mode or form of his own thought.

मुमुक्षोर्बुद्धिरालम्बमन्तरेण न विद्यते ।
निरालम्बैव निष्कामा बुद्धिर्मुक्तस्य सर्वदा ॥४४॥

Mumukṣorbuddhirālambamantareṇa na vidyate I
Nirālambaiva niṣkāmā buddhirmuktasya sarvadā II

44. The intelligence of one who strives after liberation cannot rise beyond a supporting object. But the liberated person is of desireless intelligence and verily remains constantly without any support (in his meditation).

Supporting object—Meditation free from dependence on a supporting object is already commended in XVIII, 40. The *Mukti Upaniṣad* says, 'The essence of all without any support' (*Sarvasāraṁ nirālambam*, I, 33). The Self is without any attributes or conditions that may require the support of words and meanings, assertions and denials, all relativist creations and experiences. The Self transcends the cobwebs of relativist thinking. This is real *ātma-anubhava*. Objectless meditation of the *Self* beyond all relativities abolishes the distinction of the triad : meditative subject, object of meditation and meditation. This is called *triputīkaraṇa*, which is essential for the intuitive realization of the absolute Self. In chapter XX the intuition of the relationless, undifferentiated Self that can elicit on mental modification is fully stressed.

विषयद्वीपिनो वीक्ष्य चकिताः शरणार्थिनः ।
विशन्ति झटिति क्रोडं निरोधैकाग्र्यसिद्धये ॥४५॥

Viṣayadvīpino vīkṣya cakitāḥ śaraṇārthinaḥ I
Viśanti jhaṭiti kroḍaṁ nirodhaikāgryasiddhaye II

45. Encountering the tigers of sense-objects, the frightened ones at once seek shelter for achieving control and concentration and penetrate into the interior of the cave (of the mind).

Frightened ones—Not the wise ones.

निर्वासनं हरिं दृष्ट्वा तूष्णीं विषयदन्तिनः ।
पलायन्ते न शक्तास्ते सेवन्ते कृतचाटवः ॥४६॥

Nirvāsanaṁ hariṁ dṛṣṭvā tūṣṇīṁ viṣayadantinaḥ I
Palāyante na śaktāste sevante kṛtacāṭavaḥ II

46, Encountering the lion of the desire-free, the elephants of sense-objects silently run away. When they are unable to do so, they serve him like sycophants.

Sycophants—Sense-objects and sense-experiences that ordinarily cause perturbations of the mind become ingredients of self-realization and are hence not shunned at all by the wise one.

न मुक्तिकारिकांधत्ते निःशङ्को युक्तमानसः ।
पश्यञ्छृण्वन्स्पृशञ्जिघ्रन्नश्नन्नास्ते यथासुखम् ॥४७॥

Na muktikārikāṁ dhatte niḥśaṅko yuktamānasaḥ I
Paśyan śṛṇvan spṛśan jighrannaśnannāste yathāsukham II

47. The person whose mind is absorbed in the Self is bereft of doubts does not take resort to the means of emancipation (yogic practices). He happily lives in the world, observing, hearing, touching, smelling and eating.

Observing etc.—The same words denoting outward activities are repeated from XVII,8,12 and borrowed from the *Gītā*, V,8. The emancipated one is untainted by these normal functionings of the senses.

वस्तुश्रवणमात्रेण शुद्धबुद्धिर्निराकुलः ।
नैवाचारमनाचारमौदास्यं वा प्रपश्यति ॥४८॥

Vastuśravaṇamātreṇa śuddhabuddirnirākulaḥ I
Naivācāramanācāramaudāsyaṁ vā prapaśyati II

48. The wise one who has achieved pure consciousness by just bearing the truth of the Self and who is tranquil (in the Self) makes no difference between action, proper or improper, and inaction.

This stanza echoes the *Gītā* doctrine of inaction or *naiṣkarmya*, (III,4, XVIII, 49).

यदा यत्कर्तुमायाति तदा तत्कुरुते ऋजुः ।
शुभं वाप्यशुभं वापि तस्य चेष्टा हि बालवत् ॥४९॥

Yadā yatkarttumāyāti tadā tatkurute ṛjuḥ I
Śubhaṁ vāpyaśubhaṁ vāpi tasya ceṣṭā hi bālavat II

49. The unsophisticated (wise) one does whatever comes to his lot, whether good or evil, as his actions are child-like.

स्वातन्त्र्यात्सुखमाप्नोति स्वातन्त्र्याल्लभते परम् ।
स्वातन्त्र्यान्निर्वृतिं गच्छेत् स्वातन्त्र्यात्परमं पदम् ॥५०॥

Svātantryāt sukhamāpnoti svātantryāllabhate param I
Svātantryānnirvṛtiṁ gacchet svātantryāt paramaṁ padam II

50. Through autonomy one achieves happiness, through autonomy he attains the Supreme, through autonomy he attains repose, through autonomy he reaches the supreme state.

Autonomy—transcendence of the realm of relativities. The word *svātantrya* is found in the *Maitrī Upaniṣad* where it is said that the contemplative moving upward through the age of syllable '*aum*' obtains autonomy (VI, 22).

अकर्तृत्वमभोक्तृत्वं स्वात्मनो मन्यते यदा ।
तदा क्षीणा भवन्त्येव समस्ताश्चित्तवृत्तयः ॥५१॥

Akartṛtvamabhoktṛtvaṁ svātmano manyate yadā I
Tadā kṣīṇā bhavantyeva samastāścittavṛttayaḥ II

51. As one comprehends that his Self is neither the doer nor the enjoyer, all fluctuations of the mind are extinguished.

उच्छृङ्खलाप्याकृतिका स्थितिर्धीरस्य राजते ।
न तु सस्पृहचित्तस्य शान्तिर्मूढस्य कृत्रिमा ॥५२॥

Ucchṛṅkhalāpyakṛtikā sthitirdhīrasya rājate I
Na tu saspṛhacittasya śāntirmūḍhasya kṛtrimā II

52. The wise one's conduct, though unrestrained and natural, shines; but not the artificial serenity of the ignorant one with his mind full of desire.

विलसन्ति महाभोगैर्विशन्ति गिरिगह्वरान् ।
निरस्तकल्पना धीरा अबद्धा मुक्तबुद्धयः ॥५३॥

Vilasanti mahābhogairviśanti girigahvarān I
Nirastakalpanā dhīrā abaddhā muktabuddhayaḥ II

53. The wise are free from imaginings, unfettered in intelligence and unbound. They (may) sport in great enjoyment or take resort to the mountain caves.

श्रोत्रियं देवतां तीर्थमङ्गनां भूपतिं प्रियम् ।
दृष्ट्वा संपूज्य धीरस्य न कापि हृदि वासना ॥५४॥

Śrotriyaṁ devatāṁ tīrthamaṅganāṁ bhūpatiṁ priyam I
Dṛṣṭvā sampūjya dhīrasya na kāpi hṛdi vāsanā II

54. No desire springs in the heart of the wise man encountering or honouring a learned Brāhmaṇa, a god, a place of pilgrimage, a woman, a king or a beloved person.

No desire—The wise one is *samadarśī*, sees the same in all.

भृत्यैः पुत्रैः कलत्रैश्च दौहित्रैश्चापि गोत्रजैः ।
विहस्य धिक्कृतो योगी न याति विकृतिं मनाक् ॥५५॥

Bhṛtyaiḥ putraiḥ kalatraiśca dauhitraiścāpi gotrajaiḥ ।
Vihasya dhikkṛto yogī na yāti vikṛtiṁ manāk ॥

55. The yogī is not in the least agitated even when scoffed and abused by servants, sons, wives, grandsons and relatives.

संतुष्टोऽपि न सन्तुष्टः खिन्नोऽपि न च खिद्यते ।
तस्याश्चर्यदशां तां तां तादृशा एव जानते ॥५६॥

Santuṣṭo'pi na santuṣṭaḥ khinno'pi na ca khidyate ।
Tasyāścaryadaśāṁ tāṁ tāṁ tādṛśā eva jānate ॥

56. Delighted, yet he is not delighted; afflicted, yet he is not afflicted. Only one like him can appreciate his marvellous condition.

कर्त्तव्यतैव संसारो न तां पश्यन्ति सूरयः ।
शून्याकारा निराकारा निर्विकारा निरामयाः ॥५७॥

Kartavyataiva saṁsāro na tāṁ paśyanti sūrayaḥ ।
Śūnyākārā nirākārā nirvikārā nirāmayāḥ ॥

57. Man's sense of duty is, indeed, the mundane world. This is not acknowledged by the wise who are of the form of the void, have no form nor change nor taint.

The *Jīvanmuktagītā* observes in the same strain: " I am not cognisant of any ordained activity (duty prescribed by the scriptures) whatever I understand all activity is Brahman." One who realizes this is called the liberated in life (X).

Form af the Void—Its meditation has led to the identification of the body with no-form, no change, no-duty, no-stain, transcending the human condition.

अकुर्वन्नपि संक्षोभाद्व्यग्रः सर्वत्र मूढधीः ।
कुर्वन्नपि तु कृत्यानि कुशलो हि निराकुलः ॥५८॥

Akurvannapi saṁkṣobhād vyagraḥ sarvatra mūḍhadhīḥ I
Kurvannapi tu kṛtyāni kuśalo hi nirākulaḥ II

58. Even in inaction the ignorant is distracted due to commotion (of the mind). The adept one, even when doing his duties, verily remains unperturbed.

सुखमास्ते सुखं शेते सुखमायाति याति च ।
सुखं वक्ति सुखं भुङ्क्ते व्यवहारेऽपि शान्तधीः ॥५९॥

Sukhamāste sukhaṁ śete sukhamāyāti yāti ca I
Sukhaṁ vakti sukhaṁ bhuṅkte vyavahāre'pi śāntadhīḥ II

59. Even in the practical affairs of life the man of wisdom sits contentedly, sleeps contentedly, moves contentedly, speaks contentedly and eats contentedly.

स्वभावाद्यस्य नैवार्तिर्लोकवद्व्यवहारिणः ।
महाह्रद इवाक्षोभ्यो गतक्लेशः सुशोभते ॥६०॥

Svabhāvādyasya naivārtirlokavadvyavahāriṇaḥ I
Mahāhrada ivākṣobhyo gatakleśaḥ suśobhate II

60. The wise one, even when engaged in practical life, does not have any distress like the ordinary man due to his inner disposition. Unperturbed he shines as a vast lake with all his sorrows extinguished.

Lake—Because the yogī is an infinite and tranquil reservoir of *ātmārāma* or bliss in the Self with no fluctuation of the mind-waves.

निवृत्तिरपि मूढस्य प्रवृत्तिरुपजायते ।
प्रवृत्तिरपि धीरस्य निवृत्तिफलभागिनी ॥६१॥

Nivṛttirapi mūḍhasya pravṛttirupajāyate I
Pravṛttirapi dhīrasya nivṛttiphalabhāginī II

61. The withdrawal of the ignorant is transformed into action. The action of the wise shares in the fruits of withdrawal.

Withdrawal—Everything depends upon the presence or absence of the ego-sense.

परिग्रहेषु वैराग्यं प्रायो मूढस्य दृश्यते ।
देहे विगलिताशस्य क्व रागः क्व विरागता ॥६२॥

Parigraheṣū vairāgyaṁ prāyo mūḍhasya dṛśyate l
Dehe vigalitāśasya kva rāgaḥ kva virāgatā ll

62. Often the ignorant one shows non-attachment to his possessions. What attachment or aversion is there for one whose love for the body has melted away?

भावनाभावनासक्ता दृष्टिमूढस्य सर्वदा ।
भाव्यभावनया सा तु स्वस्थस्यादृष्टिरूपिणी ॥६३॥

Bhāvanābhāvanāsaktā dṛṣṭirmūḍhasya sarvadā l
Bhāvyabhāvanayā sā tu svasthasyādṛṣṭirūpiṇī ll

63. The view of the ignorant is always addicted to either ideation or no ideation. That of one abiding in the Self in spite of his ideation of objects represents no ideation.

Ideation—As man abides in his true Self or pure consciousness his thinking (*bhāvanā*) in respect of objects is no thinking in view of his complete absence of ego-sense.

सर्वारम्भेषु निष्कामो यश्चरेद्बालवन्मुनिः ।
न लेपस्तस्य शुद्धस्य क्रियमाणेऽपि कर्मणि ॥६४॥

Sarvārambheṣu niṣkāmo yaścaredbālavanmuniḥ l
Na lepastasya śuddhasya kriyamāṇe'pi karmaṇi ll

64 The sage who moves about child-like without desire in all undertakings and is pure has no involvement even in action being done.

All Undertakings—The word (*Sarva-ārambha*) is borrowed from the *Gītā*, XII, 16, XIV, 25, XVIII, 48.

स एव धन्य आत्मज्ञः सर्वभावेषु यः समः ।
पश्यन् शृण्वन्स्पृशञ्जिघ्रन्नश्नन्निस्तर्षमानसः ॥६५॥

Sa eva dhanya ātmajñaḥ sarvabhāveṣu yaḥ samaḥ I
Paśyan śṛṇvan spṛśan jighrannaśnannistarṣamānasaḥ II

65. Blessed surely is that knower of the Self who is the same under all conditions and whose mind is free from thirst, while perceiving, hearing, touching, smelling and eating (in the realm of senses).

Perceiving etc.—This echoes the *Gītā* phrases, v, 8.

क्व संसारः क्व चाभासः क्व साध्यं क्व च साधनम् ।
आकाशस्येव धीरस्य निर्विकल्पस्य सर्वदा ॥६६॥

Kva saṁsāraḥ kva cābhāsaḥ kva sādhyaṁ kva ca sādhanam I
Ākāśasyeva dhīrasya nirvikalpasya sarvadā II

66. For the wise one, always changeless (free from the fluctuations of the mind) like the sky, where is the world, where is its reflection, where is the goal and where is the means?

Reflection—For one who sees the Self in the world and the world in the Self, the world has no deceptive appearance or reflection, as in a mirror, of the finite, ever-changeful mind.

स जयत्यर्थसन्न्यासी पूर्णस्वरसविग्रहः ।
अकृत्रिमोऽनवच्छिन्ने समाधिर्यस्य वर्तते ॥६७॥

Sa jayatyarthasannyāsī pūrṇasvarasavigrahaḥ I
Akṛtrimo'navacchinne samādhiryasya vartate II

67. He renounces all goals of desire and becomes the embodiment of perfect bliss pertaining to his essential nature. Glory to him who abides in his natural samādhi in the unlimited Self.

Unlimited—Natural samādhi is not only boundless but

also continuous. Its continuity is sustained by the perennial joy which is the essence of the Self. This echoes the *Upaniṣadic* statement, *Raso vai saḥ* ("That is the essence of bliss").

Natural—The *Gītā* also stresses that "as the yogī obtains the supreme delight in the Self, he no longer falls away from the truth of the Self". Thus *ātmayoga* becomes spontaneous and continuous (*Bhagavadgītā*, VI, 20-21). This is *sahaja samādhi*.

बहुनात्र किमुक्तेन ज्ञाततत्त्वो महाशयः ।
भोगमोक्षनिराकाङ्क्षी सदा सर्वत्र नीरसः ॥६८॥

Bahunātra kimuktena jñātatattvo mahāśayaḥ l
Bhogamokṣanirākāṅkṣī sadā sarvatra nīrasaḥ ll

68. At this point, there is no need of saying more. The wise man who realizes the truth is free from the desire of both enjoyment and emancipation and devoid of passion everywhere and at all times.

महदादि जगद्द्वैतं नाममात्रविजृम्भितम् ।
विहाय शुद्धबोधस्य किं कृत्यमवशिष्यते ॥६९॥

Mahadādi jagaddvaitaṁ nāmamātravijṛmbhitam l
Vihāya śuddhabodhasya kiṁ kṛtyamavaśiṣyate ll

69. What remains to be done by one who is pure intelligence, who forsakes the phenomenal world, beginning with mahat or cosmic consciousness and *so on*, which is manifested through mere name?

Phenomenal world—The allusion here is to Sāṁkhya system according to which *mahat* or cosmic consciousness first springs from nature or *Prakṛti* and then in order the ego-sense, the mind, the ten organs of sense and of action, the five subtle elements and the five gross elements,all constituents of the gross universe. According to the Vedānta all this is the result of illusion or superimposition by the deluded self. The Self, according to Aṣṭāvakra, is unborn, immutable and indivisible and abides in the truth. This is clarified in the next verses. The *Avadhūta gītā* has a similar verse : "Nothing of the phenomenal world beginning with *Mahat* or cosmic consciousness and so on appears to me" (II,45).

भ्रमभूतमिदं सर्वं किञ्चिन्नास्तीति निश्चयी ।
अलक्ष्यस्फुरणः शुद्धः स्वभावेनैव शाम्यति ॥७०॥

Bhramabhūtamidaṁ sarvaṁ kiñcinnāstīti niścayī l
Alakṣyasphuraṇaḥ śuddhaḥ svabhāvenaiva śāmyati ll

70. All this world springs from ignorance. Nothing exists in reality. The man of pure intelligence having known this for certain and realized that the Self alone is effulgent and pure, to whom the Unknown is manifest becomes tranquil by nature.

Self-effulgent—The Self as *cinmātra* produces and encompasses the phenomenal world. Nothing exists except the resplendent self, beyond conceptualization that makes the phenomenal world, including the mind, manifest.

शुद्धस्फुरणरूपस्य दृश्यभावमपश्यतः ।
क्व विधिः क्व च वैराग्यं क्व त्यागः क्व शमोऽपि वा ॥७१॥

Śuddhasphuraṇarūpasya dṛśyabhāvamapaśyataḥ l
Kva vidhiḥ kva ca vairagyaṁ kva tyāgaḥ kva śamo'pi vā ll

71. For one who has envisioned the Self as pure luminousness and does not perceive the phenomenal world, where is the rule of life, where is non-attachment, where is renunciation and where is control of the senses?

स्फुरतोऽनन्तरूपेण प्रकृतिं च न पश्यतः ।
क्व बन्धः क्व च वा मोक्षः क्व हर्षः क्व विषादिता ॥७२॥

Sphurato'nantarūpeṇa prakṛtiṁ ca na paśyataḥ l
Kva bandhaḥ kva ca vā mokṣaḥ kva harṣaḥ kva viṣāditā ll

72. For one who does not perceive (phenomenal) Nature, but discerns the self shining in infinite forms, where is bondage, where is salvation, where is joy and where is sorrow ?

Shining— The pure, indivisible, effulgent consciousness manifests itself as infinite existence – the endless world of names (*nāma*), forms (*rūpa*) and functions (*karma*). Only when the self is released from the flüctuations of the mind, this can be immediately apprehended by pure intelligence, and then the illusion of the phenomenal world fades away.

बुद्धिपर्यन्तसंसारे मायामात्रं विवर्तते ।
निर्ममो निरहङ्कारो निष्कामः शोभते बुधः ॥७३॥

Buddhiparyantasaṁsāre māyāmātraṁ vivartate l
Nirmamo nirahaṅkāro niṣkāmaḥ śobhate budhaḥ ll

73. In the phenomenal world that lasts until (the dawn of) self-knowledge, only illusion prevails. The wise man shines without ego-sense, egoism and desire.

Illusion—The word māyā is used here, denoting absence of knowledge of the all-encompassing, luminous Self—the source and matrix of cosmic manifestation. The relativist consciousness is saturated with *māyā*. Man must live in the non-dual, absolute consciousness so that what the *Upaniṣads* call *māyā* or *anṛta* i.e. mere illusion may not prevail.

अक्षयं गतसन्तापमात्मानं पश्यतो मुनेः ।
क्व विद्या च क्व वा विश्वं क्व देहोऽहं ममेति वा ॥७४॥

Akṣayaṁ gatasantāpamātmānaṁ paśyato muneḥ l
Kva vidyā ca kva vā viśvaṁ kva deho'haṁ mameti vā ll

74. For the sage who sees the self as immutable and free from the vestiges of sorrow, what is knowledge, what is the universe, what is the body and what are ego and egoism?

The absolute Self pervades all that exists, all material or immaterial existences in the realm of relativity.

निरोधादीनि कर्माणि जहाति जडधीर्यदि ।
मनोरथान्प्रलापांश्च कर्तुमाप्नोत्यतत्क्षणात् ॥७५॥

Nirodhādīni karmāṇi jahāti jaḍadhīryadi I
Manorathān pralāpāṁśca kartumāpnotyatatkṣaṇāt II

75. If one of defective intelligence forsakes such practices as the control of the mind, instantaneously do the wishes and fancies take over control.

The teaching here is that without Self-knowledge the yogic practices of regulation of the mind are of little avail.

मन्दः श्रुत्वापि तद्वस्तु न जहाति विमूढताम् ।
निर्विकल्पो बहिर्यत्नादन्तर्विषयलालसः ॥७६॥

Mandaḥ śrutvāpi tadvastu na jahāti vimūḍhatām I
Nirvikalpo bahiryatnādantarviṣayalālasaḥ II

76. The man of deficient intelligence, even hearing about the truth of the self, does not forsake this delusion. Outwardly he appears devoid of mental fluctuations through his efforts, but inwardly he craves for sense-gratification.

Self-knowledge is here posited as the means of the uprooting of desires that cannot be suppressed by yoga-exercises.

ज्ञानाद्गलितकर्मा यो लोकदृष्टयापि कर्मकृत् ।
नाप्नोत्यवसरं कर्तुं वक्तुमेव न किञ्चन ॥७७॥

Jñānādgalitakarmā yo lokadṛṣṭyāpi karmakṛt I
Nāpnotyavasaraṁ kartuṁ vaktumeva na kiñcana II

77. One whose actions have dropped off due to self-knowledge may be undertaking some work in the eyes of the world. He, however, has no occasion to do or say anything whatsoever about it.

The natural relinquishment of work for the man of self-knowledge is mentioned by *Māṇḍūkya Upaniṣad.*

Say anything—i.e. he is free from the notion that he is the real doer.

क्व तमः क्व प्रकाशो वा हानं क्व च न किञ्चन ।
निर्विकारस्य धीरस्य निरातङ्कस्य सर्वदा ॥७८॥

Kva tamaḥ kva prakāśo vā hānaṁ kva ca na kiñcana I
Nirvikārasya dhīrasya nirātaṅkasya sarvadā II

78. To the wise man who is ever unperturbed and fearless, where is darkness, where is light, and where is renouncement ? There is nothing whatsoever.

क्व धैर्यं क्व विवेकित्वं क्व निरातङ्कतापि वा ।
अनिर्वाच्यस्वभावस्य निःस्वभावस्य योगिनः ॥७९॥

Kva dhairyaṁ kva vivekitvaṁ kva nirātaṅkatāpi vā I
Anirvācyasvabhāvasya niḥsvabhāvasya yoginaḥ II

79. To the yogi whose nature is non-existential and undefinable what is patience, what is discrimination (of conscience) and what is courage ?

न स्वर्गो नैव नरको जीवन्मुक्तिर्न चैव हि ।
बहुनात्र किमुक्तेन योगदृष्ट्या न किञ्चन ॥८०॥

Na svargo naiva narako jīvanmuktirna caiva hi I
Bahunātra kimuktena yogadṛṣṭyā na kiñcana II

80. To him there is neither heaven nor hell, nor even liberation in life. Briefly, in the yoga-vision nothing exists.

नैव प्रार्थयते लाभं नालाभेनानुशोचति ।
धीरस्य शीतलं चित्तममृतेनैव पूरितम् ॥८१॥

Naiva prārthayate lābhaṁ nālābhenānuśocati I
Dhīrasya śītalaṁ cittamamṛtenaiva pūritam II

81. The wise man neither wishes for gain nor grieves

at loss. His tranquil mind is verily filled with the nectar (of immortal bliss).

न शान्तं स्तौति निष्कामो न दुष्टमपि निन्दति ।
समदुःखसुखस्तृप्तः किञ्चित्कृत्यं न पश्यति ॥८२॥

Na śāntaṁ stauti niṣkāmo na duṣṭamapi nindati I
Samaduḥkhasukhastṛptaḥ kiṅcit kṛtyaṁ na paśyati II

82. One who is free from desires neither has praise for the good nor blame for the wicked. He is contented and is the same in joy and sorrow. He discerns nothing to be achieved.

धीरो न द्वेष्टि संसारमात्मानं न दिदृक्षति ।
हर्षामर्षविनिर्मुक्तो न मृतो न च जीवति ॥८३॥

Dhīro na dveṣṭi saṁsāramātmānaṁ na didṛkṣati I
Harṣāmarṣavinirmukto na mṛto na ca jīvati II

83. The wise one has neither enmity with the world nor love of self-realization. Freed from happiness and sorrow, he is neither alive nor dead.

निःस्नेहः पुत्रदारादौ निष्कामो विषयेषु च ।
निश्चिन्तः स्वशरीरेऽपि निराशः शोभते बुधः ॥८४॥

Niḥsnehaḥ putradārādau niṣkāmo viṣayeṣu ca I
Niścintaḥ svaśarīre'pi nirāśaḥ śobhate budhaḥ II

84. Shining is the life of the wise man who is free from any expectation, who is without attachment to children, wife and others, without desire for sense-objects and without care even for his own body.

तुष्टिः सर्वत्र धीरस्य यथापतितवर्तिनः ।
स्वच्छन्दं चरतो देशान्यत्रास्तमितशायिनः ॥८५॥

Tuṣṭiḥ sarvatra dhīrasya yathāpatitavartinaḥ I
Svacchandaṁ carato deśānyatrāstamitaśāyinaḥ II

85. Contentment ever abides in the heart of the wise one who subsists on whatever comes to his lot. He roams about at his pleasure sleeping wherever the sun sets.

Roams about—The wandering sage is referred to here.

पततूदेतु वा देहो नास्य चिन्ता महात्मनः ।
स्वभावभूमिविश्रान्तिविस्मृताशेषसंसृतेः ॥८६॥

Patatūdetu vā deho nāsya cintā mahātmanaḥ ।
Svabhāvabhūmiviśrāntivismṛtāśeṣasaṁsṛte ॥

86. The great one has no care whether the body dies or lives. Resting on the foundation of the self, he forgets the cycle of births and deaths.

अकिञ्चनः कामचारो निर्द्वन्द्वश्छिन्नसंशयः ।
असक्तः सर्वभावेषु केवलो रमते बुधः ॥८७॥

Akiñcanaḥ kāmacāro nirdvandvaśchinnasaṁśayaḥ ।
Asaktaḥ sarvabhāveṣu kevalo ramate budhaḥ ॥

87. The wise one, alone and unattached to all things, rejoices. He is without any possession, moves about at pleasure, is free from the conflict of opposites and dispells all his doubts.

By himself—*Kevala* or alone or absolute is a term derived from Patañjali.

Dispelled his doubts—The phrase is derived from the Muṇḍaka Upaniṣad (II,2,9).

निर्ममः शोभते धीरः समलोष्टाश्मकाञ्चनः ।
सुभिन्नहृदयग्रन्थिर्विनिर्धूतरजस्तमः ॥८८॥

Nirmamaḥ śobhate dhīraḥ samaloṣṭāśmakāñcanaḥ ।
Subhinnahṛdayagranthirvinirdhūtarajastamaḥ ॥

88. There shines the wise one who has no ego-sense and looks upon a clod of earth, a stone or a piece of gold as of equal worth. The knot of his heart is perfectly cut asunder and he is purged of the attributes of *rajas* and *tamas*.

A clod of earth etc.—This echoes the well-known phrase of the *Gītā*, VI, 8, XII, 24. In XII, 24 the term *dhīra* also occurs.

Knot of his heart—This is reminiscent of the famous final passage relating to human perfection in the *Muṇḍaka Upaniṣad* (II, 28) from which, as already noted, the term 'dispelled all doubts' is derived in the preceding verse. The *Kaṭha Upaniṣad* also makes mention of all the knots that fetter the heart being cut asunder (II,3,15). Aṣṭāvakra adds, following the *Bhagavadgītā*, another condition of human perfection viz. freedom from the sway of the *guṇas*.

सर्वत्रानवधानस्य न किञ्चिद्वासना हृदि ।
मुक्तात्मनो वितृप्तस्य तुलना केन जायते ॥८९॥

Sarvatrānavadhānasya na kiñcidvāsanā hṛdi I
Muktātmano vitṛptasya tulanā kena jāyate II

89. He is indifferent to every thing; no desire lingers in his heart. Who can be compared with the contented and liberated one?

जानन्नपि न जानाति पश्यन्नपि न पश्यति ।
ब्रुवन्नपि न च ब्रूते कोऽन्यो निर्वासनादृते ॥९०॥

Jānannapi na jānāti paśyannapi na paśyati I
Bruvannapi na ca brūte ko'nyo nirvāsanādṛte II

90. Who but the one free from all desires knows not while knowing, sees not while seeing, and speaks not while speaking?

भिक्षुर्वा भूपतिर्वापि यो निष्कामः स शोभते ।
भावेषु गलिता यस्य शोभनाऽशोभना मतिः ॥९१॥

Bhikṣurvā bhūpatirvāpi yo niṣkāmaḥ sa śobhate I
Bhāveṣu galitā yasya śobhanāśobhanā matiḥ II

91. May be a prince or a beggar, he shines who is

unattached; from his attitude towards existence the sense of good and evil has vanished.

Prince—For Janaka the kingdom is no cause of bondage. According to the *Bhagavadgītā* "It was even by works that Janaka and others attained to perfection. Thou (Arjuna) shouldest do works also with a view to the maintenance of the world" (III, 20).

क्व स्वाच्छन्द्यं क्व संकोचः क्व वा तत्त्वविनिश्चयः
निर्व्याजार्जवभूतस्य चरितार्थस्य योगिनः ॥९२॥

Kva svācchandyaṁ kva saṅkocaḥ kva vā tattvaviniścayaḥ ।
Nirvyājārjavabhūtasya caritārthasya yoginaḥ ॥

92. To the yogī who is guileless and simple and realises the supreme goal of life, what is wilfulness, what is restraint, and what is determination of the Truth of the Self?

Determination—The yogī's intuitive apprehension (*vijñāna*) of the Self yields a profound certitude in comparison with which the philosophical knowledge of the Self is a pale affair.

आत्मविश्रान्तितृप्तेन निराशेन गतार्तिना ।
अन्तर्यदनुभूयेत तत्कथं कस्य कथ्यते ॥९३॥

Ātmaviśrāntitṛptena nirāśena gatārtinā ।
Antaryadanubhūyeta tatkathaṁ kasya kathyate ॥

93. How and for whom can be depicted the inner experience of one who is desireless and contented with his repose in himself, and who transcends all his sufferings ?

How—This is because the Self is unknowable and unutterable (*avyakta*).

सुप्तोऽपि न सुषुप्तौ च स्वप्नेऽपि शयितो न च ।
जागरेऽपि न जागर्ति धीरस्तृप्तः पदे पदे ॥९४॥

Supto'pi na suṣuptau ca svapne'pi śayito na ca ।
Jāgare'pi na jāgarti dhīrastṛptaḥ pade pade ॥

94. The wise one is not asleep in deep slumber nor lies down in sleep, nor again is he awake in the waking state. He is contented in all states (of consciousness).

Slumber—The three states of consciousness, given in the *Māṇḍūkya Upaniṣad*, are mentioned here, viz. waking, dream and slumber. The yogī, whose Self abides in the fourth stage (*turīya* or ecstasy), is the eternal, non-involved witness of the three states and achieves continuous, unalloyed bliss. The *Kaivalya Upaniṣad* says, "The world which shines in the states of waking, dream and slumber, knowing that it is Brahman who I am, one is released from all bondages" (17). Śaṅkara observes : "He who sees nothing in the waking state, as though in dreamless sleep; who, though perceiving reality experiences it as non-dual; who though engaged in work is inactive; that one and no one else, knows the Self. This is the truth" (*Upadeśasāhasrī*, 5).

ज्ञः सचिन्तोऽपि निश्चिन्तः सेन्द्रियोऽपि निरिन्द्रियः ।
सबुद्धिरपि निर्बुद्धिः साहंकारोऽनहंकृतिः ॥९५॥

Jñaḥ sacinto'pi niścintaḥ sendriyo'pi nirindriyaḥ I
Subuddhirapi nirbuddhiḥ sāhaṅkāro'nahaṁkṛtiḥ II

95. The man of self-knowledge is devoid of thought as he thinks, and of sense-organs as he uses them. Endowed with a good intellect he is without intelligence. Endowed with ego, he is without ego-sense.

For the yogī the sense-organs, the mind, the ego-sense and the intelligence are all successively merged in the real Self which alone becomes the prime cause and the eternal witness, transcending the universe and free from any stains (XVIII, 35). The metapsychology of the *Kaṭhopaniṣad* and of the *Bhagavadgītā* is used here in the stratification of the means of higher knowledge, the pure, effulgent Self standing at the top of the hierarchy.

न सुखी न च वा दुःखी न विरक्तो न सङ्गवान् ।
न मुमुक्षुर्न वा मुक्तो न किञ्चिन्न च किञ्चन ॥९६॥

Na sukhī na ca vā duḥkhī na virakto na saṅgavān l
Na mumukṣurna va muktā na kiñcinna ca kiñcana ll

96. He is neither happy nor unhappy; he is neither a recluse nor a man of company, neither liberated nor aspiring after liberation. He is not this nor that.

The man liberated in life has no separate self that can be defined by name, form and activity. He becomes universal and inexpressible.

Not this—This echoes the well-known phrase of the *Bṛhadāraṇyaka Upaniṣad* : *neha nānāsti kiñcana* (IV,4,19). He is not *that* because he is the indivisible Self; he is also not *that* because the Self is undefinable.

विक्षेपेऽपि न विक्षिप्तः समाधौ न समाधिमान् ।
जाड्येऽपि न जडो धन्यः पाण्डित्येऽपि न पण्डितः ॥९७॥

Vikṣepe'pi na vikṣiptaḥ samādhau na samādhimān l
Jāḍye'pi na jaḍo dhanyaḥ pāṇḍitye'pi na paṇḍitaḥ ll

97. Neither in distraction he is distracted; nor in samādhi is he in meditation. He is not dull even in dullness, nor is he learned even though possessing learning.

In distraction—His intelligence uniformly shines with the radiance of the pure Self.

Samādhi—He has no ego-sense. He is very different from what he outwardly appears. He is alert when he is visibly impassive in his contemplation.

Verses 94-98 have found their echo in Narahari : "His speech is silence, his movement is stability, his waking is sleep, his sleep is waking, his day is night and night is day. His action is Brahman, his world the embodiment of bliss, his smelling is nothing. Who can depict the nature of the wise one who has got beyond the path of the world fashioned by the *guṇas* hard to surmount? (*Bodhasāra* XXXIV, 7).

मुक्तो यथास्थितिस्वस्थः कृतकर्त्तव्यनिर्वृतः ।
समः सर्वत्र वैतृष्ण्यान्न स्मरत्यकृतं कृतम् ॥९८॥

Mukto yathāsthitisvasthaḥ kṛtakartavyanirvṛtaḥ l
Samaḥ sarvatra vaitṛṣṇyānna smaratyakṛtaṁ kṛtam ll

98. The emancipated one is established in the Self under all conditions and released from the notions of action and duty. Owing to his absence of desire, he is the same under all circumstances and does not ponder over what he has or has not done.

Same—The term *samaḥ* is the same as used in the *Bhagavadgītā* in V, 19 (Brahman is flawless and the same in all") and XVIII, 54 ("Regarding all beings as alike"). The *Avadhūtagītā* correspondingly uses *samarasam* (sameness of feeling) or equipoise along with *jñanāmṛtam* (nectar of knowledge) verse after verse in chapter III (3-42).

न प्रीयते वन्द्यमानो निन्द्यमानो न कुप्यति ।
नैवोद्विजति मरणे जीवने नाभिनन्दति ॥९९॥

Na prīyate vandyamāno nindyamāno na kupyati l
Naivodvijati maraṇe jīvane nābhinandati ll

99 He is neither pleased with eulogy nor enraged by dispraise. Nor is he agitated by (the fear of death) nor takes delight in life (due to his identification with the absolute Self).

Agitated—This is reminiscent of the *Gītā's* anudvignamanāḥ (II, 56),

न धावति जनाकीर्णं नारण्यमुपशान्तधीः ।
यथा तथा यत्र तत्र सम एवावतिष्ठते ॥१००॥

Na dhāvati janākīrṇaṁ nāraṇyamupaśāntadhiḥ l
Yathātathā yatratatra sama evāvatiṣṭhate ll

100. The wise one, whose mind is serene, is eager neither for the crowd nor for the solitude of the forest. He remains the same everywhere and under all conditions.

This verse may be read with II, 21. Man who is established in the absolute Self is conscious only of the One—without a second, whether in the crowd or in the wilderness.

Aṣṭāvakra identifies *cinmātra* or pure, stainless consciousness with a perfect state of sameness. The wise one remains the same in all his apparent routine of activities under all conditions. There are neither praise nor blame, neither desire for life nor fear of death, neither society nor solitude, neither bondage nor liberation for him. "He is not this nor that" (XVIII, 96). All this is equivalent to the *Bhagavad-gītā's* celebrated aphorism, *nirdoṣaṁ hi samaṁ brahma.* "Ātman is the flawless state of sameness". *Ātmādvaita* is an ontological ethical doctrine of complete equilibrium. Beyond happiness and misery, good and evil, life and death, existence and non-existence which all pertain to the phenomenal realm is the state of equilibrium or natural self-abidance (*svāsthya*). The indivisible, complete and subsistent Self transcends the illusory notion of attachment and non-attachment, distraction and samādhi, bondage and salvation (XVIII, 96,97). It is obvious that Aṣṭāvakra rises above the relativist oppositions of *Jīva* and Brahman, *bandha* and *mokṣa, dvaita* and *advaita* of *Vedānta-vāda.* This proceeds from intuitive illumination, *vijñāna* or *pratibhā* in his ontic mysticism. Man must discern the truth of the Self as the whole, the perfect and the beloved beyond nature and beyond all dualisms through his mystical insight.

Chapter XV

JANAKA ON THE MAJESTY OF THE SELF

This brief but magnificent chapter extols the majesty of the pure, unborn Self. Self-majesty transcends, first, man's threefold ends, desire, wealth and piety ; secondly, the duality and non-duality of the Self as expounded by metaphysical discourse and speculation; thirdly, the sense of time, space and eternity; and, finally, the context of life, death and the world (XIX, 1-3). The Self, absolute and supreme, outreaches the four states of consciousness, as defined by the *Māṇḍūkya Upaniṣad*, as well as yogic *samādhi* and dissolution (*laya*) of consciousness (XIX, 5, 7).

The Self is the non-attached, eternal witness of the changing phenomena of life and death, desires and goals, earthly relations and obligations, good and evil, past and present time and location. It is beyond both the gross or sensual and the subtle or spiritual experiences. Neither the differences of the states of waking, dream, slumber and transcendence nor the experiences of the absorption and obliteration have any relevance for the one who is purely *citsvarūpa* beyond form and change—the sole and universal eternal reality. The majesty of the supreme Self or Brahman transcends not only *yoga* but also the suprarational illumination (*vijñāna*)of the Self (XIX, 8). In the *Chāndogya Upaniṣad* VII, 24, 1-2), we have the term *Svamahiman* only once. It does not occur at all in any other major *Upaniṣad*. In the *Nṛsiṁhatāpanī Upaniṣad* we come across a similar delineation of the primal glory *mahiman* of the supreme Self (II, 4).

अष्टावक्र उवाच

तत्त्वविज्ञानसन्दंशमादाय हृदयोदरात् ।
नानाविधपरामर्शशल्योद्धारः कृतो मया ॥१॥

Janaka uvāca
Tattvavijñānasandaṁśamādāya hṛdayodarāt l
Nānāvidhaparāmarśaśalyoddhāraḥ kṛto mayā ll

Janaka said:

1. I have extracted by means of the pincers of the knowledge of the Self the thorns of diverse intellectual opinions from the deep recesses of my consciousness.

Intellectual opinions—Fluctuations of mind (*Saṅkalpa-vikalpa*) often proceed from scriptural learning and intellectual disquisition as distinguished from the direct apprehension of the Self. The Self cannot be attained by discursive reasoning (*pravacana*).

क्व धर्मः क्व च वा कामः क्व चार्थः क्व विवेकिता ।
क्व द्वैतं क्व च वाऽद्वैतं स्वमहिम्नि स्थितस्य मे ॥२॥

Kva dharmaḥ kva ca vā kāmaḥ kva cārthaḥ kva vivekitā l
Kva dvaitaṁ kva ca vā'dvaitaṁ svamahimni sthitasya me ll

2. To me established in my own grandeur, where is righteousness, where is desire, where is wealth, where is conscience ? And where is duality and where, again, is non-duality ?

Righteousness and Desire—The pairs of opposites woven by nature or *guṇas* in the phenomenal world that are transcended are : righteousness and enjoyment; conscience and prosperity; and duality and non-duality.

Non-duality—The truth of the Self transcends the notions of duality and non-duality. There is no need of the boat as the shore is reached. As duality fades away the need of contemplation on the Self is outgrown. This is natural self-abidance. The *Yoga-vāsiṣṭha Rāmāyaṇa* points out that neither duality nor non-duality comprise the truth. Each is "not unborn but really born", i.e. the product of human mind and imagination (*Utpattiprakaraṇa*, XXI, 97-98). The *Avadhūta Gītā* observes: "Some prefer non-duality. Others prefer duality. They do not understand the truth which is equipoise and is neither duality nor non-duality (1, 36)."

क्व भूतं क्व भविष्यद्वा वर्तमानमपि क्व वा ।
क्व देशः क्व च वा नित्यं स्वमहिम्नि स्थितस्य मे ॥३॥

Kva bhūtaṁ kva bhaviṣyadvā vartamānamapi kva vā ।
Kva deśaḥ kva ca vā nityaṁ svamahimni sthitasya me ॥

3. To me established in my own grandeur, where is the past, where is the future and where is the present ? Where is space and where is eternity ?

Past, Future and Present—The sense of time that involves the contradictions between past, present and future and the sense of location (*deśa*) that assumes the opposition between a 'here' and a 'there' are transcended.

Eternity—This demands the concept of transience. The silence of the Self transcends the pair of opposites, eternity and ephemeralness.

क्व चात्मा क्व च वानात्मा क्व शुभं क्वाशुभं यथा ।
क्व चिन्ता क्व च वाऽचिन्ता स्वमहिम्नि स्थितस्य मे ॥४॥

Kva cātmā kva ca vānātmā kva śubhaṁ kvāṣubhaṁ yathā ।
Kva cintā kva ca vācintā svamahimni sthitasya me ॥

4. Where is the Self, and where the non-self, where is good and where is evil ? Where is meditation, and where is non-meditation for me established in my own grandeur ?

क्व स्वप्नः क्व सुषुप्तिर्वा क्व च जागरणं तथा ।
क्व तुरीयं भयं वापि स्वमहिम्नि स्थितस्य मे ॥५॥

Kva svapnaḥ kva suṣuptirvā kva ca jāgaraṇaṁ tathā ।
Kva turīyaṁ bhayaṁ vāpi svamahimni sthitasya me ॥

5. To me abiding in my own grandeur where is dream where is slumber and where is waking ? Where is the fourth state (of ecstasy), and where is anxiety ?

The four states of consciousness, according to the *Māṇḍūkya Upaniṣad*, are again mentioned here. These comprised the core of introspective psychology and Self-knowledge of the period of the *Aṣṭāvakragītā*. The *Jīvanmukta*

Gītā gets rid of these floating states of consciousness, even of the most elevated state. In the *Avadhūta Gītā* we read, "How can there be a fourth state of consciousness when the three are not there? How can there be direction without the three-fold division of time? The ultimate reality is verily the abode of the supreme peace. I am the nectar of supreme knowledge, the sameness of feeling to all things and like unto the sky (III, 20).

क्व दूरं क्व समीपं वा बाह्यं क्वाभ्यन्तरं क्व वा ।
क्व स्थूलं क्व च वा सूक्ष्मं स्वमहिम्नि स्थितस्य मे ॥६॥

Kva dūraṁ kva samīpaṁ vā bāhyaṁ kvābhyantaraṁ kva vā I
Kva sthūlaṁ kva ca vā sūkṣmaṁ svamahimni sthitasya me II

6. To me established in my own grandeur, where is distance, where is nearness, where is outside and where is inside? And where is the gross and where is the subtle?

This is the vision of the all-full and all-perfect, wherein the discrimination between the near and the far, the interior and the exterior and the gross and the subtle is lost.

क्व मृत्युर्जीवितं वा क्व लोकाः क्वास्य क्व लौकिकम् ।
क्व लयः क्व समाधिर्वा स्वमहिम्नि स्थितस्य मे ॥७॥

Kva mṛtyurjīvitaṁ vā kva lokāḥ kvāsya kva laukikam I
Kva layaḥ kva samādhirvā svamahimni sthitasya me II

7. To me established in my own grandeur, where is death and where is life, where are the manifold worlds, and where are worldly relations? And where is dissolution of consciousness and where is *samādhi*?

The notions of time and duration in the background of changes of life and death, and the notion of space in the background of discrete worldly existence, relations and activities are both transcended. In the fullness and continuity of self-abidance, neither the effort of dissolution of consciousness nor of *samādhi* persists. Self-abidance becomes easy and spontaneous *samādhi*. From another angle, *samādhi* becomes the effulgent self that can no longer be bedimmed by any concept of the mind and experience of the phenomenal world. The differentiations familiar in meditation between self and not-self (IX, 4), duality and non-duality (IX,2), transcendence and waking (IX, 5), dissolution and absorption (IX, 7) fade away. This is the core of the experience of the self's glorious majesty the deep-ocean stillness that is not to be stirred by any breeze of impulse, thought or feeling (II, 23, 24). The verse admirably stresses that in the transcendence of the Self all the distinctions known to thought melt away.

अलं त्रिवर्गकथया योगस्य कथयाऽप्यलम् ।
अलं विज्ञानकथया विश्रान्तस्य ममात्मनि ॥८॥

Alaṁ trivargakathayā yogasya kathayāpyalam l
Alaṁ vijñānakathayā viśrāntasya mamātmani ll

8. To me completely poised in my own Self there is no need of any discourse about the threefold goals of life, about *yoga* and about wisdom.

The chapter ends with the profound revelation of the all-sufficiency of wisdom of the Self, beyond the values of life, beyond *yoga* or means of acquisition of the supreme wisdom, and beyond the supreme wisdom itself.

Chapter XX

JANAKA ON THE TRANSCENDENCE OF THE SELF

The relationlessness of the Self, absolute and supreme, is expounded in this chapter through a dialectical juxtaposition of opposite empirical determinations, all of which are surpassed. There is neither *jīva* nor Brahman, neither relation nor absoluteness, neither bondage nor emancipation, neither unity nor duality in the transcendent Self which is beyond all relativities, all formulations and denials. All distinctions and differences, known to thought and imagination, are defied by a series of grand paradoxical utterances so that the mind receiving shock after shock is moulded and sharpened to reach beyond words and the cobwebs of logic and intellectualism towards the pure, transcendent aloneness, wonder and bliss of the Self (*paramasvāsthya*).

Transcendence is amplified and reinforced by the following categories or principles of the Self or citsvarūpa, verse by verse : pointlessness or stainlessness (*nirañjana*); absence of duality of opposites (*gatadvandva*); indefinability (*arūpita*); indivisibility (*nirvibhāga*); aloneness (*kaivalya*); non-particularisation (*nirviśeṣa*); freedom from natural attributes (*niḥsvabhāva*); taintlessness (*vimala*); actionlessness (*niṣkriya*); non-conceptualisation (*nirvimarśa*); non-limitation (*nirupādhi*); immutability (*kūṭastha*); absolute bliss, tranquillity and goodness (*śiva*); and non-origination (*akiñcanabhava*).

With the nullification of the basis of a phenomenal body and mind phenomenality is completely abolished. Verses 6 and 7 of the chapter are crucial as revelations of the non-dual nature of the Self (*advaya-svasvarūpa*) beyond name and form, ignorance and knowledge, bondage and liberation, end and means, beyond all subjective human experience. It may be mentioned here that these two stanzas are closely followed by Gauḍapāda in his *Māṇḍūkya Kārikā* which even repeats some of the words here : "There is no destruction nor creation, no one in bondage no seeker, no aspirant for liberation, none liberated. This is the absolute truth" (II, 32). Śaṅkara's commentary on this verse of the *Kārikā* is equally relevant for XX,6-14. The Self which is all that exists thunders out the thrilling world-shattering truth of *Ātmādvaita Vedānta* that even liberation and bondage (XX,6), *jīva* and Brahman (XX,11), unity and duality (XX,14), end and means (XX,7) are unreal pairs of opposites belonging to the phenomenal realm. The supreme paradox of Indian metaphysics, so profoundly and poetically presented by Aṣṭāvakra, is to demolish by the transcendental unity of the Self or Brahman (*advayasvasvarūpa*, XX,6) all the subtle logical distinctions and fine conceptualisations that in the path of self-introspection yet screen rather than mirror the ultimate reality. At the end of the path nothing remains but the Self, That or the Unknowable. He who discards the notion that he has known Ātman or Brahman knows it, and none else. "The Self is beyond speech, understanding and contemplation. Giving up contemplation altogether, man should conform to his essential nature and abide in the unborn, taintless Self (XII,7,8)". Aṣṭāvakra's bold paradoxical formulae completely annihilate the fascination of reason.

अष्टावक्र उवाच

क्व भूतानि क्व देहो वा क्वेन्द्रियाणि क्व वा मनः ।
क्व शून्यं क्व च नैराश्यं मत्स्वरूपे निरञ्जने ॥१॥

Janaka uvāca

Kva bhutāni kva deho vā kvendriyāṇi kva vā manaḥ ll
Kva śūnyaṁ kva ca nairāśyaṁ matsvarūpe nirañjane ll

Janaka said :

1. To my signless Self what are the gross elements (of nature) and what is the body, what are the organs of senses, what is the mind, what is void and what is the state that transcends hope.

The pure Self is here the eternal knower and witness of the happenings of nature, body and mind as well as of the internal experiences of the mind's emptiness and transcendence of expectation. It here reaches completeness (*pūrṇam*, I, 12, XVIII, 35). Freedom from expectation is mentioned in XVIII, 84.

Void—The Buddhist principle of emptiness is contradicted here by the principle of the all-encompassing Self, whole and perfect. In the *Avadhūtagītā* we read, "The reality is neither void nor non-void" (III, 45).

क्व शास्त्रं क्वात्मविज्ञानं क्व वा निर्विषयं मनः ।
क्व तृप्तिः क्व वितृष्णत्वं गतमोहस्य मे सदा ॥२॥

Kva śāstraṁ kvātmavijñānaṁ kva vā nirviṣayaṁ manaḥ ।
Kva tṛptiḥ kva vitṛṣṇatvaṁ gatamohasya me sadā ॥

2. To me ever transcending the duality of opposites, what is scripture and what is knowledge of the Self, what is mind dissociated from objects and what is contentment.

When the mind feeding itself on pairs of opposites disappears, there is neither quest of sense-objects or knowledge nor opposition between satisfaction and dissatisfaction. The Self attains its perfect serenity (*Śāntam*, XVIII, 1).

Duality of opposites—There is a basic conflict of diverse pairs of opposites in the phenomenal world springing from the mutually contending guṇas. Both the seer of the *Gītā* and Aṣṭāvakra refer to the delusion of the fundamental duality of wish (*pravṛtti*) and aversion (*nivṛtti*) which has to be overcome by the acknowledgement of the real as above all opposites (XVI, 8; *Gītā* II, 45, VII, 28). Aṣṭāvakra particularly stresses the need of getting beyond the opposites of what is done and what is not done in the world of experience (IX, 1,4). All goals of life, *dharma*, *artha*, *kāma* and *mokṣa*, involve, according to him, a struggle of opposites of duties and their non-fulfilment (XVI, 5). Man must transcend all opposites involved in his dutifulness, springing as it does from desire and attachment, by his abidance in the absolute Self. Even the desire for self-knowledge (*ātmavijñāna*) and the duty of attainment of *mokṣa* have to be abandoned. The *gatadvandva* here is the *nirdvandva* and *dvandvātīta* of the *Gītā* (II, 45, IV, 22, XV, 5).

Contentment—First, the enquiry, then the mind, and finally, the spring of desire fade away.

क्व विद्या क्व च वाऽविद्या क्वाहं क्वेदं मम क्व वा ।
क्व बन्धः क्व च वा मोक्षः स्वरूपस्य क्व रूपिता ॥३॥

Kva vidyā kva ca vāvidyā kvāhaṁ kvedaṁ mama kva vā l
Kva bandhaḥ kva ca vā mokṣaḥ svarūpasya kva rūpitā ll

3. What is knowledge and what is ignorance, what is the ego and what is the world, what is mine, and what is bondage, and what is liberation, what is definition of the essential Self?

The Self experiences complete and permanent unity (advaya, XX,6). The notions of I and It, ignorance and knowledge, bondage and liberation disappear.

The *Avadhūtagītā* says, "I am never born, nor do I die; in me there is no activity, neither holy nor sinful. I am all-pure Brahman, devoid of all differentiating, limiting and mutually conflicting qualities (*guṇaṣ*) Then how should there be in me anything like bondage or liberation? (I,59)".

Definition—The real Self is unthinkable (*acintyam*) and undefinable (XII, 7, XVIII,79).

क्व प्रारब्धानि कर्माणि जीवन्मुक्तिरपि क्व वा ।
क्व तद्विदेहकैवल्यं निर्विशेषस्य सर्वदा ॥४॥

Kva prārabdhāni karmāṇi jīvanmuktirapi kva vā l
Kva tadvidehakaivalyaṁ nirviśeṣasya sarvadā ll

4. To myself, who am ever free from particularisation, what is the ripening action pertaining to previous births, what is liberation in life and what is aloneness at death?

The Self having lost its individuation is no longer gripped by the law of *karma* and the condition of liberation in life or liberation at death, both of which involve the body-sense, ego-sense and activity (*ahaṁkāra*).

Particularisation—According to Aśvaghoṣa the original nature of the mind is free from particularisation. "When the oneness of the totality of things is not recognised, then ignorance as well as particularisation arises, and all phases of the defined mind are thus developed" (*Discourse on the Awakening Faith in the Mahāyāna*, pp. 55-57).

Ripening Action—The Vedānta divides actions into triple categories : (1) actions, the seeds of which were planted by actions of previous births but which have not germinated but have remained as a set of latent dispositions and trends (*sañcita-karma*); (2) actions which proliferate, fructify, accumulate and entangle the individual as the result of ignorance (*āgāmi-karma*) ; and (3) actions the germs of which have been assembled through previous births and which are yielding fruit in present life (*prārabdha-karma*). The destiny of the individual cannot escape from the good and evil consequences of past actions in spite of his attainment of the supreme wisdom. The *Jīvanmukta* who has lost his sense of doership and duty does not make a fresh beginning of his *karma* cycle, but endures the inescapable consequences of actions of previous births as embodied in the dual events of his life. Śaṅkara observes : "The work that fashioned this body prior to the dawn of self-knowledge is not destroyed by that knowledge until it yields its fruits-like an arrow shot at an object. The arrow that is short at an object with the idea that it is a tiger does not, when the object is perceived to be a cow, check itself ; it goes on and and pierces the object with all its force" (*Vivekacūḍāmaṇi*, 451-452). In spite of his absorption in the Self, the *Jīvanmukta* cannot check nor nullify the ripening of previous *karmas* into the fruits of actual happening although he considers these latter as completely unreal and inconsequential. "His actions merely follow the lot of his life" (XVIII, 13).

Liberation in life—Even liberation in life or at death is rejected because the notions of the body and of life and death are surmounted by the Self, unborn, changeless and free. Freedom and bondage are simultaneously denied. In *Mukti Upaniṣad* we read that *videha-mukti* and *kaivalya-mukti* (meaning bodiless liberation) are the same (I, 31, 1).

The wise one abides in eternity, and as the shell of his body drops away at his death there is no change in realm of eternity ; while as long as he lives and moves in the world, he transcends the realm of phenomenality. Only the momentum of his actions in past births drives him in the world like a dry leaf carried hither and thither by the wind.

In XVIII, 21, we read that the *jīvanmukta* moves about "like a dry leaf blown by the wind of the *saṁskāras*".

क्व कर्ता क्व च वा भोक्ता निष्क्रियं स्फुरणं क्व वा ।
क्वापरोक्षं फलं वा क्व निःस्वभावस्य मे सदा ।।५।।

Kva kartā kva ca vā bhoktā niṣkriyaṁ sphuraṇaṁ kva vā I
Kvāparokṣaṁphalaṁ vā kva niḥsvabhāvasya me sadā II

5. To myself who am ever devoid of natural attributes, what is the doer and what is enjoyer, what is inaction and what is manifestation, what is direct apprehension (of the Self) and what is the fruit thereof ?

The wise one no longer witnesses the upsurge of any impulses (*vṛtti*) derived from human nature and has no sense of being the doer, the enjoyer and the knower. The self abides in its pristine nature—*jñānasvarūpa* or pure intelligence.

Devoid of natural attributes—Freedom from human nature is a new category of Aṣṭāvakra. Dattātreya in the *Jīvanmuktagītā* uses a similar phrase, '*svabhāva-guṇa-varjitam*', devoid of the natural attributes of man (rooted in *prakṛti*) (XVII).

Apprehension—In the immediate experience of the Self as continuous, all-pervading intelligence (*sakṛt prakāśaṁ ajaṁ ekaṁ avyayam*) the mode of experience disappears. Luminousness is the very nature of the Self. Alone the Self exists and shines by itself. See II, 8, XVIII, 22.

क्व लोकः क्व मुमुक्षुर्वा क्व योगी ज्ञानवान् क्व वा ।
क्व बद्धः क्व च वा मुक्तः स्वस्वरूपेऽहमद्वये ।।६।।

Kva lokaḥ kva mumukṣurvā kva yogī jñānavān kva vā II
Kva baddhaḥ kva ca vā muktaḥ svasvarupe'hamadvaye II

6. To my indivisible, essential Self, what is the world and what is the aspirant for liberation, what is the *yogī* and what is the wise man, what is the non-free and what is the free man?

The complete unity of the Self nullifies the experience of the world and the status of man, whether seeker of knowledge or *yogī*, whether in freedom or in bondage.

क्व सृष्टिः क्व च संहारः क्व साध्यं क्व च साधनम् ।
क्व साधकः क्व सिद्धिर्वा स्वस्वरूपेऽहमद्वये ॥७॥

Kva sṛṣṭiḥ kva ca saṁhāraḥ kva sādhyaṁ kva ca sādhanam
Kva sādhakaḥ kva siddhirvā svasvarūpe'hamadvaye ll

7. To my indivisible essential Self, what is creation and what is withdrawal, what is end and what is means, what is the seeker and what is the accomplishment?

It is stressed again that non-duality of the Self excludes all notions of creation and destruction, and of end, action and means.

क्व प्रमाता प्रमाणं वा क्व प्रमेयं क्व च प्रमा ।
क्व किञ्चित्क्व न किञ्चिद्वा सर्वदा विमलस्य मे ॥८॥

Kva pramātā pramāṇaṁ vā kva prameyaṁ kva ca pramā ll
Kva kiñcit kva *na kiñcidvā sarvadā vimalasya me* l

8. To the Self ever taintless, what is the knower and knowledge, what is the means and the object of knowledge and what is knowledge, what is something and what is nothing.

Non-duality cannot be attained with the fusion of the basic triadic categories of the knower, the object of knowledge and the knowing in contemplation (II,15). Nothing then exists except self-effulgence.

Knowledge—The Self is, in the first place, indemonstrable and relationless, beyond proof and beyond relativity; secondly, the Self itself comprises the knower, the object of knowledge and the means of knowledge.

Something and nothing—For the all-encompassing Self nothing exists outside itself. The Self is merely relationless existence.

क्व विक्षेपः क्व चैकाग्र्यं क्व निर्बोधः क्व मूढता ।
क्व हर्षः क्व विषादो वा सर्वदा निष्क्रियस्य मे ॥९॥

Kva vikṣepaḥ kva caikāgryaṁ kva nirbodhaḥ kva mūḍhatā ।
Kva harṣaḥ kva viṣādo vā sarvadā niṣkriyasya me ॥

9. To me ever actionless, what is distraction and what is concentration, what is inertia and what is delusion and what is joy and what is sorrow?

The completely impassive Self transcends the distinction between fixation and distraction, delusion and inertia, joy and sorrow.

Actionless—Inactivity (i.e. cessation of *samādhi*) and absence of distraction are linked together. In the *Bodhasāra* we read, "Activity is true worship, when every activity is for the sake of the Self (*śiva*), inactivity is true worship when it is a mode of silent meditation (of the Self).

क्व चैष व्यवहारो वा क्व च सा परमार्थता।
क्व सुखं क्व च वा दुःखं निर्विमर्शस्य मे सदा ॥१०॥

Kva caiṣa vyavahāro vā kva ca sā paramārthatā ।
Kva sukhaṁ kva ca vā duḥkhaṁ nirvimarṣaya me sadā ॥

10. To me who am ever free from (discursive) reasoning, what is relation and what is absoluteness, what is happiness and what is misery?

Abandoning analytical or discursive reasoning, the Self devoted to intuitional illumination (pratibhā), does not distinguish between existence and transcendence.

Freedom from reasoning—This is a new category of Aṣṭāvakra. The *Taittirīya Upaniṣad* uses the cognate term *amanvānasya*, i.e. one who does not reflect (II,7,1).

Relation and Absoluteness—Plotinus thus observes in respect of the ultimate reality beyond relation and absoluteness. "Generative of all, the Unity is none of all, neither thing nor quality, nor intellect nor soul, not in motion, not at rest, not in place, not in time, it is the self-defined, unique in form or better, formless, existing before Form or Movement or Rest, all of which are attachments of Being and make Being the manifold it is" (Enneads,E.T., VI, 9).

क्व माया क्व च संसारः क्व प्रीतिर्विरतिः क्व वा ।
क्व जीवः क्व च तद्ब्रह्म सर्वदा विमलस्य मे ॥११॥

Kva māyā kva ca saṁsāraḥ kva prītirviratiḥ kva vā l
Kva jīvaḥ kva ca tadbrahma sarvadā vimalasya me ll

11. To me who am ever taintless, what is illusion and what is the (ephemeral) *saṁsāra*, what is attachment and what is repulsion, what is *jīva* (empirical self) and what is That Brahman?

Self-abidance (*svāsthya*) is a blessed state which is oblivious of the distinction between bondage and freedom, *jīva* and *Brahman*—deluding experiences of the phenomenal world.

That i.e. transcendent Brahman which is unutterable. *Jīva* as it abides in the Self or Brahman becomes devoid of human attributes, conditions and relativities, and cannot also be denoted. As the *Muṇḍaka Upaniṣad* says, 'He who realizes Brahman through knowing becomes Brahman (*brahmavid brahmaiva bhavati*, III,2,9).

Like the *Aṣṭāvakragītā*, both the *Tejobindu Upaniṣad* (IV, 65-79) and the *Avadhūtagītā* (V,VI) assemble similar strings of paradoxical statements with a view to denote the transcendence of the non-dual self. These resemble much the *Aṣṭāvakragītā* in their shattering, iconoclastic, non-dual mood and temper.

क्व प्रवृत्तिर्निवृत्तिर्वा क्व मुक्तिः क्व च बन्धनम् ।
कूटस्थनिर्विभागस्य क्वस्थस्य मम सर्वदा ॥१२॥

Kva pravṛttirnivṛttirvā kva muktiḥ kva ca bandhanam l
Kūṭasthanirvibhāgasya svasthasya mama sarvadā ll

12. To me ever-abiding in the immutable and indivisible Self, what is impulsion and what is withdrawal, what is liberation and what is bondage?

Self-abidance (*svarūpa*) is not sullied by the human condition of attachment or detachment, bondage and salvation.

Liberation and bondage—The *Jīvanmuktagītā* stresses the same thought : "He is said to be liberated in life who is free from the opposite ideas of bondage and liberation" (XVI).

क्वोपदेशः क्व वा शास्त्रं क्व शिष्यः क्व च वा गुरुः ।
क्व चास्ति पुरुषार्थो वा निरुपाधेः शिवस्य मे ॥१३॥

Kvopadeśaḥ kva vā śāstraṁ kva śiṣyaḥ kva ca vā guruḥ I
Kva cāsti puruṣārtho vā nirupādheḥ Śivasya me II

13. To me who am *Śiva* (the supremely blissful, tranquil and good) and unconditioned, what is teaching and what is scripture, what is disciple and what is master, and what is the ultimate goal of life?

Teaching and scripture—In spiritual progress the distinction between instruction or scriptural injunction and the seeker of knowledge, between the Guru or master and the pupil is one of the last pairs of opposites that are surpassed.

Śiva—The Self is often called *Śiva-svarūpa* or *Śiva-caitanya* ever unconditioned and undivided, and beyond the relativity of the phenomenal world. *Śiva* combines several principles : absolute tranquillity, goodness or auspiciousness and bliss of the non-dual Self.

Śiva is "pure and embodies all-bliss of the self", says Śaṅkara, while commenting on the *Māṇḍūkya Upaniṣad*(7,12). In *Śvetāśvatara Upaniṣad*, the all-pervading Brahman "is the Lord (*Bhagavān*) and therefore the omnipresent Śiva" (III, II). Again in IV, 14 and IV, 17, where the Brahman or the universal Self is depicted as the One, embracer of everything, immanent in everything, blissful and exceedingly subtle, it is called *Śiva*. In V,14 the same *Upaniṣad* observes : "Him who is to be grasped by pure consciousness, who is called incorporeal, who makes existence and non-existence, Śiva, the maker of creation and its parts, the Divine, they who know Him have left the body behind".

Śiva focuses the notions of the non-dual Self (*advaita*) as supremely blissful, tranquil and good According to the *Vedānta*, self-knowledge or the realization of *Śiva-svarūpa* is the cessation of all ills of life, and hence the absolute good. The *sohambhāva* or *śivohambhāva* is also associated with perfect tranquillity and auspiciousness—*Śivaṁ Śāntam* of the *Upaniṣads*. In the *Śāṇḍilya Upaniṣad* we read, *Dattātreyaṁ śivaṁ śāntaṁ sarva-sākṣiṇaṁ, devadevam.* (III, 1-4). *Śāntaṁ, śivam, advaitam* go together in the famous description of the one Self into which the world (*prapañca*) is dissolved, as given in the *Māṇḍūkya Upaniṣad* (7). This seems to be Aṣṭāvakra's implication here, as he also conjoins *nirupādhi* with *Śiva* in the verse. He uses the term *niṣprapañca* in XVIII, 35 for the Self. *Śiva* has come to mean the most serene, good and benign one—the One, all-God, God of gods or the supreme Self. In a sense *Śiva* is the nexus between the Self as the incomprehensible beyond (XV, 8) and the Self as *Bhagavān*, *Jagadīśvara* or creator of the universe (I, 19, IV, 6, XI, 2). In the *Śvetāśvatara Upaniṣad*, produced in a mystical milieu, Brahman is identified with *Śiva* whose name is also *Hara*, *Rudra* and *Bhagavat* (I, 10; III, 2 and 11).

क्व चास्ति क्व च वा नास्ति क्वास्ति चैकं क्वच द्वयम् ।
बहुनात्र किमुक्तेन किञ्चिन्नोत्तिष्ठते मम ॥१४॥

Kva chāsti kva ca vā nāsti kvāsti caikaṁ kva ca dyayam I
Bahunātra kimuktena kiñcinnottiṣṭhate mama II

14. What is existence and what is non-existence, what is the dual and what is the non-dual? Nothing of me springs up. What more can be said?

With the realisation of the primordial, unborn and undivided Self, the notions of existence or non-existence, unity or duality, embodying empirical determinations of the mind, are silenced. The unborn and unthinkable Self is the Supreme, beyond definition and denotation, affirmation and denial. The Self is absolute transcendence.

The dual and the non-dual—The notions of unity and duality are derived from relativist worldly relations and experiences. The unborn Self is beyond *dvaita* (dual) and *advaita* (non-dual, See also XIX, 2). The *Tejobindu Upaniṣad* remarks, "By no means is there known a distinction of dualism and non-dualism. This distinction is the work of *māyā* due to the notion of the external. The conviction, 'I am Brahman' will arise only if the thought, "I am the body" becomes painful. When the non-self becomes the stealer of the Self, the only guard of the gem of the Self is the Absolute

Brahman who is composed of everlasting bliss" (98-102). The *Avadhūtagītā* says : "Some prefer non-duality, others prefer duality. They do not understand the reality which is the state of sameness, devoid of either duality or non-duality" (I, 36). Again, "The world is manifest as sameness without parts or intervals. Oh, *māyā* is a great delusion, an imagination of duality and non-duality" (I, 61). The *Kulārṇava Tantra* observes in the same manner : "Some prefer the non-dual, others the dual. Know the essence of my knowledge, it is devoid of the attributes of duality and non-duality".

Nothing of me springs up—The grammar here is worthy of note. It is a marked characteristic of the epic style to use the *ṣaṣṭī vibhakti* in a free manner, sometimes in the sense of *caturthī* and sometime in that of *pañcamī*.

From or out of the self nothing proceeds (*mama kiñcit nottiṣṭhate*) i.e. the Self is all that was, that is and that will be. The Self is indivisible and immutable. It is unborn and non-dual. If it does originate, it originates from itself (XIII, 1). Gauḍapāda in his *Māṇḍūkya Kārikā* similarly says: "No *jīva* is ever born. There does not exist any cause which can produce *jīva*. This is the highest truth that nothing eer springs from that" (*yatra na kiñcit jāyate*, III, 48). Śaṅkara in his commentary on this passage says, "No cause can ever exist which may produce the Ātman which is by nature unborn and non-dual. In other words no *jīva* can ever be born, as the cause which may produce it does not exist".

Aṣṭāvakra throughout the text emphasises that the Self as it encompasses the universe does not come from anywhere nor goes anywhere (outside the Self), *na gantā na agantā* (II. 12). It does not spring out of anything except the Self), *akiñcana-bhavaṁ* (XIII, 1) and also produces nothing (outside the self). XX,4. "Wherefrom can there be birth, action and ego-sense for the Self who is one, immutable and still"? (XV, 13). Aṣṭāvakra obviously is the founder of the *ekajīvavāda* and *ajātavāda*, as these absolutist doctrines were called in the later centuries. Before the advent of Buddhist idealism he seems to have been the first thinker who recovered the absolutist (*advaita*) trend of the *Upaniṣads* in his doctrine of the absolute and unborn Self a most courageous, iconoclastic and clear manner. He obviously anticipates Gauḍapāda's *kārikā* in which the latter agrees with those who hold that there is no coming into being and further elaborates this seminal notion: "The non-dualists hold that the existent cannot have generation and the non-existent also cannot come into being as existent. Thus disputing among themselves they as a matter of fact support the ajāti or the absolute non-evolution of what exists" (*Māṇḍūkya Kārikā*, IV. 2,4).

Our sage teaches boldly for the first time that there is no birth of the Self, there is no *creation* at all. Like the boundless space which is intelligence (*cidākāśa*), it has neither duality nor unity, neither bondage nor liberation,. neither beginning nor end. Let us quote at the end one noble verse : "O, marvellous am I. I adore myself who though with a body am one. I have neither coming from anywhere nor going anywhere and encompass the entire universe" (II, 12).

Aṣṭāvakra's philosophy or *tattva-darśana*, as adumbrated in the last chapter, pertains to truth, i.e. the truth of the Self and Life. Transcendence is the ultimate truth of the cosmic Self, existence and freedom (*jīvanmukti*). The great bane of modern Western thought is empiricism rooted in eighteenth and nineteenth century scientific development. Modern Western philosophy, grounded in science, merges itself in scientific empirical thought. Modern religion in the West also loses itself in a dogma of God which does not completely fulfil man's desire and capacity for transcendence in thought and feeling. Aṣṭāvakra rejects the notion of *Iśvara* or God as belonging to empirical thinking. The Self is the ultimate, transcendent reality. The Ātman is itself. It is self-established beyond empirical thought and imagination; and if it be identified with God must embody the truth of the all and the beyond-human-and-cosmic. Not mind, speech and concept but immediate apprehension reveals the truth of the Self as surpassing the phenomenal and the empirical realm. The distinctions of *dvaita* and *advaita*, relativity and transcendence, direct illumination and revelation are empirical and must disappear, It is the ever undefinable and transcendent Self which realizes the ultimate truth of transcendence and its omnipotence.

The ultimate is the transcendent. Not empirical speculation but intuitive insight, practice of yoga and *Śraddhā* or unswerving devotion to the truth of the self and life open the gates to the ultimate reality. The Atman of Indian philosophy from the time of the *Upaniṣads* to the present time, the *nous* of Greek philosophy from Parmanides, and Heraclitus to Plato and the intuition of Whitehead, Bergson, Hocking and modern Existentialist philosophy comprise a persistent endeavour to break away from the emrpirical dimension in the quest of truth. The *Aṣṭāvakragītā* belongs to this glorious tradition. At the same time it is unique in defining philosophy or *samyagdarśana* as the state of ineffable wonder and bliss and making it highly fruitful for man's life and freedom with their conditions and goals. The acme of Aṣṭāvakra's teaching is this : "O pure intelligence, do not agitate your mind with (the thoughts of) affirmation and denial. Silencing these abide happily in your own Self—the embodiment of bliss itself" (XV. 19). Aṣṭāvakra magnificently transcends the *advaita* of the *Upaniṣads* and presents supreme Self as the same in bondage or liberation, relativity or the transcendence, distraction or samādhi. The *Aṣṭāvakragītā* is sung with the feeling of inexpressible wonder and joy of the Self.

Adoration to the Self for whom there is neither source nor becoming, neither the past nor the present nor the future neither space nor eternity, neither illumination (*vidyā*) nor illusion (avidyā). The only-lonely (*kevala*) is silent (*mauna*). The silence of the Self is its own inherent and preferred attitude. *Maunaṁ iti vākhyānaṁ śāntaṁ śivaṁ advaitaṁ sarvasākṣin.*

Om Saccidānanda Rūpa Paramātmane Namaḥ. Om Tat Sat. *Tat Paraṁ Brahma.*

प्राच्यप्रतीच्यलोकाना-
मुपदेष्टारमीश्वरम् ।
तापत्रयस्य हन्तारं
विश्वात्मानं नमाम्यहम् ॥१॥

यो विश्वकृत् विश्वदृगप्यचिन्त्यो
विश्वात्मको विश्वमुखश्च वन्द्यः ।
वेदान्तसिद्धान्तलसत्स्वरूपः
सोऽहं परो बोधमयो न चान्यः ॥२॥

सोऽहं ब्रह्मेति यज् ज्ञानं यदत्यन्तं हि निर्मलम् ।
तदात्मानुभवोल्लासो मुन्यष्टावक्रवर्णितः ।

ततः सर्वात्मसंसिद्धिहेतवे मुनिसत्तमम् ।
राधाकमलसंज्ञोऽहं याचे विश्वविमोचनम् ॥

GLOSSARIAL INDEX

A

Ābhāsa, reflection, empirical or finite consciousness. I,13.

Abhāva, non-existence, XVIII, 4.

Abidance in self, *svasthaḥ*, *svāsthya*, *svapada*, *svarūpa*, VII, 3,4; IX,7; XII, 1-7; XVII, 14; XVIII, 33,63, 98; XX,1,3,
natural condition, XII,8; XVI, 11; XVIII, 41, 63, 70; XX, 3, 6, 7.
(Gītā, *svastha*, XIV, 24).

Abhimāna, ego-feeling, XVI, 10.

Abjuring speech, thought and effort in the quest of the self, XII, 1-3, 7 ; XVIII, 40-42, 63, 64, 67 ; XIX, 4, 7; XX, 10-13.

Acintya, self as unthinkable, XII, 7.

Action, karma, no efficacy of, I, 6; X, 8; XII, 1; XVIII, 48, 51, 57-58 ; 77, 98; XIX, 3, XX, 4.

Adhivāsita, coveter, XVII, 4.

Adhyāsa: super-imposition i.e, attribution of something unreal to something real XII, 3.

Adṛṣṭi, aimlessness, XVIII, 63.

Advaya, *advaita*, *eka*, self as non-dual, I, 7, 12; II, 7; III, 6; IV, 6; XVIII, 43; XIX, 2; XX, 6, 14.

Ajñāna, *advidyā*, ignorance, cause of manifestation of the phenomenal world, I, 9; II, 7; X, 5; XII, 6.

Akiñcana, without any possession, XVIII, 87.

Akiñcanabhava, unborn self (not springing out of anything), XIII, 1; XX, 14.

Amṛtam, perennial bliss, XVIII, 81.

Ānanda-paramānanda, self as supreme bliss, I, 10.

Anantarūpa, self as infinite, XVIII, 72.

Anara, self as beyond human, XVII, 16.

Anātma, not-self, XIX, 4.

Anavadhāna, indifference, XVIII, 88.

Anirvāya, self as undefinable, XVIII, 79.

Ārambha, action, XVIII, 64.

Arthasannyāsa, renunciation of all goals of life, XVIII, 67.

Arūpita, indefinability of the self, XX, 2.

Asaṅga, self as unattached, I,5, 12; (Gītā, XV, 3).

Jñānasvarūpa, self as the embodiment of pure knowledge, XV, 8.

Joy of the Self, I, 10, XV, 6; XVI, 2, XVII, 3 ; XVIII, 12, 59 (*Gītā*, *ātmaratiḥ*, III, 17).

K

Kaivalya, *kevala*, aloneness or absoluteness of the self, III, 9 ; XI, 6 ; XVII, 18; XVIII, 87.
    videha (at death), XX, 4.

Knowledge, triad (*tritaya*), of, unreal, II, 15. XX, 8.

Kāma, pleasure. See Goals of life.

Karma, action. See Action.

Knots of the heart, *hṛdaya-granthi*, XVIII, 88.

Kūṭastha, self as the immutable, witness of the movements of the body, senses and mind, I, 13 ; XX, 11 (*Gītā*, VI, 8 ; XII, 3 ; XV, 16).

L

Laya, melting or dissolution of the phenomenal world and consciousness, ways of attainment of, V, 1-4 ; rejected, VI, 1-4 ; XIX, 7.

Lepa, involvement, XI, 4, XVIII, 18, 64 (*Gītā* IV, 14; V, 7, 10, XIII, 31, XVIII, 17).

Liberation, *mukti*, *mokṣa*, causing fear, III, 8,
    means of attainment of, desirelessness and non-attachment, VIII, 2-4 ; detachment from sense-organs and sense-objects, I, 2, VII, 3, XV, 2,
    cultivation, of certain virtues, I, 2.
    dispassion, *vairāgya*, X, 3, 8,
    indifference, *nirveda*, IX, 1, 5, 8.
    in life and at death, XX, 4.

Life, desire for, to be extinguished, IX, 2,
    and death, transcended, II, 22; XVII, 6;
    XVIII, 83, 86; XIX 7.

M

Majesty of the self, beyond all relativities, XIX, 2-8.

Māyā, World-illusion, III, 11, XVIII, 73: XX, 11
    (Gītā, VII, 14, 15 XVIII, 61).

Meditation, *dhyāna*, hindrance to self-knowlege,
    XVIII, 3, 7;
    to be abandoned, XV, 19, 20; XVIII, 16, 17, XX, 28, 33,

Mind, *mānasa*, *citta*, producing the phenomenal world,
    I, 10, II, 23-24; XX, I,

Niḥśaṅka nirātaṅka, self as free from fear, XVIII, 41, 78;

Nairāśya, transcendence of expectation, XX, 1, XVIII, 84.

O

Ocean of Self, the phenomenal world being waves or bubbles, II, 23, 24, 25, III, 3, V, 2; VI 2; VII, 1-3; XV, 7, 11.

Oblivion of world, XVI, 1, 4, 11.

Origin of the self from nothing (*akiñcanabhava*), XIII, 1.

P

Para, self as the beyond or transcendent, II, 1, III, 5, VI, 4, XV, 6-8; XVIII, 16, 37, XX, 14 (*Gītā*, IV, 40, VIII, 20, 22; XIII, 22).

Parmātmā, the Supreme Self, II, 3; XIV, 3.

Parameśvara, self as the Supreme Lord, I, 19,

Parigraha, possession, XVIII, 62. (Gītā, XVIII, 53)

Phenomenal world illusory, XVIII, 69, 73.

Pravṛtti, impulse, XVIII, 69.

Prakṛti, primal nature, II. 1. XV, 8; XVIII, 69.

Prārabdha-karma, actions begun in previous births. XX, 4,

Praśamaupaśama, tranquillity, IX, 2; X, 8; XI, 8; XVIII, 3.

Prince or beggar, same when unattached, XVIII, 91.

Pleasure, enemy of self-knowledge, III, 7.

Protam, self as diffused, I, 16 (*Gītā*, VII, 7).

Priya, self as beloved, XVIII, 35.

Puruṣa, person, XIV, 3.

Pūrṇa, self as full, I, 12; V, 4; XVII. 2; XVIII, 35, 67.

Prakāśa, self's nature as luminousness, II, 8.

Prayer, rejected as expansion of word, XII, 1.

Puruṣārtha, life's supreme goal i. e., *mukti*, XIII, 2. See Goals of Life.

R

Renunciation, *tyāga* IX, 1, 8; XVIII, 2.
of the goals of life, XIII, 2; XVI, 5; XVII, 6; XVIII, 12; XIX, 2, 8;
of both good and evil, happiness and sorrow, XIII, 5-7.

Resolution of the triad of knowledge, knower and object of knowledge ,II, 15.

Reverence, *Śraddhā* XV, 8 (Gītā, VI 21; IX. 23; XII, 2; XVII, 1, 17),

Rope as snake, metaphor of world illusion, I, 10; II, 7, 9; V, 3.

Rajas, principle of human energism, XVIII, 88.

S

Sādhyadarśī, self that does not seek after goals, XI, 4.

Salutation to self, II, 11-14.

Sākṣī self as the eternal and universal witness of the phenomenal world, I, 3, 5, 12; XIV, I; XV, 4 (*Gītā*, IX, 18).

Sama, self as the same in all human conditions, V, 4; VI, 4; XV, 6; XVIII, 82, 98, 100 (*Gītā*, II, 15; V, 18; VI, 29-32).

Samadarśī, equal-minded, XVII, 15.

Samādhi meditation as bondage. I 15; XII 3, 7; XV, 20; XVI, 2; XVIII, 97; XIX, 7,

Saṁsāra, world, rooted in desire and attachment, IX, 8; X, 3; XV, 7, 8; XVIII, 57.

Śānta, self as tranquil, VII, 3, 4, XVIII, 1.

Sarvam, all as Self; XV, 15, XVIII, 9.

Sarvārambha, all beginning, XVIII, 64 (*Gītā*, XVIII, 48).

Sarvagatam, all-pervading self, I, 20 (*Gītā*, III, 15; XIII, 32).

Self as the boundless ocean, with the mind creating wave-like forms and appearances, II, 4, 23-25; III, 2; V, 2; VI. 2; VII, 1-3; XV, 18.

as marvellous (II, 11-14, 25);

as unsurpassingly beautiful, III, 4;

as beyond thought, XII, 7;

identified with the universe, IV, 4;

as boundless space contrasted with finite space in pot representing the world, VI, 1;

neither gains nor loses with the appearance or disappearance of name and forms, VII, 2; XV, 11;

is all that exists, XV, 15; XVIII, 8, 9;

in all and all in the self, III, V; XV, 6 (*Gītā*, VI, 29).

abidance in, XII, 1-8;

as the embodiment of transcendent bliss, XV, 19; XVI, 2; XVII, 1, 81;

attributelessness of, XX, 1-14;

filling the whole universe alone, XVII, 2;

its grandeur, XIX, 2-8;

beyond the three states of consciousness, XVIII, 94; XIX, 4;

absolute transcendence, XV, 8; XX, 14;

T

Void (Buddhist), XX, 1,
speculations on non-existence, XVIII, 42, 63 ;
form of the self, XVIII,57,
naturally void-minded, XIV, 1, 4 ; XVIII, 24.
Void-mindedness, *Śūnyacitta*, essential for self-knowledge, XIV, 1, 4 ; XV, 1, 4 ; XV, 19-20 ; XVIII, 24, 63.

W

Wisdom, *vijñāna*, given up, XIV, 2, XIX, 8.
Witness, *sākṣī*, self as the eternal and universal, I, 3, 5, 7, 12, XIV, 3, XV,4 (Gītā, IX, 18).
World, as a magic show, VI, 5 ; X, 2
as transient, worthless and miserable, IX, 3, X, 6-8;
as unreal and non-intelligent, X, 5 ;
as due to desire, VIII, 1, 3, 4 ; X, 3, 4 ; XV, 2 ;
as mere illusion (*māyā*), III, 11, XV, 17; XVIII, 72 ;
as due to the sense of duty, XVIII, 57 ;
as created and impelled by mind and imagination, I, 9 ; VII, I, 3 ; XVIII, 7 ;
not perceived, 1, 7, 10, II, 7; III, 13 ; XVIII, 15, 68, 71, 72 ; XX, 8.

Y

Yathāsukham, living in True happiness, XIII, 1, 3, 7.
Yoga, *yogī*, excellences and defects, IV, 2; XIII, 4 ; XVIII, 9-13, 55-56, 92 ; XIX, 8.
Yogābhyāsa, practice of yoga, XII, I, XVII, 1.
Yogadṛṣṭi, yogic vision, XVIII, 80.